NORSE GODDESS MAGIC

"In this important and original work Alice Karlsdóttir, a leading expert on Norse religion, makes new and dramatic teachings available and applies these methods in a practical way in order that the ancient Norse goddesses can speak directly to those who seek their ageless wisdom. This book is something that can guide practitioners in all traditions in a process of esoteric discovery of what lies hidden in often obscure and scant mythological references. She concentrates on the often neglected goddesses of the Norse pantheon, especially the goddess Frigg. The teachings pioneered by this author show the way to move from the known to the unknown and shine a light that illuminates the darkness."

STEPHEN FLOWERS, PH.D.,
AUTHOR OF *ICELANDIC MAGIC*
AND *LORDS OF THE LEFT-HAND PATH*

"Karlsdóttir's accessible, practical, and engaging guide to the goddesses of the Norse tradition covers not only the mother goddess Frigg but many of the lesser-known deities as well. By studying myth, reading ancient texts, and engaging in trancework you can experience these ancient archetypes yourself and strengthen your connection with them. Karlsdóttir explains the necessary steps to enter the trance state and embark upon an enjoyable journey and safe return. She introduces thirteen Norse goddesses, among them healers, protectors, counselors, and messengers. *Norse Goddess Magic: Trancework, Mythology, and Ritual* is a wonderful addition to any library and will enrich your knowledge of mythology, magic, and the Divine Feminine."

"Alice Karlsdóttir brings the thirteen Norse goddesses of the Aesir alive within us through her research but especially through her teachings of trance. She shows us how to experience each goddess personally and the values each has to teach. The values taught by each goddess take the meaning of compassion, nurturance, and protection to a much deeper level of our soul, the soul of the family, the community, and of our Great Earth Mother."

NORSE GODDESS MAGIC

TRANCEWORK, MYTHOLOGY, AND RITUAL

ALICE KARLSDÓTTIR

Destiny Books
Rochester, Vermont • Toronto, Canada

Destiny Books
One Park Street
Rochester, Vermont 05767
www.DestinyBooks.com

Destiny Books is a division of Inner Traditions International

Library of Congress Cataloging-in-Publication Data
Karlsdóttir, Alice.
  [Magic of the Norse goddesses]
  Norse goddess magic : trancework, mythology, and ritual / Alice Karlsdóttir.
    pages cm
  Originally published under the title: Magic of the Norse goddesses : mythology, ritual, tranceworking. Smithville, Tex. : Runa-Raven Press, 2003.
  Includes bibliographical references and index.
  Summary: "A practical guide to the magic of the feminine side of the Norse pantheon" — Provided by publisher.
  ISBN 978-1-62055-407-4 (pbk.) — ISBN 978-1-62055-408-1 (e-book)
  1. Goddesses, Norse. 2. Mythology, Norse. 3. Trance. I. Title.
  BL863.K37 2015
  133.4'3—dc23

                                                                    2014042245

Printed and bound in the United States

10 9 8 7 6 5 4 3 2

Text design and layout by Virginia Scott Bowman
This book was typeset in Garamond Premier Pro and Neue Hammer Unziale used as the display typeface

To send correspondence to the author of this book, mail a first-class letter to the author c/o Inner Traditions • Bear & Company, One Park Street, Rochester, VT 05767, and we will forward the communication.

This book is dedicated to David Byron Bragwin James, who was the best of teachers in so many areas— metaphysics, poetry, languages, fine wines, and everything in between. He was also the dearest and most charming of friends. May he feast with his gods and ancestors (and may he give a chuckle now and then for those of us still striving in Midgard).

Abbreviations

OE	Old English
Gmc.	Germanic
OHG	Old High German
ON	Old Norse
ch.	chapter
st.	stanza

A Note on Special Characters

In writing certain words in languages such as Old Norse or Old English, certain special written characters are used. When representing these words in the current set of characters used in English, please note these correspondences:

Þ, þ = th

Ð, ð = dh

Contents

PART ONE

Looking for a Goddess

*Discovering Mythology and
Understanding Tranceworking*

PART TWO

Frigg and Her Women

*The Lore and Trance Methods
for Finding the Goddesses*

Acknowledgments

This book began as a project for the Rune Gild and probably would not have been completed without the help and inspiration of that organization and its Yrmin-Drighten, Edred Thorsson. I would also like to thank my first teacher, David Byron Bragwin James, who instructed, inspired, and encouraged me when I was just beginning to explore these areas and who helped me find my way back to the old ways. Thanks also go to Tina Bindman and Carl McLaughlin, Macha ni Padraiga, Lynn "the Moose" Stone, and June for letting me bend their ears about my ideas over the years; to Kveldulf Gundarsson for etymological help; to Christopher Ransom for the photography; to Joseph "Chepe" Lockett for helping me with my score; to James Chisholm for nagging me to finish when inspiration lagged; and to Kean for being there, in this world and beyond.

The Balance between Trance Knowledge and Lore Knowledge

When I first wrote this book, the Heathen community was focused on research and attempting to re-create traditional practices, and there was a paucity of information on the Germanic goddesses. The idea of using more subjective practices, like meditation or tranceworking, to supplement what was available in the lore was less common and sometimes viewed with skepticism or mockery. Now it seems that the pendulum has swung in the other direction. More and more people have been using less traditional methods to fill out their understanding of the gods and goddesses and some types of *seiðr* (a magical technique involving trance states, prophesying, shamanic traveling, and talking to spirits) are being actively practiced and even standardized by some groups.

Sometimes it seems that subjective experience and opinion are almost given prominence over the traditional lore, which I think is a mistake. There are many things missing from the information that has survived from the original Heathen times, but when it's there, we should use it. When doing subjective work like tranceworking, there is always the danger of becoming too attached to one's personal view of a god or goddess and losing one's objectivity. I have even seen some people get into arguments because their personal picture of a goddess didn't match someone else's. This is unfortunate. Not everything you see or learn in a trance is necessarily a valid revelation. It may be a message or insight meant for you alone, but not necessarily meaningful or true for the rest of the world. Sometimes it may just be a product of your own personal mental landscape, or you may have been influenced by some event or condition in your everyday life.

The real benefit to people using trance, meditation, and other subjective forms of magic is to be able to work together to compile and compare what's learned, to find common themes and unexpected insights. It's always exciting to talk with someone who has a fresh perspective or who has had an experience that matches one of your own. Sometimes you just need someone who will honestly tell you when you're off track. But the greatest good comes from forging emotional links and understanding, and ultimately strengthening the bonds between the people of Midgard and their gods. The rainbow bridge still shines brightly, beckoning those who are willing to cross over to the other worlds.

The Role of Tranceworking in the Heathen Community

> It is time to chant   from the seer's stool
>   at the Well of Urð;
> I saw but stayed silent,   I saw and thought,
>   and heard Hár's words.
>
> HÁVAMÁL, ST. 111

This book grew out of a personal need to better understand the Norse gods and goddesses. However, in the process of trying to flesh out the somewhat scanty information available on many Norse deities, I discovered the art of tranceworking and its role in spiritual study and worship. I am therefore sharing not only the lore I was able to learn but also the means I used to acquire it.

Although Norse goddesses serve as my examples, the methods I describe can be used to explore gods or goddesses from any tradition. Because information on female deities is often scarce in the Germanic traditions, I chose thirteen goddesses to explore in detail. I also deliberately selected many who are obscure to show just how much can be done, even with very little information.

I strongly feel that the historical and archaeological information available on Pagan gods and goddesses should be supplemented, at least by practicing Pagans, with less traditional methods. This is the only way we can reclaim our religions and those practices lost to us through the years. Practices such as meditation, tranceworking, and ritual can imbue cold, dry facts with emotional links and make religion more personal and meaningful. Moreover, a living, vital religion must continue to grow and develop and not remain a carbon copy of the past.

PART ONE

Looking for a Goddess

Discovering Mythology
and Understanding Tranceworking

FIFTEEN YEARS AGO if someone had told me that I would be writing about going into trances, I would have laughed. I had never been very good at what is sometimes called passive or lunar magic—divination, scrying, aura-reading, channeling, meditation, dreamworking, and tranceworking. When I participated in guided meditations at workshops or festivals, I would never get "in"; I would still be trying to relax my back when everyone else had traveled to Avalon and back. I thought that this type of visionary work was something you either had a knack for, or you didn't.

So why am I now presuming to advise others on how to journey to other worlds? Because I believe that the very fact that I don't have a natural aptitude for faring forth makes me the very person to write on this subject. Let's face it: Naturals who trance off after a few drumbeats don't need to read things like this; they already know instinctively what to do. It's the rest of us, those who have trouble with trances and who perhaps think that this means we can't experience these sorts of adventures, who need to study and practice. Because, surprisingly enough, I discovered that the ability to do tranceworking is something that can be learned and developed, just as you develop muscles by exercising.

I never felt particularly motivated to do tranceworking until I began to practice Norse Heathenism more actively. My ritual group liked to work with both male and female deities at every ritual. As I helped develop and write these rituals, I discovered, as so many others have, that there is a lot more information on Norse gods than there is on Norse goddesses. I researched these goddesses as best I could, poking into every esoteric book I could lay my hands on, but still found my harvest of information woefully inadequate. There we would be, with a two-page call to Thor and about three lines to his giantess lover Jarnsaxa.

However, just because I couldn't find much material on the goddesses does not mean they weren't worshipped. On the contrary, assuming that a religion reflects the culture within which it developed and judging from what we know of Norse society, women played a strong role; therefore, it makes sense that the female deities would be equally strong in their world. Great mortal heroes like Sigurd and Helgi took good strong women for their mates. Would the great Thor, then, have some weakling for his wife?

I knew that much of the information was probably missing because for many centuries the Christian churches had proscribed Heathen religions, and because most of the Old Norse lore was passed down orally, it disappeared along with its last practitioners. It is logical that information on female deities, who were the least compatible with the new order, would be the first to go. So, despite my conviction that goddesses had been an important part of Heathenism in the past, it didn't seem that there was anything I could do about the scarcity of facts except scrape together the few names and characteristics I could find and make do. If I had been working as an archaeologist or a medieval historian, the matter would have had to die there.

ALTERNATIVE PATHS TO WISDOM

Germanic Paganism, or Heathenism as many practitioners prefer to call it, refers to the religious practices of an ethno-linguistic group of tribes that originated in Northern Europe and shared similar languages, mythology, and culture. The term *Germanic* was first used in classical times by Roman authors referring to barbarian tribes. In modern times the term is generally used to refer to ethnic groups including Scandinavians, Germans, Austrians, Dutch, Flemish, English, Frisians, and others. The Heathen period began at some time in the Iron Age and lasted until the medieval period when the Germanic peoples were

Christianized, which occurred at different times in different regions. In general West Germanic Paganism was practiced in Central Europe during the sixth to eighth centuries, Anglo-Saxon Paganism flourished in Britain from the fifth to eighth centuries, and the Norse religion in Scandinavia (Norway, Denmark, Sweden, and Iceland) reached its height during the Viking Age (793–1066 CE) but lasted as late as the twelfth century in some places.

But Heathenism is more than history—it is a religion. One can delve into it by conducting historical, archaeological, and anthropological research as well as by using other methods, including dreams, divination, the arts, prayer, and mysticism. I also wondered how the original followers of Heathen religions found out about their gods and goddesses in the first place. I mean, there aren't any stories about Odin handing out any stone tablets. Presumably the store of lore about the gods, goddesses, and other beings of the Nine Worlds was accumulated from people's spiritual experiences. Back then people believed in dreams and visions and took them seriously. These people were my ancestors, and my religion doesn't have a fall from grace or a privileged priest class. If someone two thousand years ago could find out what Frigg was like, I could certainly do the same.

Some occultists question the spiritual value of these practices, viewing them as an indulgence in a person's own consciousness, which is liable to degenerate into self-delusion and fantasy. Perhaps this might hold some truth; used improperly and unwisely, tranceworking can definitely manifest these and other problems. Then again, like many jobs considered "women's work," perhaps these practices are devalued simply because they have traditionally been associated with women and considered their special preserve, at least in Western tradition. At any rate, tranceworking is certainly an avenue that merits further exploration and that can benefit anyone who is interested in real contact with his or her gods.

1

The Importance of Mythology

Why should we bother to work with gods and goddesses in the first place? Almost every religion includes some form of mythology, from the earliest and most primitive practices to the more modern and "scientific" variants, which tend to disguise their myths as symbology or history. It is obvious that these god figures and their stories, whatever one chooses to call them, are important and meaningful to humanity, a vital and intrinsic part of our spiritual lives. Myths also usually prove to be one of the most provocative and revealing aspects of the inner life of a people.

Our present-day interest in mythology is a relatively recent phenomenon. Once a particular mythology and the religion it is a part of lose power and credibility, there is a tendency to try to push those myths into a background far from us, suitable only for indigenous peoples. We endeavor to objectify myths and provide logical and scientific explanations for them. In the nineteenth century, with the upsurge in nationalism among the various European nations, renewed interest in mythology was sparked as part of national culture. There was also a tendency in that scientific age to equate all the mythological figures with natural phenomena, reducing each tale to a primitive attempt to explain the workings of the universe.

In the twentieth century the new science of psychology brought myths renewed respect, and they came to be viewed as symbols and archetypes of the great human unconscious and of the workings of the human psyche. The study of comparative religion also sparked renewed interest in mythology. Still, we moderns are hesitant to hint at anything that smacks of the "spiritual" in our society, and we continue to use scientific terms and explanations to skirt the issue of the importance of myth in humanity's spiritual life. We call the divine tales of primitive people "myths," while we call our own modern myths "theology."[1]

MYTHOLOGY'S ROOTS AND MEANING

What is mythology, then? Why should we bother to study it, and what relevance does it have to our spiritual lives? Briefly, a myth is a story in narrative form that recounts the acts of gods and goddesses or of heroes and is set in the divine and magical realms of the other worlds. Myths are expressions of spiritual or psychic truth, not rational or scientific truth, and are often incorporated into rituals. Often, they have as their theme the origin of things. Their purpose is to make incomprehensible universal truths intelligible to human beings and to help articulate and explain a culture's beliefs, rituals, collective experiences, and values. They are thus a vital component of human civilization.

Myths communicate through the language of symbols, using them to represent abstractions. These symbols lend a sense of compression to most myths, embodying the essence rather than the detail of experience; mythological symbols usually seem to imply more than is being said.[2] Myths are characterized by vivid and graphic imagery, metaphor, and imaginative qualities. They usually display a certain freedom of fact, form, and time, for they deal with primordial, nonlinear time, rather than chronological events.[3]

Myths tell a sacred history; they relate events that took place in the "beginning time." They usually recount how a reality, either big or small, was created, or how something came to be. Myths describe the acts of supernatural and legendary figures, revealing the creative and sacred nature of such beings. Myths describe instances when the sacred has penetrated the mundane world. The purpose of telling myths is to allow people to reexperience that beginning time, to meet with the gods and learn again their lessons of creation.[4] By knowing myths, one knows the origin of things and can therefore control and shape them at will. Myths provide a past basis for our own current actions and give us the confidence of precedent; they give us a model for life within our universe. Myths give us a voice when our own inspiration fails us.[5]

Myths often deal with paradox. They attempt to resolve contradiction and dilemma by blurring polarities and breaking through extreme oppositions. Rather than presenting absolute truths, myths try to identify mediating forces to resolve conflict.

Myths do not relate rational, scientific, idea-oriented knowledge but instead offer experiential knowledge: sensual, ethical, and emotional.[6] Their meaning is accessed by intuition, rather than by linear reasoning. Mythology accepts and preserves the unknown and the unquantifiable, the outer reaches of the universe, that which can't be examined and mathematically analyzed. Myths are not meant to represent factual, rational truth; they are not meant to be taken literally. They are a conscious deception conceived to impart a different kind of truth.

Myths embody a culture's deepest truths, those that give purpose, direction, and meaning to life.[7] They confirm a people's belief in reality, truth, and the significance of life, the knowledge that something real and meaningful does indeed exist in this universe. Myth is a refusal to accept that our mundane world is all there is, an acknowledgment that the physical world is not quite enough. Myths arise from an interest in reality that is not satisfied by facts alone. They free us from everyday experience, stir up our intellect and emotions, and give us full freedom of human expression.

It is not important that myths confirm scientific fact but that they make the world more comprehensible and manageable to people. Myths help people deal with the realities of existence, including hardship and death, and give them guidance in conducting their lives.[8] Myths explore and explain the social order and offer a system for interpreting individual experience within a universal perspective.

Myths are also a powerful cultural and social force, teaching and reinforcing social values. They legitimize and validate society by relating human needs to mythic archetypes. Myths create cohesiveness and unity among members of a community and provide a sense of continuity; they reinforce systems of meaning held in common by all. Containing the seeds of a collective memory, they reinforce the values and ideals of a group's ancestors. They can also defuse potentially tense situations by enacting conflict in a safe and socially acceptable way. Myths offer the opportunity to focus a community's efforts on cooperative and productive responses to problems.[9]

RITUAL AND MYTHOLOGY

Ritual and mythology are closely related; one implies the presence of the other. Ritual is a form of magic; its purpose is to focus the imagination. Ritual springs from the human need to periodically reenact the myths, to go back to the beginning time and re-create the world, so to speak. By repeating the actions of a myth in ritual, people seek to live the myth and share in the power of the sacred.

Ritual makes the sacred accessible to human experience. It frees people from the restriction of time. When they reenact myth, they cease to live in the everyday world, and the beings of the myth are made present to them.[10] Further, ritual fills a deep human need to respond to those numinous upwellings of joy and wonder that overtake us from time to time, a need to perform concrete, material actions in the physical world to reflect those feelings of awe and inspiration. Ritual allows us to be participants in the universe instead of merely spectators.

The use of god-forms and mythology is often viewed as childish and somewhat primitive by scientific and sophisticated moderns, but this is perhaps because they are not considering the true function of mythological figures. Most people don't think of their gods and goddesses as real people living up on a sacred mountain somewhere anymore than Christians or Jews or Muslims believe their god is an old man sitting on a throne out in space. Rather, the use of god-forms is an attempt to symbolize the great forces perceived to exist in the universe, to somehow get a grasp on them and display them in such a way that we can understand and interact with them.

Although these sensory interpretations are highly subjective, they are a mask for real, objective energies. These god-forms symbolize in human terms the true nature of the gods behind them. By consenting to the use of these god-figures, the gods are able to communicate and interact with humanity, to make themselves present in our world and allow us to interact with them in theirs through trance and ritual. A society's myths provide links with the gods, a channel through which we can communicate, a path between the worlds that both gods and humans recognize and can use. They help us comprehend the Divine.

Mythology and god-forms also provide a valuable emotional link with what might otherwise be seen as a set of abstract concepts. Effective magic and ritual is dependent on a certain level of emotional energy, as well as thought and will. It's very hard to get emotionally worked up about an abstraction or a symbol, whereas it's very easy to feel real affection and kinship for a red-bearded god who rides a goat-driven chariot or a beneficent earth mother with wondrous golden hair. While some individuals can be truly moved by the beauties of prime numbers, most of us need a more personal touch to become fully engaged in an experience. Mythology, with its powerful symbols and sensory images and its use of archetypes and primal events, has the power to stir the human soul and aid us in discovering our own spirituality.

2

Exploring Norse Mythology

If we accept that gods and goddesses are an important part of religion, and that when exploring deities for spiritual rather than purely intellectual purposes we can use subjective techniques to supplement more traditional studies, how do we then proceed? How can we go about reconstructing a tangible personality from a mere name? There are actually many methods available. The following outline, which is based on my own experience, is just one example of what can be done.

Assume that you want to learn more about a particular Norse goddess. The best way to start is to do as much traditional research as you can and then supplement that with knowledge derived from other methods. Primary texts are the best source of information. Read through the Eddas and sagas, noting down anything pertaining to the particular goddess you are working on, including things only vaguely related to her. Next, read historical and archaeological texts for clues, such as inscriptions on stones or objects related to the deity. It also helps to read books depicting the folklore of Germanic cultures—the older the better—to find any places, plants, or animals associated with or named after that goddess.

DETERMINING
THE AUTHENTICITY OF SOURCES

However, even primary texts are not always entirely reliable. So it is wise to find out when a given work was written and by whom. Was it written by a genuine Heathen or by a Christian? What sort of Christianity was practiced in that time and place? If the Heathen material might be distorted, you need to know what kinds of outside influences to look out for. It's also useful to check out any Christian letters or edicts of the period, especially the writings of clergy. Whenever you find some priest condemning the worship of a particular god, you can bet that god is one of the more important deities of that era. And if the priest goes on to complain in detail about the specific acts he's upset about, you have a nice list of ritual practices that you can incorporate into your work.

Secondary texts on Norse culture and mythology are also useful, especially in terms of gaining a broad overview, providing bibliographies, and learning what conclusions other writers and scholars have formed about your goddess. You have to be even more careful in evaluating these sources, however. It's particularly important to note the date a book was first published and the background of the author in order to judge how reliable the opinions in that book are. Scholarship goes through fads, just like music or fashion, and it is important to know which philosophies were popular when a particular book was written. For example, during the nineteenth century, many scholars were enamored of the idea that all Pagan gods personified natural forces. Therefore, although many gods and goddesses are indeed associated with the sun, the moon, thunder, and so on, some writers drew some pretty far-fetched conclusions about the nature of many of the deities.

It is also a good idea to read the author's biography, which is usually provided somewhere in the introduction, on the flyleaf, on the dust jacket, or on the back cover. The background and expertise of each writer will give you a clue as to how accurate her writing is. An author with a degree in Germanic languages will probably know a great deal about the etymology of a goddess's name; however, that same author may be a devout Christian and have prejudiced views when it comes to Heathen ritual practice. Some books, too, are just plain off the wall, written by someone trying to cash in on the current fad for runes. But it won't hurt you to read a book, and if you arm yourself with knowledge, you can draw informed conclusions about what you read.

DELVING INTO WORKS OF IMAGINATION

You should also include imaginative works in your reading, such as mythology books written for children and other folk stories from the Germanic countries. Because you are after artistic and symbolic as well as intellectual information, you shouldn't restrict yourself to factual or scholarly texts; select some books chiefly for their ability to spark your imagination. Reading fairy tales, especially older or more traditional ones, serves another purpose; the images and style of folktales attune your mind to the world of myths and prepare you for the more visionary work to come.

Because names were very important to the Germanic people, you might next try to find any etymological meanings that can be gathered from the names and bynames of the goddess at hand. This does not mean you have to be a language scholar. For example, I am by no means an expert in Germanic languages, although I have a reading knowledge of German and a little Old English and Old Norse, so my research in this area is probably not conclusive. Still, I was able to find some useful information. I used dictionaries in Icelandic, Old Norse, and German to try to ferret out some of the meanings; I read the conclusions drawn by other writers on the subject, many of whom are language scholars; and, finally, I asked some of my friends who are language scholars to help me out (see, you don't have to know everything yourself to do this!).

After doing all this work, it is surprising how much information you can accumulate about these obscure deities, although some of it is admittedly trash. Go ahead and read it all, good and bad, noting which facts are repeated by more than one source, tracking down where some of the more unusual ideas came from, and deciding whether you think the author who proposed a particular idea knew what she was talking about. Don't feel that you necessarily have to throw out an idea just because it shows up in only one or two places; remember, the majority isn't always right. Keep in mind that you are reading not only to gather as many facts as possible but also to stir your imagination with stories, ideas, and images.

LOOKING FURTHER AFIELD

You needn't limit yourself to information specifically about your particular goddess, either. Consider her relations as well: family, friends, servants, associates, and even enemies. What other deities usually appear or are named in connection with this goddess? If nothing is known about her but her husband's name, use what you know about him to ferret out clues. For example, what kind of wife would Thor have? You can also use comparative mythology to help you out. What kinds of deities are traditionally paired in other similar cultures? If your goddess is married to a sky deity or a weather god, might she therefore be an Earth or fertility goddess?

After accumulating and evaluating all these facts and ideas, you might need to mull things over for about two to four weeks. During this stage try to spend some spare time thinking about the goddess and what you've read, testing conclusions in your head, and letting your own ideas about her begin to gestate. Also note down any dreams you might have during this period, especially anything that seems significant to your deity. You might begin to meditate or daydream about the goddess, and this can be done in a very casual or playful manner. Try out different physical images of her to see which one seems right. Create some scenarios in which you imagine her in various situations, and observe how she acts under different circumstances. Try to build on the knowledge you have by letting the deity you're studying interact with gods and goddesses you already know a lot about. What would this goddess and Odin talk about? How would she get along with Freyja? You can even go a step further and try to imagine what it would feel like to be this goddess, or perhaps to be one of her representative animals.

This is the point at which some people will say, "Well, you're just making it all up, aren't you? This isn't a goddess, it's just one of your own thoughtforms, a fantasy figure you've invented to amuse yourself." I can only reply that any version of what a god or goddess has done or looks like was "made up" by someone. How did we learn that Thor has a red beard and hair? Did someone decide that a thunder god should be a redhead? Did Thor appear to someone in a vision or a dream? I speculate that all these things happened to a lot of people over a long period of time and that there were probably other secondary characteristics proposed by a few that were rejected by the rest of the people because they didn't seem right. And after worshipping Thor for many, many years, enough people had experienced him in the same way to be able to say collectively, "This is what Thor is like."

The tricky part in these reconstructions is figuring out how to separate legitimate revelations from your own personal fantasies. This isn't easy to do, because it's difficult to be objective about your own pet ideas. I can only urge you to be as open and, at the same time, as skeptical as possible. Give yourself the freedom to brainstorm, to read anything, no matter how absurd; to let your imagination run wild and try out any idea that comes to you, no matter how unusual; to be willing to try anything that seems appropriate. It's also important to keep a record of your research, your dreams and daydreams, and your trances, because when you're done letting your fancy have a field day, the critic in you will have to go over it all with a mind like a razor and a heart of stone.

Because many of the goddesses are so poorly defined in most sources, you will have to reconstruct for yourself what they looked like, how they talked, and what sorts of adventures they might have had, and it's tempting to let ideas from some book or movie or dream creep in to your vision of the goddess. Some ideas are genuine revelations, but many are just whims. How do you tell the difference?

TAKING CONCRETE STEPS

A good way to start is by making an outline of all the concrete facts you do know. These are the facts gathered from the oldest and most trustworthy sources, or the ones that appear repeatedly in the more reliable authors' work. What physical characteristics are typically associated with this deity (for example, Thor's red beard or Sif's hair)? Consider the goddess's possessions and dwellings. What symbols are associated with her: plants, trees, rocks, animals? What sorts of places, seasons, and weathers are linked with her (for example, Thor is associated with thunderstorms and the goddess Holda with pools and wells)? You might also consider things like colors, numbers, and sounds. Use these outlines as a framework for your more speculative work, and don't ignore obvious, well-established facts. If the *Prose Edda* says that Fulla has long golden hair, don't try to make her a brunette. You'll find few enough facts as it is; don't discount those you come across in legitimate sources.

Next, write down all the actions your goddess performs in any myths or stories known about her. Leave out all the adjectives, adverbs, and editorial comments made by the various writers and just look at what she actually does—the bare bones of the stories. It's also important to note any other characters who are present. Who does what to whom, and who else is there contributing to or watching the action? Break down the different sides or functions of the goddess. Is she a simple deity, associated with only one basic function, or is she many-sided and complex? What other gods share her various functions, and how are they similar to and different from those of your chosen goddess? Consider what gifts she contributes to Midgard and what sorts of gifts and deeds would please her in return.

WRITING AN INVOCATION

After you have put together all the facts, the ideas from other sources that you have decided are legitimate or at least worth investigating further, and the impressions from your daydreams and musings that you believe are possibly valid, you should have at least a dim picture of the goddess you want to work with. Now you are ready to write an invocation to her using names, adjectives, and attributes gathered from your various sources. You may not have very much material, but you can at least put together a few sentences.

Address the goddess by some of her names, making sure to pick ones that express the qualities you wish to call forth. Include relational titles like "wife of Thor," "mother of Hnoss," or "friend of Frigg." If you know of a few physical traits or possessions, throw those in: "Redbeard," "Hammer-wielder," "Sif of the golden hair," "One-eyed god." Finally, include phrases indicating function: "champion of Asgard," "best of skalds," "keeper of the apples of youth." Don't be afraid to include a few things you may have come up with on your own that particularly struck you, especially if they evoke some strong emotional response, but don't go too far afield at this point. You may eventually decide that some of these phrases are inappropriate, but for now you want to have a starting point for the next step in your process—tranceworking.

3

Defining Trance and Its Many Manifestations

Before attempting tranceworking, it is important to thoroughly explore all intellectual and rational sources of information to build up an understanding of the cosmology and the myths. This will give you a structure rooted in reality to which you can add more subjective information. Without this structure, you run the risk of being sidetracked by illusion or personal fantasies. Supported by this rational understanding, however, tranceworking can fill in the gaps left by too many careless centuries and add an emotional and spiritual level of understanding to your relationship with the goddesses.

Tranceworking involves many levels of experience. Although some of these levels are purely private and relevant only to the individual, others involve real archetypes, touching on the collective unconscious and reaching back into the time of myth. These images often duplicate the experiences of others and can be shared and agreed on. The events of the trance state are thus both personal and objective, and often what begins in the imagination later manifests in the real world.

TRANCE: AN ALTERED STATE
OF CONSCIOUSNESS

Tranceworking, pathworking, guided meditation—one hears these terms used over and over in all forms of Paganism and magic. Just what is tranceworking? People use the term *trance* to describe anything from a catatonic stupor to mild daydreaming.

The definitions of *trance* and other related words indicate a state in which bodily functions, senses, and feelings are temporarily suspended and the mind—removed and separated from the stimuli of the outer world—becomes fully occupied with its own inner landscape. An archaic Scottish meaning for the word was "passageway."[1] These definitions suggest many of the characteristics of tranceworking—a lessening of physical sensations in order to concentrate deeply on the act of passing between the worlds, a turning of the attention inward to experience a state of nonordinary reality.

Many people expect a trance to be such a spectacular and awesome experience that they don't realize it when they attain one. In reality, we already experience some types of trance states in our everyday life—daydreaming, meditating, being deeply absorbed in a play or film, or being under the influence of intoxicants. If you have ever driven your car to work and arrived without being able to remember how you got there, you have been in a trance. If you have ever read a book and at some point realized you didn't remember what you had just read, you have been in a trance. Most people going into even a formal trance still have some awareness of the physical world outside them but choose to direct their attention away from that world toward other realities.

TRANCEWORKING
AND ASTRAL PROJECTION

Tranceworking is very similar to the traditional magical practice called astral projection. In both cases, one sends the consciousness out of the body to explore places that are not accessible to the physical form. Astral projection involves a person separating a part of the self from the body, and this "self" then travels through this world or through others, eventually returning with the memory of where it's been and what it has experienced. Astral projection most often refers to the practice of separating the astral body from the physical body, leaving the two joined only by a thin connection of etheric energy, sometimes referred to as the "silver cord." Other methods involve projecting the consciousness alone—what some occultists call the "mental body"—without creating an etheric body to travel in. W. E. Butler, noted twentieth-century occultist, refers to the "body of light," an artificial, mentally produced vehicle of consciousness that is a type of thoughtform, which the magician creates and to which he transfers his consciousness.[2]

Shamans have traditionally utilized trances to see and interact with nonmaterial forms of being. Michael Harner, author of *The Way of the Shaman,* describes the shamanic altered state as being similar to a waking dream in which, although dreamers can control and direct the action, they still do not know what they will encounter.[3] The shaman's experiences in the other world are considered to be fully real, not fantasy.

For any Norse purists out there, rest easy in the knowledge that early Norse Heathens also practiced forms of tranceworking. Some of these types of workings were part of the magical practice called *seiðr.* This type of magic was historically associated with the group of gods and goddesses called the Vanir. The Vanir goddess Freyja was a mistress of the art and is said to have taught it to the leader of the Aesir, Odin. It was most often practiced by women and was characterized by the act of soothsaying while in a trance state. Other workings, such as "faring forth" from the body and "sitting out" at night to speak with other beings or the dead, also bear resemblances to tranceworking.

Faring forth is a form of astral projection in which the practitioner travels from her body, usually in the "hide" (similar to the astral body) of an animal or with the aid of her "fetch" (a semi-independent part of the soul that usually appears in the form of an animal or a person, most often a woman).[4] Sometimes the fetch alone is sent to work the will of the seið-worker. Faring forth involved travel both in the everyday physical world of Midgard and through the other Eight Worlds of Norse cosmology and could be used to carry out magical acts, communicate with other beings, or gain information. While the hide or fetch of the worker was gone, the person's body would appear to be in a deep sleep or trance.

There is a detailed description in *Eirik's Saga Rauða* (4) of a *völva*, or prophetess, performing a soothsaying trance. The völva arrived at a farmstead wearing a distinctive costume made of several animal skins, ate a ritual meal made from the hearts of various animals, and then sat on a platform while one or more helpers chanted special songs to aid her tranceworking and to enlist the support of helpful spirits. From this trance she learned the answers to various questions concerning the future of the land and the people.

WESTERN TRANCEWORKING

Western occultists have long used a type of tranceworking to explore the kabbalistic Tree of Life and the tarot. This practice, usually called pathworking, involves going into a trance state and exploring the different spheres and paths on the Tree of Life or "stepping into" a tarot card to experience what it has to offer. Pathworking can also be used to explore any comparable system of symbols. Scrying, another similar practice, involves going into a light trance while gazing at a fixed point, such as a crystal, a black mirror, a bowl of water or dark liquid, a candle flame, or the smoke of incense. One then observes the mental pictures that come to mind, usually in order to learn something about the future.

Also bearing some similarities to tranceworking are the nineteenth-century passion for spiritualism and the current New Age interest in channeling, or going into trance and allowing an entity or spirit to communicate with and through you, as well as the more structured Wiccan practice of "drawing down," where you open yourself specifically to a goddess or god and allow the deity to speak through you. Finally, tranceworking is closely related to hypnosis. The physical and mental sensations are very similar, and most of the methods for hypnotic induction can be used for tranceworking rituals.

Having presented all these different practices to show the breadth and diversity of tranceworking and related practices, I am going to describe what I mean by tranceworking in the following chapters. What I usually experience while researching gods and goddesses is a light trance, which is akin to the drowsy state preceding sleep or a lucid dream—the kind where you suddenly realize you're dreaming while you're still asleep and can exert some degree of control over your actions and the direction of the dream. In these trances I am not in a total stupor; I am still aware of the outside world, but my attention gradually pushes the outside world into the background as I become involved in the trance. It is similar to channeling or drawing down, in that I am seeking to communicate with another being. But rather than opening my own consciousness to allow someone else in, I send my consciousness out to meet other beings on their own turf. Also, these tranceworkings are not used to visit just any entity I run across; I plan ahead of time which goddess I am going to try to reach and research her in advance, attempting to fill my mind with images of her before I begin the trance. I also usually perform a brief ritual and invocation to my chosen deity to guide my trance journey to the desired destination.

In these workings I definitely send some part of my consciousness out "somewhere," but it is not the kind of astral travel in which an etheric body is separated from the physical one. The trances at this initial phase are not meant specifically for healing or divination but rather are merely an attempt to interact with a particular goddess and acquire information about her for future rituals or magical workings. However, I have often received healing or advice as a by-product of these journeys. The practices of pathworking or guided meditation are most similar to what I have been doing.

The point of all this discussion on tranceworking is to explore the many types of methods that have been used by Pagans and occultists over the years and to show that the term may mean many different things. I want to be clear about what sorts of trances I will be referring to in the following chapters. I also want to give people an idea of what kind of experience they might have if they try out any of my suggestions and what types of sensations to expect. Once you know what sort of trance state you're aiming for, the next step is to learn how to achieve it.

4

How to Do Trancework

Because tranceworking is so similar to self-hypnosis, many of the same induction methods can be used. Classical occult texts on astral projection are another source of hints on what conditions might be helpful in achieving a trance state. The best method is to carefully prepare and record your own experiences, noting things like weather conditions, outside noise, your physical state, and the events of the day, especially those immediately preceding the trance. Write down the details of your own induction, including what methods you used and your reaction to them. When you review these notes later on, you will begin to discern patterns that will help you figure out which methods work best for you.

Many people find that certain weather conditions affect their trance. In general, weather that is dry, clear, calm, and mild (say, in the middle to high 70s) provides optimal trance conditions; weather that is hot, muggy, damp, or stormy inhibits trances. Fortunately, thanks to modern technology, we can artificially create our own weather right inside our homes. An air conditioner is a great boon for eliminating both heat and mugginess. Even if you tend to keep your house as cold as an icebox in the winter, you'll probably want to turn up the heater just before attempting a trance, especially since the body tends to get colder than usual during a trance session. Lightning and thunder are generally disruptive to a trance, and there's not much you can do about that except wait it out or pick another night.

The time of day can affect a trance as well. It usually seems easier to achieve a trance state at night, perhaps because there are fewer outer disturbances then. Some occultists believe that the night also contains fewer psychic disturbances, since most other people are asleep. Various phases and astrological signs of the sun and moon also might affect your trances. If you record such details over a period of time, you'll soon get an idea of which conditions are best for you. I personally find it harder to get good results during a waning moon.

Your own personal condition can greatly affect your trance results; in fact, I find that this is the most important factor affecting the trance. First of all, it is best to be in good physical health and in fairly good shape. You shouldn't be too tired or sleepy, and you should be moderately well fed, although it's wise not to eat too close to the time you trance (allow an hour or so, as you do with swimming). Avoid alcohol or any kind of drug beforehand, particularly depressive drugs. However, I have found that sometimes a small dose of caffeine—say, a cup of tea—can be helpful shortly before a trance, particularly if I'm tired (not too close, though, or you'll wind up having to go to the bathroom in the middle of everything).

Besides your physical condition, your emotional and mental state can also affect your success in trancing. Strive to be fairly serene emotionally, in a state of assurance, confidence, and harmony. If you have some pressing or disturbing matter on your mind, or even if some trivial incident fires you up emotionally shortly before a trance, those feelings will start to intrude on your concentration once you begin your journey. Likewise, if you become mentally stimulated shortly before a trance, you will find it much harder to quiet your thoughts and your inner dialogue when you start to go under.

PREPARING FOR A TRANCE

Therefore, it's best to spend a little time before the actual trance preparing yourself. Try to pick a day when you will be rested and not too stressed; eat a light and healthy supper early in the evening, maybe along with a cup of tea. You might bathe or shower beforehand, or just wash your face, brush your teeth, and comb your hair. Then try to sit quietly for a quarter of an hour or so, perhaps listening to soothing music. Avoid watching TV, reading, or chatting with others, even about light or trivial matters; those thoughts will stick in your mind and interfere with your concentration once you try to trance.

If you have any physical problems—aches and pains in your lower back, a bad knee, or the like—take steps to ease the discomfort before you actually start the trance; it's very disruptive to have to interrupt your induction process to do backstretching exercises before you can go on. Try doing any standard relaxation exercise and you'll soon feel where your troublesome areas are. For some reason, the minute you start to quiet your mind, your body feels obliged to speak up about its various problems.

Different cultures throughout the world and throughout history have employed a variety of aids to trance and magic: various drugs, sleep deprivation, sensory deprivation or sensory overload, and even physical suffering, to name a few.[1] For the level of tranceworking I am talking about here, I don't think any of these are necessary or advisable. Most of the time drugs, fatigue, stimulation, and pain interfere with the ability to trance. What you want is to take care of the needs of your body and mind as completely as possible so that nothing will interfere with your concentration.

HELPFUL AIDS TO TRANCEWORKING

Some other traditional aids to tranceworking that are more helpful are various forms of music and dancing, particularly very rhythmic, monotonous music. Shamans of many cultures have long used drums and dancing as aids to getting into and staying in trance, though there is little evidence that drumming was a traditional trance method among Norse seið-workers. The one hint that such an instrument was used is found in a passage from the Lokasenna (24), where Loki taunts Odin with "beating on a *vet* like a völva." It's not clear what a *vet* was, but it seems to have been some sort of musical instrument that could be struck or tapped. It could also have been some other sort of surface, like the lid of a container of some sort, for no drums have yet been excavated from Norse archaeological digs.[2] Ritual chanting, which was used by the old Norse wisewomen, among others, can also be useful, as can soft, barely audible music or a spoken phrase repeated over and over, like a mantra. Incense can also be a powerful trigger; I have always used it in my trance rituals and now I find that just a whiff of certain incenses can put me into the beginning stages of trance.

This is another area where you need to experiment to see what helps you and what doesn't. Unlike religious rituals or magic, where you might want to include only those things that fit the tradition with which you're working, trance journeys are so personal and so difficult to accomplish that just about anything safe and legal that helps you go into trance is fair game. Drumming was not a traditional trance method among Norse seið-workers, for example, but if you're following a Norse path and you find that drumming helps you achieve a trance state, you might as well try it.

You will want to do the actual trance in a room with a comfortable temperature, perhaps a tad warmer than you'd usually keep it, because tranceworking tends to make the body cold. Your setting should be dimly lit, fairly quiet, and safe from interruption or intrusion. Because you are going to withdraw your attention from the outside world, you will not be able to protect yourself as you normally would. Therefore, unless you have a trusted companion to keep watch for you, you should probably avoid doing a trance outdoors in a public park or campground, or in any other location where you will not be private and secure.

A RITUAL BEFORE THE TRANCEWORKING

In addition to being physically safe, you also want to make sure you are psychically safe. Once you are ready to begin the trance, you should first set up a ritual space. This can be a very simple or a very elaborate procedure, but you should do some kind of beginning ritual to give yourself a safe place in which to open yourself psychically; otherwise, you run the risk of letting in undesirable forces while your soul is journeying and your physical body is left unattended and vulnerable. A very simple type of opening ritual from the Norse tradition is to light a candle, signifying the beginning of the ritual, and then do a form of hammer-hallowing. A sample opening ritual might go as follows:

- Chant *Ansuz—Laguz—Uruz* and light a single candle to begin the ceremony. These are the names of three runes whose initials together spell *alu* ("ale"). Together they form an old rune charm for general vitality, magical force, and inspiration.
- Sit before the candle and relax, composing yourself and centering your energies and will on the ritual. As you do this, chant *Woden—Wili—We* three times. These are the names of Odin and his two brothers, often thought to be aspects of Odin, in their roles as shapers of the universe. The names can be roughly translated as "divine inspiration," "will," and "holy space." They are used here to call upon Odin as the god of magic and inspiration, since you are about to perform a magical ritual. They also symbolize the fact that you are about to shape your own private universe, as these three god-forces shaped the greater universe.
- Stand and face the North. With your ritual knife or sword, wand, hammer, or the first two fingers of your right hand (or any other magical tool suitable for hallowing the rite at hand), draw a hammer shape before you. Start at a point overhead and draw the vertical bar toward the ground, stopping at roughly the same level as your solar plexus. Then begin the horizontal bar at a point to your left and continue across to the right (see fig. 4.1).

   The hammer is used as a symbol of Thor, the guardian of the homes of the gods and goddesses and of Midgard, our world. Thor's hammer protects the worlds of order from the forces of chaos. It is used here to protect the boundaries of your sacred space from unwanted and chaotic influences.

   As you draw the hammer, say or chant: "Hammer in the

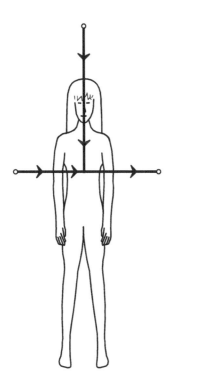
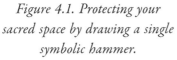

Figure 4.1. Protecting your sacred space by drawing a single symbolic hammer.

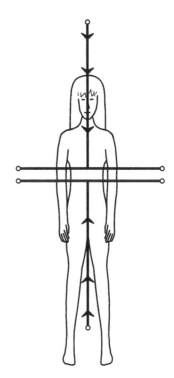

Figure 4.2. Protecting your sacred space by drawing a double symbolic hammer.

North, hold this place from ill, hallow this place for good."

- Repeat this process in the East, South, and West. You might also draw a hammer above and below you, visualizing a kind of globe of protection around you. I prefer to draw the hammers above and below in a vertical manner, so that the shaft of the hammer is coming straight down toward the head or up toward the torso, and the head of the hammer extends horizontally toward either side (see fig. 4.2).

This is just one simple version of a common ritual done by some Germanic Pagans. You can substitute any similar ritual to set apart and protect a magical or ritual circle. I would recommend using those symbols and ceremonies with which you are most familiar and which make you feel most secure and comfortable. Again, this is not a public ritual, but a very private one, in anticipation of your tranceworking. This type of practice is hard enough to achieve, so anything you can do to make yourself more secure should be done. If you feel you need a very elaborate circle-casting, use whatever is necessary to achieve a safe sacred space for you. Whatever you use, be sure to perform some sort of rite to set apart a ritual space before you begin the trance.

A CALL OR INVOCATION

The next thing you should do is to recite a call or invocation to the god or goddess you intend to visit on your trance. This can be an elaborate, poetic invocation you've already written out or a simple, impromptu one you make up on the spot. The kind of call you use depends on your skills as a poet and writer, how much information you have on the deity, and the nature or style of the god or goddess you are addressing. For example, Odin is the god of poetry; you probably want something pretty snappy for him. On the other hand, Frigg, his wife, is a mother goddess involved with the family, the home, and practical skills and crafts, so with her you might be able to get away with something more simple and homespun. A simple invocation is better than an elaborate but poorly done one, so if you're not especially good at wordcraft, don't feel you have to concoct something too elaborate for you to execute well.

The invocation serves several purposes. By reiterating the qualities and aspects of the deity, you are reminding yourself of what that god or goddess is like and setting the scene for your imaginative mind to build upon. You are also shaping the direction of your trance, ensuring that you will journey to the destination you intend to reach, rather than wandering off just anywhere on the astral plane.

Once you have defined both your sacred space and the purpose of your ritual, you're ready to start the trance. In hypnosis the steps of creating a trancelike or hypnotic state are called an induction (from the word *induce*). This is a process geared toward focusing and enhancing the concentration and imagination until an altered state of consciousness is reached. The three basic elements of induction are the reduction of sensory reception, the restriction of movement, and the guiding and directing of the attention. By these steps the attention is shifted from the outside world to the inside, and as the conscious mind relaxes, the inner thoughts can arise.

INDUCING A STATE OF RELAXATION

The first step in a trance, therefore, is to focus the attention on one's breathing and inner sensations and away from one's external surroundings, and to achieve a state of relaxation. Sit or lie in a comfortable position so that you are not cramped or uncomfortable in any way. Wear clothing that will not restrict or bind you, especially in the area around the midsection. Since doing a tranceworking tends to make you cold, you should wear warm clothing and perhaps lie on or cover up with blankets or quilts. If you are a purist who uses only ritual garb, then by all means consecrate yourself some ritual socks and sweaters, but cover up with something. If you have any physical problems, like a knee that needs propping up with a pillow, do whatever you need to achieve freedom from physical discomfort and distraction.

As you rest in your comfortable position, close your eyes and breathe deeply in a regular rhythm, but avoid holding your breath, either in or out, for any length of time. Just let yourself breathe naturally and easily. Next relax your body. Empty yourself of tension and distracting thoughts and think of sleep, drowsiness, ease. Many people like to go through the entire body, relaxing it part by part, starting at either the feet or the head, a practice known as progressive relaxation. This can be effective if you're very tense, but it is also very time-consuming and so boring that it can put you to sleep before you begin your trance. I used to use this method, as I have a tendency to be very tense physically. I also had a hard time achieving a trance state and felt that I could use all the help I could get. However, I found that this method took so much time and effort that I often didn't have enough energy to do much trancing afterward. I would recommend that you try progressive relaxation as you are beginning to experiment with tranceworking to get an idea of the kind of state you are trying to achieve and to give your body an opportunity to learn how to relax. Then, if you later feel the process takes away from your trance, you can pare it down to a brief relaxation exercise.

FOCUSING YOUR ATTENTION

Once you are relaxed, your next step is to begin to restrict and guide your attention. There are many ways to do this; your best bet is to sample them all and choose the ones that are most effective and comfortable for you. What they all have in common is that they restrict your thoughts and senses to the point where your conscious mind gets so bored that it finally turns off and gives your inner thoughts the opportunity to manifest themselves. In a nutshell, boredom induces trance. In fact, the time-honored practice of daydreaming when bored out of one's senses is actually a type of trance.

The traditional movie hypnotist, with his evil eye or swinging watch, exemplifies a fairly standard practice: eye fixation. Staring at one single object for a long enough period of time has the effect of inducing a trance state; however, this doesn't require a magic ruby ring or amulet—any object will do, especially bright ones. Some examples include a human eye (when someone else is guiding your trance or hypnosis), a picture on the wall, a flower, a candle flame, any bright object like a piece of jewelry or a watch, a bowl of water or dark liquid, a crystal, a flashlight, a mirror, the tip of someone's finger or the tip of a fountain pen, a symbol painted on a card (like a tarot card, a rune, or a kabbalistic symbol), or even cracks on the ceiling.

Another popular method is that of inducing eyestrain by rolling the eyes or looking upward. Apparently, turning the gaze upward as if looking at an object about forty-five degrees above the head is supposed to be effective in inducing trance. I have a magician friend who swears by it, but I could never get it to work and found it uncomfortable, distracting, and annoying. In this, as in all aspects of tranceworking, you should be guided by your own personal choice and what works best for you.

This stage of trance is where drumming, chanting, rhythmic dancing, or incense fit in. These serve the same purpose for the ears, nose, and body as gazing at a single object does for the eyes: you listen to a single repetitive pattern over and over, or make the same movement again and again, or fill your nostrils with a single smell, until your mind gets tired and bored and shuts off your inner dialogue. In fact, lying perfectly still with your eyes closed while you breathe rhythmically not only helps to relax you, it also serves the double purpose of restricting your sensory input.

Once you begin to enter a state of mild trance, which will feel no more mysterious than lying in bed and getting drowsy before sleep, you can conjure various imagery to increase your relaxation and further turn your attention inward. Since nothing amusing is going on outside anymore, the mind decides it might as well entertain itself. Again, there are many, many images and methods, and you can pick and choose among them. For some people, only a few relaxation exercises and images will send them right out; for others, like me, it takes a repeated layering of images and techniques to achieve a trance state. Fortunately, there are so many different methods that you can surely find enough to eventually enable you to enter a trance.

Some of the more common images include counting backward (even medical anesthetists use this) or reciting the alphabet; repeating a simple phrase, such as "deeper and deeper, deeper and deeper" or the ever-popular "You are getting sleepy . . . very sleepy . . ."; imagining yourself walking down a set of stairs (or, for the more technologically minded, riding down an escalator or elevator), perhaps while also counting backward; imagining yourself floating on water, or up in the air, or down through the air; imagining yourself riding a bike or a horse; imagining a succession of colors, usually starting at one end of the spectrum— say, red—and ending at the other, with violet; and visualizing any other images of moving either up or down.

DEEPENING YOUR TRANCE

As you deepen your trance, you can combine these images with more imaginative and individualized visions taken from your personal life or religious mythology: rippling water; rain on a windowpane; a sunset; waving grass; a rainbow; a favorite place, real or imagined; or mythological places or scenes. You can eventually create a whole special imaginary place where you can go each time you enter trance before venturing out into the other worlds, a place that comforts and appeals to you and one that can grow and develop each time you do trance or meditation work. This place should be one in which you can be alone and one that makes you feel good and positive, where you feel safe to be totally receptive and responsive. Having a safe and happy place inside you can be useful on other occasions, such as taking a brief meditative rest in your special spot during the breaks between college entrance exams or on a plane; I assure you it can be more restful and reinvigorating than a nap or a quick martini.

Some of the feelings and sensations you might experience when entering a trance state include a sense of deep relaxation, peace, and increased receptivity. You may have a sense of limpness, stiffness, numbness, cramps, or tingling in your arms and legs. Some people feel great bodily heaviness, while others have the sensation of lightness or floating. You generally will experience a sense of detachment, feeling out of touch with an environment that seems very distant and disinclined to make any effort to do anything whatsoever except lie there and experience this trance state.

I'll pause a moment here to point out some other aspects of the trance state. You might have already noticed from reading the above descriptions that a person entering trance or hypnosis is extremely vulnerable and receptive. As the outer world recedes and diminishes in importance, the inner world expands and becomes more influential. If you are doing a guided meditation with a hypnotist or a trance leader, her words and images will occupy a much more prominent place in your inner world than they would if you were fully conscious. In the hands of a responsible and trustworthy therapist or magical colleague, this can be very helpful and beneficial; her images can help you better understand your inner world or more successfully journey to the other realms you seek.

However, if the person guiding your meditation is clumsy, unethical, or neurotic, her images can unduly influence and disturb you. Keep in mind that if, while you were in a trance, someone told you to go out and shoot someone, you certainly would not go right off and do that. But you are very open to suggestion while in a trance state, and you can pick up the germ of an idea from someone that can trouble you for a long time to come if that image is a negative or disturbing one.

The point of all this is to be careful with whom you do guided meditations. Many times at festivals, psychic fairs, or other such events, a complete stranger will offer to do guided meditations for other people. While most of these people are very responsible, you don't necessarily know what they're going to say while you're in a trance. I participated in at least one such guided meditation (the purpose of which was to encounter some aspect of the goddess) where the leader began injecting bits of her own political philosophy once the trance was under way—things that had nothing whatsoever to do with the matter at hand. I don't even think this leader was deliberately doing this, but the effect was very disturbing. That was one time I felt it was to my advantage that I was difficult to put into a trance, since I wasn't fully "under" when these asides started cropping up.

Therefore, I would recommend being a bit cautious about throwing yourself open to just anyone. Try to talk to the person leading the trance to see what she is like, or perhaps talk to others who have done a tranceworking with that leader before. If you are dealing with someone you already know and trust, that's fine. Also, if you use any of those taped guided meditations, I would advise first listening to the whole thing while you're fully conscious, preferably while you're walking around a room or doing something equally trance-inhibiting, to make sure that you want to experience it while in a receptive state.

EMERGING FROM THE TRANCE STATE

Whatever steps you use to induce the trance, you should repeat each one in reverse order when you're ready to come out of it: walk up the stairs if you initially walked down them, count forward instead of backward, float back up if you floated down. Be sure that you complete the return journey and don't just sit up or drift into sleep, as the former will tend to shock your system a bit while the latter can lead to eventual confusion between the worlds that you visit in trance and your own physical, mundane world. The return, while it should mirror the departure, can be much faster and more cursory, because, contrary to the fears of some, it's usually extremely easy to come out of trance; the hard part is getting into one in the first place. The very last thing you should do is experience the sensation of yourself being once more in your physical body, lying or sitting there on the floor or bed and breathing rhythmically. Then you can open your eyes and sit up. You should generally feel relaxed and refreshed, often filled with a sense of great well-being. If nothing else in the trance worked, the mere fact that your conscious mind was shut off for a while is usually an extremely refreshing experience.

You will also want to end your ritual and leave your sacred space. You should do this as quickly as possible so that you can record the results of your tranceworking while they're still fresh in your mind. Also, it's best to get out of the ritual space and into the mundane world as soon as possible to ensure that you are fully awake and alert. If you used incense or drumming or some other aid, you should stop it soon after you sit up from the trance to help you come fully awake. It's also a good idea to make a toast and libation to whichever deities or beings you were visiting, thanking them for any gifts or advice, or at the least for the opportunity to get to see something of them. A sample closing might go like this:

- Make a toast or libation to any beings or deities you encountered.
- Stand and sprinkle a little bit of the libation in the direction of the North, using either your fingers, a wand, or a small tree twig (evergreen is traditional in Norse ritual and magic), saying, "Hail to the North!"
- Repeat the above process in the East, South, and West. End up

facing north again, and sprinkle your altar, too, for good measure. Drink or pour out the rest of the libation.

- Repeat the chant *Woden—Wili—We* three times.
- Repeat the chant *Ansuz—Laguz—Uruz,* and blow out the candle.

Once your ritual is over, immediately write down what you remember about your trance experience. Trances, like dreams, must be written down as soon as possible or you will forget most of what happened. Do not stop and do anything else if you can at all avoid it, or that very rich and detailed experience you just had will soon fade to a few vague images. You may want to jot down a rough sketch of what happened, including the more significant and impressive images you saw while you were trancing, then wait and flesh it out more fully later on. But write something, or you'll forget—I promise you.

When you're done writing down your experience, get right up and turn on some lights. Put on the television or some music—loud, attention-getting stuff, none of this soothing mood music. Walk around, dance, talk with other people if there are any there, or telephone a friend. Many people feel cold and hungry when they come out of trance. Eating and drinking not only satisfies your physical need, it is an excellent way of coming out of trance. Eating nice, rich, solid things is best: meat is very good, if you eat it, and also chocolate or any nice type of stew or soup. I personally find that a shot of liquor works very well in bringing me to full wakefulness, but if you can't or won't drink alcohol, this is certainly not necessary. The main thing you want to accomplish is to redirect your attention from the inner to the outer world.

5

A Visit to Fensalir

An Example of Trancework

What follows is an example of one of my trances—the induction, the journey itself, and the return. This is not intended to be taken as the only way, or even the best way, to enter a trance; it just represents one method that happens to work for me. I have developed this pattern over several years by trial and error, trying out various methods as I learned about them and discarding those that didn't work for me. Anyone who decides to attempt tranceworking should sample the different methods and include in her repertoire those that seem best for her, as well as any other symbols and actions that are personally meaningful.

I am lying in my bed in my girlhood bedroom in my parents' house. I relax my body and breathe regularly and rhythmically, in and out, and feel myself in my body in that bed, feel the mattress and sheets underneath me, feel the familiar furniture around me in the background.

When I am fairly relaxed and fully conscious of being in that room, I open my eyes and rise, walk toward my closet, slide open the door, and reach down and pull up the trapdoor in the floor of the closet. I turn and climb down the five ladderlike steps leading into the crawl space beneath the house and begin to crawl through the darkness on my hands and knees. Finally, I come to a soft, white feather bed covered with a fine white muslin sheet. I lie down on the bed on my back and pull the sheet up over my face.

I begin to breathe regularly, in and out, in and out, and soon begin to feel myself floating slowly and gently downward, rocking slightly to and fro, and my bed, my sheet, my body, and the air all around me are light and clean and white, like laundry just brought in from hanging in the sunlight. And as I breathe in and out, I change the color of my bed, my sheet, and my body to red, the color of a ripe apple, and the air all around me is also red as I float farther down and down. And as I breathe in and out, I change the color of my bed, my sheet, and my body to orange, the color of a ripe orange, and the air all around me is also orange as I float farther down and down. And as I breathe in and out, I change the color of my bed, my sheet, and my body to yellow, the color of a lemon, and the air all around me is also yellow as I float farther down and down. And as I breathe in and out, I change the color of my bed, my sheet, and my body to green, the color of new grass, and the air all around me is also green as I float farther down and down. And as I breathe in and out, I change the color of my bed, my sheet, and my body to blue, the color of the sky on a clear summer day, and the air all around me is also blue as I float farther down and down. And as I breathe in and out, I change the color of my bed, my sheet, and my body to indigo, the color of a piece of lapus lazuli, and the air all around me is also indigo as I float farther down and down. And as I breathe in and out, I change the color of my bed, my sheet, and my body to violet, the color of grape juice, and the air all around me is also violet as I float farther down and down.

And now I softly and gently feel myself reaching the ground again, and the bed, the sheet, my body, and the air all around me are now a soft, warm, enveloping black. I pull the sheet off my face, sit, and rise up from my feather bed, walking slowly in the dimness. I soon see a flight of stone stairs with a smooth wooden bannister, winding clockwise and downward. I begin to walk down these stairs, holding on to the rail and breathing regularly in and out, counting backward one number at each step, beginning with ten and ending with one.

When I reach the bottom I find myself in a large hallway lit with many candles, which are set in sconces along the walls. There are many doors and passageways branching off in all directions. I know where some of these lead, but others are strange to me. I walk along until I reach the door I'm seeking. It is a small wooden door with a rounded top, the kind found in fairy-tale cottages. I open it and walk through the doorway. I walk along a short, dim passage and down several short steps to arrive at a subterranean stream that runs through an underground passage. Here there is a dock to which is tied a small wooden rowboat.

I untie the ropes holding the boat to the dock, lie down inside the craft, and soon begin to float, feetfirst, through the dark underground tunnel carved through walls of rock. I travel gradually upward and to the right. Eventually I emerge from the tunnel, floating on an open stream. As I travel on, I pass a changing landscape of lovely meadows and fields and forests. My boat finally drifts to the bank lying to my left and stops. I rise and get out of the boat.

Here I find Sleipnir, the eight-legged horse of Odin the Allfather, saddled and waiting for me. He can travel through all the Nine Worlds and has come to guide me on my journey to Asgard. He is a dappled gray, the color of smoke, and he looks somewhat whimsical with so many legs, and very friendly and gentle. I climb onto his back with no difficulty and we gallop away together. As I ride, the sound of Sleipnir's eight hooves sound like drumbeats. We travel over fields and forests and all the lands of the earth, journeying northward. We then pass over raging rivers into Jotunheim, the land of etins, or giants. Here we travel through a dense and dark forest and then over endless barren plains.

We finally reach the flaming colors of Bifrost, the rainbow bridge, and Sleipnir gallops across it without hesitation. Heimdall the Watcher hails me silently from his home in the distance. Passing over the bridge, Sleipnir continues at a more moderate pace, and I see the homes of Asgard, many fine houses surrounded by gardens, courtyards, and fields. Ahead in the distance I see the broad halls of Valhalla, recognizable by its roof of gleaming golden shields and its many wide doors.

Sleipnir halts in front of one of the entrances, and I dismount and enter the hall, where I see all the heroes feasting, laughing, singing, and generally carousing and enjoying themselves. Up on the dais in the high-seat I see Odin with his ravens perched on the back of his chair, or on his shoulders, and his wolves lying at his feet. He surveys the hall with pride and sober content but is not making much of a racket himself. There are servants, Valkyries, and heroes all over the place, swarming to and fro on various business.

Standing by a side door I see a woman and know that she is Frigg, Odin's wife and the mistress of Asgard. The realization comes to me that she has *planned much of the food and entertainment I have just witnessed. She beckons me to come with her. I follow her outside and across a courtyard or garden in which there are flowers, various trees, and a fountain with splashing water. Soon we arrive at a square-shaped, low-roofed stone house; this is Fensalir, Frigg's home. The grounds surrounding this dwelling are very quiet after the noise of Valhalla. There is an air of peace, order, and rightness.*

We enter by a side or back door, and I see that the inside of the building is made of cool stone and marble and looks much larger than the outside led me to believe. There is a stone pool in the center of the spacious hall and an array of seats, nooks, and alcoves in which women sit working on various projects or talking quietly. From this central hall there are many doors and hallways leading out to other parts of Fensalir, where these women live with Frigg. They are her women, her attendants, but it is more like a women's college.

Frigg sits in a large, comfortable chair in one area of the room and talks to me. She is of medium stature, with light-brown hair done up in an intricate braided coronet, and she wears blue-gray and white clothing that is both simple and utterly elegant. Her tiny touches of jewelry, embroidery, and other ornamentation are exquisite and subtle. Her eyes are blue-gray and deep-set, very mild and kind, and yet piercing. Her face has strong lines, high cheekbones, and a strong chin. She has a ring of golden keys at her waist and wears assorted small knives, needles, and other domestic implements, which hang from chains from various brooches on her garments.

Around her chair are pieces of needlework, spinning, papers and books, baskets, and all sorts of handiwork and knickknacks. The room is very clean and neat. Nevertheless, it is filled with bits of projects and pieces of partly finished work lying here and there, left by Frigg or her attendants, for they are always doing something here. There is a fireplace or hearth with a gentle fire in it and some tea or soup or something cooking over it in a covered kettle. Frigg washes my hands and face with some water and combs my hair while talking or singing to me, or sometimes just being quiet. I sit at her feet and lean my head against her lap. Her presence is very comforting and loving, very motherly. Finally, she sees me out the door and points me to where Sleipnir waits near an entrance to the garden; I do not reenter Valhalla. As I ride away, Frigg waves from her doorway.

I return the way I came, riding on Sleipnir over the wilds of Jotunheim and the fields of Midgard, floating in my boat back to the rocky passage that leads underground, walking back through the halls and back up the stone stairs to where my feather bed lies. I lie on it again, cover myself with the black sheet, and float rather quickly, and yet gently, up through the violet air, and the indigo air, and the blue air, and the green air, and the yellow air, and the orange air, and the red air until I am lying once more under a white sheet. I leave the bed and crawl back underneath the house until I arrive at the trapdoor, and climb the stairs, close the trapdoor, slide the closet door shut, cross the room, and lie back down in my bed. I breathe regularly, in and out, and feel my body in the bed in my parents' home. But as I breathe I begin to feel my body lying on the floor and hear the sounds in the home I live in now, and smell the smells in that home, and feel myself breathing in my body, now, today, and when I feel myself to be fully back, I open my eyes and sit up.

6

Challenges of Tranceworking

Tranceworking and astral travel are considered to be dangerous by some, unless done with proper training and supervision. While I do not think tranceworking is necessarily dangerous, there are a number of cautions and safeguards that should be taken into consideration.

Tranceworking is an activity that is best attempted after one has had some experience with other forms of ritual and magic. You should at least be competent in some sort of basic circle-casting ritual and should always do your trances within the protection of a sacred space. It is also helpful to have practiced visualization exercises, since trances are dependent on one's powers of visualization and imagination. Dreams are very similar to trances; thus any kind of dreamwork is good practice, particularly lucid dreaming, where you are aware that you are dreaming and can guide the action of the dream but still remain in the dream state. The ability to control and shape your dreams is also useful when you're on a trance journey. Above all, you should have enough experience to feel fairly confident and fearless about your journeys.

As I've said before, you should always create a ritual space before attempting a trance, and close that space afterward. It is also wise to pick a specific destination, at least until you are very, very good at trance journeys. Having a particular god or goddess in mind when you set out ensures that you will be journeying into a safe space, under the protection of a deity. I often find that the goddess I am trying to contact is expecting me, as if I'd made an appointment with her when I decided to do the trance. You should also put some thought into which deities you visit. When starting out, it's best to pick gods and goddesses who are highly accessible, friendly, and beneficent. Sometimes the more ambiguous deities can be a little disturbing or hard to contact, and you want to ensure your success as much as possible on your early journeys.

AVOIDING PITFALLS

You might want to call in a magical helper of some sort to accompany you on your initial expeditions. As you will see from my own trance descriptions, I was always met by Sleipnir, the god Odin's horse, which could travel through the various worlds. Having a trusted guide greatly increases your confidence on your journeys and makes the initial stages more interesting. Later, after you gain more experience, you can try journeying alone, although it often seems harder to reach your desired destination that way. You can take the shape of an animal or envision an ideal trance self for these journeys. After all, this is an imaginary body, so you can fulfill your deepest fantasies. I personally always see myself as taller and stronger, with the beautiful reddish hair and flawless complexion I ought to have had. When I began tranceworking my trance self was older than my actual age, but she is now somewhat younger, although I'm afraid she's not the one who has changed.

If you are walking down a path in your journeys, you should not step off it for any reason. If you wander into a landscape or region that makes you feel at all uneasy or that looks ugly or threatening, just turn around and go right back; you can always start again, or try it some other night. The point of these trances is to make yourself feel empowered and glad, not to scare yourself silly. Often, if you are going to visit a particular god or goddess, that deity will appear and help you if you get hung up somewhere. Sometimes you will meet the deity on your way to her abode and wind up traveling with her to some other location altogether. Be aware that your imagination can shape this trance world, just as it does in a lucid dream. You can imagine yourself able to fly, jump over forests, fight magnificently, or turn into an animal. Once, when I felt scared and wanted to return very quickly, I conjured up an image of a very fine outboard motor that ran on mead to speed my little boat.

I sometimes experience various physical sensations while in a trance, usually when I've had enough and am ready to come back. I get muddled and vague and have trouble communicating or listening. I feel the trance world starting to fade, and sometimes my own body starts getting a bit transparent. Usually the deities I am with will notice this first and comment on it; very often they will tell me point-blank to go home and come back again later. I often experience slight cramping in the calves of my legs and a sense of restlessness and discomfort when I have been in trance too long; it's as if the body can only do this for a certain period of time. When you start feeling uncomfortable in the trance, simply say good-bye and head back as swiftly as possible.

After my initial problems with achieving the trance state, I became convinced that my objective was to try to achieve the best, deepest trance state possible. However, in practice I have found that deeper is not necessarily better. If I go into too deep a trance, I find that my body becomes too heavy and I can't move in the trance world; I can't maneuver my body, act, or communicate. On the other hand, if the trance is too shallow, I find I am not free enough to interact with the beings of the trance world; I'm unable to perceive it fully. With practice you will learn just how deep a trance you function in best; this will even vary from time to time, depending on how tired you are and how good your concentration is. That's why I find it useful to have a whole list of induction methods. On a bad night I go through one after the other until I achieve the level of trance I desire; on other nights I only use one or two steps, then set out on my journey.

Sometimes your trance starts out very well, then you get "fuzzy" and bogged down in the middle of it; at other times you feel in the beginning that you aren't achieving a very good trance at all, but it winds up being highly successful. I would advise always starting your journey, even if you feel your trance to be poor in the initial stages, just to see what happens. Even if you can't make much headway, at least you'll have some data to add to your lists of what works and what doesn't. An exception to this would be if you felt a definite sense of unease or fear; in that case, return immediately and try it another night.

When contacting your god or goddess, you will sometmes get only vague, scattered images and symbols and a few cryptic phrases. At other times you will experience an entire conversation, sometimes even a full-blown adventure, and the deity will give you all sorts of advice and suggestions. You will find that some deities are easier to contact than others. Sometimes this depends on the god or goddess—some beings are just friendlier and easier to understand than others. Other times it depends on you, on your own nature and personality. Just as you get along with some people better than others, so you will have more in common with some gods and goddesses than with others, and those deities most similar to your personality and interests tend to be easier to reach. Sometimes it takes several separate journeys to the same deity before you feel you've made real contact. I would suggest you make at least two or three attempts, because your failure might be due to the weather or your being tired rather than on your relationship with that being.

CURB YOUR ENTHUSIASM

Although tranceworking can be such an enjoyable and enriching experience that you want to return again and again, I would advise against doing trances too often. For one thing, doing a tranceworking more than, say, twice a month seems to inhibit the effectiveness of the workings, and you wind up feeling as if it's a chore rather than a pleasure. Tranceworking requires a lot of preparation to do it right and it's a little tiring physically if you do it too often. It is also best to mull over what happened on the first trances for a while before filling your head with new images. You don't want to start spending all your time in "fairyland" lest you become lost to your own world, as did some of the mortals in folk legends. If you do a tranceworking to a particular god or goddess and are not satisfied with your results, you might try a second one a week or two later. If you still don't have much success, let it wait a while and return to that deity after some time has passed.

Again, always complete the journey once you've started out, even if the return is faster and less detailed than the going in, and always end by feeling yourself in your real physical body again. Be sure to record your experiences as soon after the trance as possible. Attend to your physical needs after the trance, keep warm and eat something, and let yourself reexperience this world.

Above all, tranceworking should be an enjoyable experience, not a chore or a fearsome proposition. Just as some rituals attempt to bring the presence of the gods into our physical world, tranceworking gives you the chance to be present in the world of the gods. It is your opportunity to get to know better the gods and goddesses with whom you work and to develop a sense of understanding and friendship with them. You can learn little details about your deities that will fill out and enrich the historical and mythological records. You may often receive very wise and helpful advice, occasionally about problems you didn't even know you had or hadn't thought to ask about. In fact, don't be surprised if your god or goddess starts to talk about the problem that's really bothering you instead of the one you thought you wanted to discuss.

KEEPING AN OPEN MIND

Tranceworking is not meant as a replacement for all the historical, literary, and archaeological evidence available to us, and you should certainly not fall into the trap of deciding that any pet whim you imagine in a trance is more valid than something written in a book. You should also not take offense if you meet someone whose trance experiences differ from your own, nor try to insist that your perceptions are right and hers are wrong. Remember that your own ideas and experiences will color your trances and that not everything you see and hear is valid for anyone but yourself. However, tranceworking is a valuable addition to factual information, especially when dealing with figures for whom we have sparse information. Many of the things you learn in trances are valid, and you will often find other people who saw the same things as you did, or read something in a scholarly text that confirms what you saw or heard in a tranceworking.

Tranceworking, like ritual, allows you to build emotional links with your gods and goddesses and gives you access to the other worlds and the beings in them. Trances can enable you to learn things about the universe and about yourself. Most of all, they allow you to form bonds with your gods and your ancestors, links of love and loyalty that can bridge time in all directions.

PART TWO

Frigg and Her Women

*The Lore and Trance Methods
for Finding the Goddessess*

IT'S ALL VERY WELL TO STUDY the practice of tranceworking, but the only way to really understand it is to experience it. The next best way is to read accounts of the experiences of others to give you an idea of what you might expect.

My original intention in taking up tranceworking was not to experience the process for its own sake, although I must admit I usually find it very enjoyable and satisfying, but to gain insight and information and to grow closer to my gods and goddesses. To fully share what I've experienced, I want to show the whole process I followed, both the intellectual and the experiential.

I have therefore included descriptions of thirteen Norse deities, specifically Frigg and the twelve Asynjur, or Aesir goddesses, typically associated with her. These pieces are based on both research and interpretation and include narratives of what I experienced with these goddesses in trance and suggestions for ritual workings. I know some people dislike reading about how others have experienced a certain deity or symbol in meditation or trance because they feel it will influence their own workings, so the trance sections are set in a different typeface. That way, these people can avoid reading them until they're ready.

I also want it to be very clear as to which information came from texts and sources that can be verified and which emerged from my personal experiences. The latter, of course, you can accept or not, whichever seems best to you. I have no delusions that the way I personally experience a goddess is the way she is or should be to everybody. Still, it's often fascinating to discover how many people will come up with similar images. Hopefully, someday, by working together, we will find enough common lore to enable us to reclaim our knowledge of these lost gods and goddesses.

FRIGG AND THE ASYNJUR

In dealing with Frigg, we must take into account the other goddesses listed among the Asynjur. Snorri Sturluson gives a brief account of the goddesses below in the Gylfaginning section of the *Prose Edda*. Many of these are so similar to Frigg that they seem to be mere aspects or hypostases of her, rather than separate goddesses; but whether forms of Frigg or individual deities, Frigg, as their queen, oversees them. Hence their qualities may be said to be hers as well, as a manager is responsible for the work of all those under her.

Saga lives in a large estate of her own called Sokkvabekk, or "Sinking Brook," which stands among cool waves. She and Odin are supposed to get together every day to drink out of golden cups and exchange stories.

Eir is said to be the best of doctors. She also shows up in the Svipdagsmál of the *Elder Edda* as one of the maidens who accompany Menglod, usually associated with Freyja, on the Lyfjaberg, a hill said to cure sick women who climb it.

Gefjon, designated a maiden by Snorri, receives those women who die unmarried. In the beginning of the *Prose Edda* there is a story about how she won a large piece of land from the Swedish King Gylfi by plowing it up with four oxen, which were in reality her four sons by a giant; this would indicate that she herself was not a virgin. Loki also accuses her of having had sex with a boy in return for a necklace (although Loki might say anything).

Fulla is also a maiden, pictured with loose hair fastened by a circlet. Her name suggests that she was a goddess of prosperity and plenty. In the "Second Merseburg Charm," an old German spell, she is called Frigg's sister and appears with her as a healer. She keeps Frigg's casket of jewels and her footwear and is her special confidante and advisor.

Sjofn is greatly concerned with turning the thoughts of men and women to love. Affection or love-longing was called *sjafni,* after her name.

Lofn is reputed to be particularly gracious and kind to those who call on her. She can get the permission of Odin and Frigg for people to marry, even though it has been denied before, and this permission was called *lof* after her name, which is praised (*lofat*) among humans.

Var listens to the vows (*várar*) and contracts made between men and women and takes vengeance on those who break them.

Vor is wise and searching, and nothing can be hidden from her. Therefore, there was a saying that a woman became "aware" (*vör*) of what she came to know.

Syn guards the door of the hall and locks it against those who should not enter. She is also called on in legal assemblies for the defense by anyone who wants to deny an accusation; thus people used to say *syn* (denial) is made.

Hlin protects those whom Frigg especially favors; thus one who escaped danger was said to "lean" (*hleinir*). She is also mentioned in the Völuspá, where it says that when Odin goes to fight the wolf at Ragnarok (and subsequently is slain), another hurt would come to Hlin.

Snotra is said to be wise, gentle, and moderate, and thus a prudent man or woman was called *snotr.*

Gna is Frigg's messenger and travels through the different worlds on her errands. She rides a horse called Hofvarpnir, or "Hoof-Thrower," who can travel through air and water.

7

The Influence of the Queen of the Gods on Germanic Culture

Frigg was one of the more widely worshipped Germanic goddesses, appearing in Scandinavia, Britain, and on the Continent. Snorri names her the foremost of the Asynjur, a group of goddesses described as being equal in holiness and authority to the male Aesir (Gylfaginning, ch. 20). Nevertheless, very little is known about her worship, and until recently she has often been overshadowed by the better-known figure of Freyja.

Frigg is the wife of the Aesir's leader, Odin, and the mother of Balder the Beautiful, who was slain by his blind brother, Hod, through the machinations of the god Loki. Her name comes from an Indo-European root meaning "love" or "pleasure" and could be interpreted as "beloved," "lover," or "wife." She has a dwelling called Fensalir ("Hall of Mists," "Sea Halls," or "Marsh Halls"), which is described as "most grand" (Gylfaginning, ch. 35). The sixth day of our week, Friday, was named for her and was traditionally considered a good day for marriages.

There are some place names connected with Frigg in Sweden, particularly in Västergötland and Östergötland, where Frigg and Odin were especially revered.[1] There are even more traces on the Continent, particularly in southern Germany. Her name is also associated with a number of plant names and other natural objects. An herb known as *friggjargras* ("Frigg's grass") was used to make love potions and was also called *hionagras* ("marriage grass"). The Romans associated Frigg, as well as Freyja, with their goddess Venus, and the planet Venus has been called *friggjarstjarna* ("Frigg's star").[2]

In the Lokasenna (st. 26), Frigg is called *Fjörgyns mær* ("Fjörgynn's maiden"), which can mean either Fjörgynn's daughter or his mistress. Since Loki goes on to accuse Frigg of infidelity in the same stanza, "mistress" may be a likely interpretation. The giant Fjörgynn may form a divine pair with the giantess Fjörgyn, who is sometimes said to be the mother of Thor and who seems similar, if not identical, to the goddess Jord (ON Jörð, "earth"). Frigg is also often seen as an earth goddess, whereas Jord represents an earlier, more primal form of the earth. Frigg can be seen as the tilled, managed earth, fruitful and blessed, the earth that has become transformed by her alliance with humans.

As an earth goddess, Frigg has strong associations with water, as suggested by the name of her hall. Her German counterparts are worshipped at holy wells and streams and are often seen bathing or washing. Frigg scries in a magic mirror, a practice that also can be performed in a container of water, and her powers of divination are traditionally associated with the watery element in Western magical tradition.

Frigg can also be seen as representing the old Indo-European concept of a sky queen,[3] and in this aspect she controls the atmosphere, clouds, and wind. Whereas Odin is a deity of the high skies and stormy winds, Frigg is the air nearest the earth, the air that sustains the life on it. She owns a hawk plumage with which she can fly like a bird, soaring through the heavens. Her clothing is white, dark blue, or gray, representing the different aspects of both the clouds and the goddess. As mistress of Asgard, she is sometimes pictured wearing a golden girdle from which hangs a ring of keys, a symbol of the authority of the mistress of a household.

Frigg is very concerned with domestic affairs and crafts and thus was the special patron of the Norse housewife. An accomplished weaver and spinner (the clouds are said to be her handiwork), she is the goddess of all skills of housekeeping and husbandry. In Sweden the constellation we know as Orion's belt was called *Friggerock* ("Frigg's distaff" or "spindle"). Norwegians believed that if chains of knitting were cut through on Friday, the day holy to Frigg, the weaving would be unsuccessful.[4] Frigg is a goddess of practical, homely knowledge as Odin is a god of abstract, scholarly knowledge and magical lore.

A WISE COUNSELOR

One of Frigg's functions is ruling as queen of Heaven. She sits on the council of Aesir judges, as mentioned in the Skáldskaparmál of the *Prose Edda* (ch. 1), and she alone shares with Odin the throne of Hlidskjalf, from which they can look over all the Nine Worlds. Kveldulf Gundarsson, well-known author on Germanic Paganism and magic, emphasizes that the responsibilities of a Germanic noblewoman included acting as counselor to her husband and family and as peacekeeper and diplomat to her own household, her husband's followers, and visitors and foreign guests.[5] In fact, one of the kennings for women was *fridowebban* ("peace weavers").[6] In this role, Frigg seeks to uphold social and cultural order and stability, a good balance to her more innovative husband.

In the Vafþrudnismál (sts. 1–4) we can see an example of Frigg's role as counselor. At the beginning of the story Odin asks Frigg what she thinks of his visiting the giant Vafthrudnir to match wits with him. Frigg warns Odin of the danger involved in the venture, but because he definitely wants to go, she gives him her blessing, which seems to be a magical warding. In this brief conversation we see the respect Odin has for his wife's advice, the careful and wise counsel she gives, and Frigg's understanding of Odin's pride and need for knowledge, which spur him on to the adventure, despite the acknowledged danger.

As Odin's first and foremost wife, Frigg has precedence over his other mistresses or concubines (Skáldskaparmál, ch. 19). They include Jord, an earth giantess, mother of Thor; Rind, the reluctant mother of Vali, Balder's avenger; Grid, another giantess, mother of the silent god Vidar; and Gunnlod, from whom Odin won the mead of poetry and who is possibly the mother of Bragi, the god of skalds, or poets. However, one finds no myths showing Frigg in a jealous rage over these ladies, as the Greek Hera, for example, ranted over her husband Zeus's infidelities. Richard Wagner does present Frigg as a bit of a shrew in his operas, but there is no support for this anywhere in the Eddas. Frigg does not pursue Odin's other women or persecute their children. One presumes that she is concerned with more important matters and is secure enough in her position not to bother.

Frigg herself is sometimes accused of being unfaithful. Loki reproaches her for sleeping with Vili and Ve, the two brothers of Odin who helped him create the world (Lokasenna, st. 26). Of course, one can't always believe Loki. This accusation might allude to one of Odin's long absences, mentioned in the *Ynglinga saga* (ch. 3), when he left his brothers to rule Asgard and they allegedly shared his queen as well.

Saxo Grammaticus tells of a similar incident in the *Gesta Danorum* (book 1, ch. 7). Here Odin's absence is prompted by the infidelity of his wife Frigg, who bribes some workmen to strip down one of Odin's statues to make herself a necklace or ornament in return for her favors in bed. The kingdom in Saxo's version is taken over by a magician named Mithotyn. Finally, the real Odin returns, whereupon the false "Odin" flees and the world returns to normal. In another section of the *Gesta Danorum* (book 3, ch. 4), Saxo tells of Odin being exiled by the other gods for unseemly behavior, namely disguising himself as a woman. (Considering how often Odin is said to have done this without repercussions, it's likely that it was Saxo, rather than the Aesir, who took offense.) In this case Odin's throne is assumed by Ollerus (Ull), the winter god of hunting, skiing, and skating. Again, Odin later returns and drives away his usurper.

These stories can be viewed as representative of the winter king versus the summer king myth that appears in many cultures, showing the two rival seasons endlessly conquering and succeeding each other. In one folk custom in Germany, a man clad in furs was pelted with flowers by the May king. This might be seen as a representation of this myth, with Odin as the May king and the false Odin as the winter king.[7]

As far as Frigg's virtue is concerned, Saxo's version of the defaced statue contains many elements of doubtful authenticity and is probably an altered version of an earlier myth, perhaps even a variant of the tale of Freyja's necklace in which Frigg is confused with the Vanic goddess. In the stories that show Frigg engaging in sexual relations with Odin's usurper, her supposed infidelity would seem to be a function of her role as queen and earth goddess. In many cultures the rulership of a kingdom is only obtained by the king's consummating his marriage with the queen, or in some cases with the land itself in a symbolic marriage. In this sense Frigg is not so much being unfaithful as a wife as she is fulfilling her role as queen and, by doing so, maintaining the social and natural order. As a deity of fertility, Frigg can't let the earth go barren just because Odin won't stay home. It's her job as goddess to continue to be fruitful, just as it is Odin's to quest after wisdom.

A POLITICAL LEADER

Odin and Frigg are more interested in politics than in marital indiscretions. The seventh-century text *Origo Gentis Langobardum* tells of an occasion when Frigg influenced the outcome of a battle in Midgard in which Odin had a stake. In this tale the leaders of the Vandals ask Odin for victory in battle, but he says he will favor those whom he sees first at sunrise, possibly assuming that it will indeed be the Vandals. Frigg, however, is solicited for help by the queen of the Winniles and her sons. Frigg advises her favorites to have all their people get up early the next day. She also instructs their women to plait their hair over their chins like beards, put on armor and weapons, and march at the head of the army. The goddess next waits until Odin is asleep and then turns his bed around to face the Winniles.

When Odin awakens, the first thing he sees is a bunch of peculiar-looking warriors with extraordinarily full whiskers. "What Longbeards are these?" he exclaims. Now Frigg has him. He's not only seen the Winniles first, he's given them a new name—the Longobarden (Lombards)—and by custom is bound to give them a name-gift, the victory. Odin good-naturedly concedes that he's been cleverly tricked and from then on becomes the Lombards' special patron.[8] Perhaps this indicates that those asking Odin for victory would be advised to enlist the aid of his spouse as well. It certainly shows that Frigg has influence and power in spheres other than the home, like any good queen; it also shows that even the great Odin must sometimes yield to Frigg.

The custom in which the bestower of a name must give a gift to seal it was well established in the North; in fact, any important deal had to be sealed with gifts. Frigg's actions in the myth of the Lombards suggests that she might have been one of the deities called upon in such naming rituals, including the important one of *vatni ausa* ("sprinkling with water"), in which a nine-day-old child is named and formally accepted into the clan. Many stories tell of groups of goddesses, the family's norns,* or *dísir,* who appear at the naming of an infant to set its fate by the giving of gifts. Often one of these dísir becomes angry at something and bestows an ill future on the child, whereupon her sisters try to offset the curse with their gifts.

The story of Sleeping Beauty is an example of these kinds of myths coming down to us in a folktale. In this story the wicked fairy foretells that the girl will prick her finger on a spindle and die at the age of sixteen, after which another fairy declares that the princess will only fall asleep for a hundred years. The use of the spindle here as the means of the maiden's destruction is also reminiscent of Frigg, the goddess of spinning. With her connection to childbirth and the family, as well as her renowned foreknowledge of the future, Frigg was very likely connected with these rituals of naming and the setting of an individual's destiny, or *ørlög*. This might also indicate an association with the Norns or the dísir, with whom Frigg has more in common than Freyja, the goddess often associated with them.

In another story, from the Grímnismál, Odin and Frigg, disguised

---

*Generally the term *norns* is capitalized when referring to the three great Norns (similar to the Greek Fates), who are goddesses of sorts and control the fate of the Universe, and is lowercase when referring to the various lesser norns believed to be associated with individual people or families. You will see both usages in this book.

as an old peasant man and woman, befriend King Hrauthing's two sons, Agnar and his younger brother Geirrod, who have been lost at sea while fishing. The old couple take care of the boys through the winter and grow fond of them, Odin favoring Geirrod and Frigg, Agnar. In the spring they send the boys home, but just as their boat reaches the shore, Geirrod jumps out first, shouts a curse to his brother, and pushes the boat back out to sea, where it is carried away. When he arrives home, Geirrod finds out that his father has died and that he, as the sole surviving heir, is the new king.

Later in Asgard, Odin teases Frigg that his adopted son is a king, while hers is living with a giantess in a cave somewhere. Frigg responds that Geirrod is known to be inhospitable and cruel to his guests, a horrendous crime in the Norse code. Odin rides off to check this out and Frigg, knowing her accusation to be a lie, sends her sister and confidante Fulla to Geirrod with a message to be on the lookout for an evil sorcerer in a blue cloak and a floppy hat, who can be recognized by the fact that the dogs won't bark at him.

When Odin arrives, Geirrod has him apprehended and tied between two fires until the supposed wizard confesses what he is up to. The only one to help Odin is Geirrod's son, Agnar, named after the king's long-lost brother and just ten years old, the same age as the original Agnar was the last time anyone saw him. This boy gives Odin a drink and expresses his disapproval of Geirrod's treatment of his guest. After drinking, Odin begins a long poem about life and the universe, ending with the announcement that he just happens to be the Allfather, lord of the Aesir. Geirrod, who's been getting nervous as he begins to suspect who his prisoner really is, jumps up to free his former patron, falls on his own sword, and dies, leaving young Agnar to begin a long and prosperous reign.

So, Frigg doesn't fight any fairer than Odin, and she's a match for his wits. He must have been overjoyed to find a wife with whom he could play these games of intrigue. Their arguments are chiefly over political and social subjects, leaving domestic brawls to others.

In the Geirrod myth, Frigg gets her way by means of the kind of deceit and trickery more in keeping with Odin. However, the result of her actions is to dethrone the younger brother, who according to custom should not have been king at all, and replace him with the young Agnar. While Agnar is the usurper's son, by his name he shows that he is considered to carry the kin-soul of the elder Agnar, the legitimate heir. Thus Frigg ultimately acts to uphold social and political norms and traditions.

GODDESS OF MARRIAGE AND CHILDBIRTH

In her roles as wife and mother, Frigg is goddess of marriage and childbirth. She is usually toasted at weddings, along with Freyja and Thor. Helene A. Guerber, a British historian best known for her works on Germanic mythology, suggests that husbands and wives who truly loved each other and didn't want to be separated after death would come to Frigg's hall in the afterlife,[9] which is a pretty thought, though not supported by any evidence. In Norse society, marriage was more than the joining of two people; it was the joining of two families and represented a highly important occasion with deep social and spiritual ramifications. Frigg's role as patron of marriage stems not only from her interest in women, children, and domestic concerns but also grows out of her function as a maintainer of social laws and norms and an upholder of society itself.

Frigg is also invoked, along with Freyja, at childbirth. In the Oddrúnargrátr (st. 8), the king's daughter Borgny calls on the two goddesses together after she has finally given birth to twins with the aid of Oddrun's magic. Frigg is also petitioned by childless couples who wish for children. The *Völsunga saga* (ch. 1) tells how Rerir, king of the Huns, and his wife pray to the gods for a child, and Frigg hears their prayer and reports it to Odin. Odin subsequently sends a wish-maiden (a supernatural female being, possibly a *valkyrja*) with a magic apple to give to Rerir, whom she finds sitting on a mound. The king and his queen both eat the apple, and she later bears him a son who becomes the great hero Volsung.

Rerir sitting on the mound is an example of the old Norse practice of sitting out on a howe, or burial mound, to get help or advice from one's ancestors. This practice also seems to have had some relation to matters of inheritance and royal selection. Here again Frigg seems related to the female beings called *dísir,* often regarded as the female ancestors of a family, who protected the clan's fertility. Frigg's involvement in the matter also reflects her dual interest in private family matters and in the greater social and political order, which would be adversely affected by Rerir's failure to have an heir. The apple sent to the king is reminiscent of the goddess Idun and her golden apples of immortality and youth. To the Norse, having children was true immortality, for the souls of the clan were reborn in the descendants.

MAGICAL POWERS

Frigg, as well as Odin, possesses magical powers, notably second sight. She is said to know the fates of all people, though she never says what she knows (Lokasenna, st. 29). Perhaps she doesn't feel it advisable to tell others their fates before they've lived them out. It has been mentioned before that Frigg shares Odin's seat, Hlidskjalf, from which the two can see all that happens in the Nine Worlds; therefore, Frigg could be considered a goddess of scrying. However, she would not necessarily be good to call on during a divination, because she is so disinclined to share her information; rather, she might preside over activities designed to look into one's own soul for self-knowledge.

Frigg's reluctance to interfere in fate possibly stems from her tragically unsuccessful attempt to avert her son Balder's death in what is probably the best-known myth about this goddess (Gylfaginning, ch. 49; Baldrs draumar). In it, the beloved god Balder is troubled with foreboding dreams, and Frigg sends word into all the worlds to extract an oath from everything—fire and water, metals, stones, illnesses, plants, animals, and people—not to harm her son. After this, the gods get cocky and initiate a game in which they amuse themselves by throwing all sorts of weapons at Balder and watching them turn away without hurting him. Loki, disguised as a woman, visits Frigg and discovers that she has neglected to ask an oath from only one thing—the mistletoe, which she considered too young to take an oath. Loki then takes some mistletoe to the Thing, the lawgiving assembly of Old Norse culture, where he finds the blind Hod standing a little dejectedly to the side. Hod says he is not participating because he is blind and has no weapon, so Loki gives him the small dart of mistletoe and offers to guide Hod's aim. The mistletoe shoots Balder through and he falls down dead, whereupon the other gods are overcome by grief, not only for their fellow's death but also because he died at the hand of a kinsman on the sacred grounds of the Thing and thus no one who is present may take vengeance for him and restore the Aesir's lost honor.

Frigg is the first to recover her wits. She offers her special love and favor to anyone who will ride to the land of the dead and try to ransom Balder back from the death goddess, Hel. Hermod the Bold, another of Odin's sons, volunteers and borrows Odin's horse, Sleipnir, to ride to the Underworld. After riding nine days and nights, he arrives in the hall of Hel, where he finds Balder and his wife Nanna sitting in the high-seat at Hel's table. The next morning Hermod asks Hel to let his brother ride home with him, telling her how all things weep for the the slain god. Hel replies that if every single thing in all the worlds will weep for Balder, she will release him from death. Hermod departs again, carrying with him gifts to Asgard, including a piece of linen from Nanna to Frigg.

When the Aesir receive the good news, they send out messengers to all things, living and inanimate, asking them to weep for Balder. All things do so except for one mountain giantess called Thokk; she answers that she will weep waterless tears for Balder and that Hel shall hold what she has. The *Prose Edda* goes on to state that men believe that this giantess was really Loki in disguise. The result, however, was that Balder remained with Hel until after Ragnarok, the end of the age.

This myth is the longest and most important story dealing with the goddess Frigg and shows her at her most active. She is first of all the protective mother, doing all in her power for the well-being of her child, even going so far as to confront Death herself. Frigg must be a goddess of considerable power to be able to extract an oath from everything in all the worlds. She has influence over men and women; gods and giants and the inhabitants of the other worlds; animals, plants, and even inanimate objects and forces, such as metals, rocks, and diseases. All these entities bow to Frigg's will and do what she asks of them. Her role as the receiver of oaths possibly indicates that one of her roles was a goddess of vows; this dovetails well with her interest in social order.

But in this story Frigg also attempts to evade the laws of society and of life. She tries to alter her son's ørlög and thus attempts to change history. By her own actions she brings about the circumstances that lead to Balder's death, for the gods would never have been throwing weapons at him if Frigg had not made all things swear oaths not to hurt him. Yet in a way, she saves him after all, because he and his blind brother, Hod, both survive Ragnarok because they are safe in Hel's kingdom, and the two gods return again to rule over the new Asgard. Frigg is a goddess who battles all the odds and goes head to head with the laws of life and the universe itself to try to gain her will, and it is all for her child. In the best Norse tradition, she takes up a battle she probably knows she cannot win and yet gives her all in the attempt. Perhaps it is this failure to alter the workings of fate that causes her to refuse to speak the prophecies that she knows.

OTHER GERMANIC GODDESSES AND FRIGG

There are several German goddesses who are very closely associated with Frigg. They are possibly the same goddess going under different names.

Holda

Holda (Frau Holda, Holle, meaning "kind, gracious") is a goddess of sky and weather—when she shakes out her feather bed it snows, when she does her washing it rains, the fluffy white clouds are her linen things put out to bleach, and the gray clouds are her weaving.[10] The Dutch named the Milky Way after her—*Vronelden straet* (or *Vrou-elden-straat,*

"Frau Hulde's street").[11] She, like Frigg, is a goddess of spinning, weaving, and other housewifely skills and helps people with smithwork and baking.

One legend about Holda from the Tyrol tells of how she introduced flax to humankind. In this story, a peasant wanders into her secret cave while herding sheep in the mountains. He finds himself in a marvelous jeweled cavern. Before him stands a beautiful lady in shining robes, the goddess Holda, attended by a group of young women. She tells him to take anything with him that he likes, and he asks for the bunch of tiny blue flowers she holds in her hand. Holda tells him that he has chosen wisely and will live as long as the flowers do. She also gives him some seed to plant in his fields, and then vanishes.

At home the peasant's wife scolds him for not bringing back something more valuable, but he sows his fields with the seed and soon he has a crop of tiny blue flowers. When the blooms drop away, Holda returns and teaches them how to harvest the flax stalks and to spin, weave, and bleach the linen they produce. The peasants grow rich selling both linen and seed, and live long and prosperously.

When he has become quite old, the peasant one day notices that his flowers have finally begun to fade. He goes back to the mountains to find the cave once more and is never seen again.[12] It was thought that the goddess had taken him to live with her. Note here how the goddess does not give wealth outright but instead provides the means for the people to earn it themselves.

This story is reminiscent of the Tannhäuser legend. In this tale the goddess is called Frau Venus and lives in a cave in the Horselberg in Thuringia, where she was said to lure people into her realm and keep them there forever. A Christian knight named Tannhäuser lives with her for a time, until he begins to tire of a life of sensuality and to worry about his immortal soul. He runs away to Rome, but the pope rejects his pleas for absolution, telling him that the papal staff will break into blossom before Tannhäuser can expect forgiveness from the Christian god. The knight flees in despair and returns to the more tolerant goddess, but, after his departure, the pope's staff does indeed flower with buds.[13]

Holda is sometimes pictured with various attendants, including the spirits of the dead, particularly the souls of small children; night hags, enchantresses, and women armed with sickles; and elves or dwarves, who snarl and soil the spinning if it is done at improper times. Holda is said to dwell in a cave or hollow mountain, where she keeps the souls of dead and unborn children. She can also be found in the woods or in wells and often appears near water, bathing or washing clothes. People can reach her realm by falling down wells, as described in the Grimms' tale "Mother Holda."

Babies are said to come from Frau Holda's well or pool, which indicates that she is in charge of newborn children as well as dead ones and suggests that this goddess is involved with the process of rebirth. Holda usually appears as a beautiful and powerful deity, kind and helpful toward human beings, but she also has a dark and wild side. In this aspect she appears as an ugly old woman with a long nose, big teeth, and bristling, matted hair. Tangled hair was so strongly associated with her that a person with unkempt hair was said to "go holda." Nevertheless, her helpfulness and concern with the domestic affairs of humanity persist, despite her ugly shape, and she becomes angry and fearsome only when she finds disorder in the household.

Berchte

Berchte (Perchte, Berhta, meaning "bright") is a goddess very similar to Holda; her legends appear in the south of Germany, while Holda's predominate in the north. Berchte is also a goddess of spinning and weaving, and of agriculture. She rides around the country with her plow or wagon and her train of youngsters, called *heimchen*, thought to be the souls of dead and unborn children. Later, in Christian times, her train came to include the souls of unbaptized babies. This small entourage is armed with water jars with which to tend the plants, while the goddess plows beneath the earth.[14]

Sometimes Berchte has a falling-out with the people of the country she resides in, and then she takes her plow and her complaining children (who never seem to want to move) and goes elsewhere. She punishes those who gawk at her train as she passes or who fail to leave the appropriate gifts of food at Yule. On one occasion she struck a silly girl blind for laughing at her bedraggled children, although Berchte restored the girl's sight when the goddess passed through the area the following year.[15]

Like Holda, Berchte has two contrasting aspects and can appear as a noble and beautiful lady or an ugly hag. In the latter form she is particularly noted for her shaggy hair, long nose, and large or misshapen foot or feet, which got that way from treading her spinning wheel. Thus she is sometimes called "Big-Footed Berchte" or "Queen Goose-Foot." Jacob Grimm, the famous German philologist and mythologist, speculates that the pentagram, which resembles a bird's foot, was therefore connected with her.[16] One of the Grimm stories, "The Three Spinners" (see pages 204–7), features three magical old women, each with a deformity caused by too much spinning, which possibly derived from legends about this goddess.

In an old German poem, guests at a Twelfth Night feast are warned to eat all their food or the Stempe would trample them (and you thought Mom was kidding about cleaning your plate). This figure could be meant to represent Berchte, and the name is similar to one of Holda's nicknames, Die Trempe ("the trampling one").[17] Another interesting connection is a German folk name for flax, *stempen-har*.[18]

Interestingly, the legendary mother of the Christian king Charlemagne was called *Berte au grans pies* ("Berchte of the Big Foot"). There is a tale about how, while on her way to be married, Berte, the mother of Charlemagne, was left in the woods by a serving woman who substituted her own daughter for the bride. The true bride was eventually revealed by her skill at spinning and weaving.[19] Although scholars disagree about whether this Berte can be considered a manifestation of the goddess Berchte, the legends about that deity must have crept in to the folklore about this mythical royal personage.

The White Lady

Another form of this goddess is the White Lady, a figure that has appeared throughout Germany and other parts of Europe up until the past century (and perhaps does still). The White Lady is a beautiful woman dressed all in white, often with a ring of keys at her waist; sometimes these keys are bound with a snake. She appears in lonely, out-of-the-way places, often near pools or wells, and particularly likes to show herself to young children, animal herders, fishermen, and other solitary workers. She is particularly associated with the springtime, especially Easter, and tends to appear during the day around the noon hour.

Like Holda, Berchte, and Frigg, the White Lady is passionately interested in spinning and in flax. Among the Wends she would appear to women who were weeding flax and lecture them on the pros and cons of how to plant, raise, harvest, and spin the plants; she would occasionally wring the necks of women who would not answer her. This figure is also sometimes called "aunt-in-the-rye" or "woman-in-the-wheat" because of her habit of passing through the fields at noontime.[20] The White Lady often attaches herself to particular families, especially noble or royal ones. At night she is sometimes discovered rocking the babies of the house on her lap, and in general she functions as the "old grandmother" of the house,[21] in much the same way that Odin appears as the ancient ancestor of kingly lines.

Huldra

In Scandinavian lore there is a being who bears some similarities to Holda and Berchte in Germanic folklore, although she should not be taken as the Norse version of Holda, despite her name. This figure is a wood- or mountain-wife called Huldra (Huldre, Holle). She dresses in blue and white and appears variously as young and beautiful or old and melancholy; in some places she is said to be beautiful in front and ugly or hollow in the back. She is not directly connected to textiles, like the other goddesses, but in Norway there is a type of soft vegetable material, similar to flannel, called *huldre-web*.[22]

Huldra is the patron of cattle grazing and milking, just as the German Holda is the patron of spinning and agriculture. Huldra sometimes appears armed with a milk pail and leading her flock. She is also said to have a cow's tail, which she takes great pains to conceal. Up until recent times most young men and women in Scandinavia grazed the flocks on the mountains during the summer. There they made butter and cheeses, living alone at the *seder,* a small mountain cabin, for several weeks or months at a time. It was during these times that Huldra and her elves were apt to visit the pasture grounds.

Huldra is the queen of the *huldrefolk,* or mountain elves, which sound very much like Holda's attendants, the *holden.* Huldra's train also consists of human children, for Huldra, like Berchte and Holda, is believed to carry off the souls of infants. Like the German White Lady, Huldra is fond of music and is often heard singing sad songs. She likes to join in human dances, but she is easily recognized by her tail and will flee in embarrassment if she is discovered.[23]

HOLDA AND BERCHTE AND HOLIDAYS

Both Berchte and Holda are particularly associated with the Yule season. They travel the country at this time, between the solstice and Twelfth Night, bestowing their blessings on the land and checking up on the housekeeping and spinning. If all is in order, they reward the virtuous worker with a fine new spindle or some particularly good flax. If the worker has been slothful and sloppy, they spoil and tangle all the thread. Holda has many traits later ascribed to Santa Claus; she punishes naughty children and rewards good ones, and travels about with her muffled servant, Holle-peter, or Ruprecht,[24] like the European Saint Nicholas and his aide, Black Peter. In Franconia as late as the nineteenth century, a boy dressed in a cow's hide and carrying a bell acted the part of Eisen-Berta ("Iron Berta") and gave treats to good children and rods to bad ones.[25] The people in other areas had a procession during Yule in which a figure representing Holda and dressed in straw and other oddments entered each of the houses of the village to the accompaniment of fiddlers.[26]

In many places in Europe it was the custom to finish all the spinning by the end of Yule or run the risk of offending the goddess. In fact, she is believed to spoil any unfinished spinning she finds on the last day of the year; the wild version of Berchte is said to wipe her behind with it.[27] During the Yule season itself, no spinning is done at all, because it is a time considered holy to the goddess and is supposed to be a time of rest. This goddess seems to recognize the importance of both working and resting at appropriate times. Besides, a good housewife should be fully occupied with supervising the Yule festivities if the festival is being observed properly.

People of other German districts would fill their distaffs at the beginning of Yule and spin it all off by Twelfth Night. Here the magical act of spinning is performed during the holy nights, perhaps to draw the notice of the goddess and win her favor. The idea of finishing all old work at the end of the old year and beginning fresh in the new one ties in with the whole Germanic concept of Yule as a time between worlds when the old year that is ending overlaps with the new one being born. It is a time to abandon ordinary work and everyday concerns and to concentrate on holy things.

In some places, the Carnival season in February signaled an end to work. The time before Lent was traditionally associated with women, particularly housewives, in many Germanic cultures. At Shrovetide in England, women still hold pancake races in which contestants run through the streets flipping pancakes on skillets. In parts of Germany the Thursday before Shrove Thursday was called *Weiberdonnerstag* ("wives' Thursday"). On this day the women took a holiday from their household duties and carried a barrel of wine around the village on a cart drawn by cows, after which they retired to an inn and drank late into the night. (Marion Frieda Ingham, who wrote her dissertation on the goddess Freyja, suggests most of the drinking may have been done by the joyous throng, rather than by the women, but I would imagine they imbibed their fair share.)[28]

Although not specifically associated with Frigg or Holda and Berchte, these customs seem to have some relation to older festivals. The pancake races are a celebration of housekeeping skills (it's not easy to flip a pancake while you're running), and the Weiberdonnerstag procession with its cow-drawn cart is very similar to the procession of the goddess through the land at Yule or in spring. All the festivals have in common the participation of women who are resting from their work and running a bit wild, which is characteristic of the Yule celebrations of Holda and Berchte.

In one German legend, Berchte sticks her head in the window of a spinning room on Twelfth Night and finds it filled with merrymakers. Enraged, the goddess hands in a large number of spindles that have to be filled with thread within the hour. In the midst of the general consternation, one bold girl runs up to the attic for a roll of cloth, which the people wrap around the reels; the cloth is then covered with two or three thicknesses of spinning to make the reels appear full. When Berchte reappears, she receives the skimpy reels and walks off shaking her head; one gets the impression she is not really fooled.[29] It can be inferred that the goddess can be satisfied with only a token amount of work, because it is the gift of the holy act of spinning itself that restores the bond between herself and humans.[30]

In Austria and other parts of Europe, the figure of Berchte/Holda is represented by St. Lucia, also known as St. Lucy, Frau Lutz, or Spillelutsche ("Spindle-Lucia"). The name also appears as Spillaholle or Spillahulla,[31] showing the close ties between Lucy and the goddess Holda. Like her Heathen counterparts, this goddess-turned-saint is associated with Yule and with spinning. In Denmark her day is celebrated on December 13, the beginning of the Yule season. On that day all spinning ceases, and Lucy comes to check up on the work and to punish the lazy and reward the good. Sweden also celebrates Lucy's day. Early on that morning, the eldest daughter of the house, or sometimes the prettiest girl, rises before the others and, attired as "Lussi-Bride" in a white robe and a crown of candles decorated with greenery and red berries, proceeds to serve coffee, pastries, and *gløgg* (a truly potent alcoholic drink) to the whole household.

Both Berchte and Holda are in the habit of stopping any unwary person who is rash enough to be out on Twelfth Night and asking him to mend her wagon or plow. The goddess then gives him chips as payment, and the next morning he finds that the chips have turned to gold. This goddess appreciates those who are skilled with their hands (so remember your pocketknife when you go out on Twelfth Night).

However, Berchte has no patience with greed. In an old story, a master wheelwright is returning from work on the eve of Twelfth Day and meets the goddess and her weeping children on a riverbank. She asks him to use his hatchet to mend her broken plow and then offers him the fallen chips as payment, which he refuses. At home he finds that one chip, which had lodged in his shoe, has turned to gold. The next year one of his men, who had heard the story, waits at the same place on Berchte's Night. When she encounters him, the goddess demands to know what he is doing there at that hour and, exclaiming that she is better provided with tools that year, strikes him in the shoulder with her own hatchet.[32]

In all her encounters with humans, this goddess is looking for people with practical skills, but in none of these stories does she demand any unusual or heroic acts. In the past, spinning and mending wagons or plows were all fairly common crafts, which any moderately competent person would have known how to do. Holda and Berchte are not asking great deeds of you but only that you be able to take care of yourself in the everyday world, that you exhibit a few simple skills—any skills—and show that you are neither too proud to work with your hands nor too selfish to help a fellow being in need.

Gifts of food and drink, particularly milk, are often left out for Holda or Berchte during Yule. Certain foods are to be eaten on the goddess's night as well, usually a porridge, dumplings, or a cake of oats, and often herring as well—the standard peasant fare. This is a meal even the god Thor enjoys on occasion, as mentioned in the Hárbarðsljóð (st. 3). If Berchte finds that her special dish has been omitted, she cuts open the person's belly, takes out any other food she finds there, fills the space with straw, and sews it all back up with a plowshare for needle and a chain for thread[33] (a condition anyone who has been to a really good New Year's Eve party will recognize immediately).

This sort of thing is similar to shamanic visions in which the initiate is eaten or torn to pieces as part of a visionary experience. In *Laxdæla saga* (chs. 48 and 49) a man dreams that his *dís* (a guardian spirit, usually female) removes his intestines and replaces them with brushwood. Later he is wounded in battle and assumed to be dead, but he survives, claiming that his dís had returned and replaced his organs, which she had presumably taken for safekeeping.

HOLDA AND BERCHTE AND THE WILD HUNT

Both Holda and Berchte at times lead the Wild Hunt, a frightening procession of the dead who ride through the winter storms accompanied by fearsome black dogs and usually led by the god Wodan (Odin). The Hunt itself is often held to symbolize the storm wind howling through the skies, and the wind's bride (*windsbraut*) was the whirlwind, a force associated with Holda.[34] When the goddess leads the Hunt, her train often includes wild women, as well as hounds and other wild beasts, and usually they ride during the winter season between Yule and Easter. A Fastnacht procession in Nuremburg, Germany, in 1588 featured a Wild Hunt procession led by a figure who represented Frau Holda riding a black horse and who blew on a horn, cracked her whip, and shook her hair about madly.[35] In other parts of Germany they held the Perchtenjagd, or Perchtenlauf ("Berchte's hunt" or "run"), in which young men in masks and odd disguises, such as black sheepskins or headresses made of white cocks' feathers, went through the villages ringing cows' bells and cracking whips and generally making merry.[36] Sometimes they danced, leaped into the air, or jumped over wells or brooks.

When taking Wodan's place as leader of the Hunt, the goddess is called Frau Gode (Frau Gaue, Frau Wode, i.e., "Mrs. Odin"). Like Wodan, Frau Gode rides during "the Twelves"; that is, the twelve nights of Yule. If people leave their doors open, she sends in a dog that sits by the hearth and disturbs everyone's sleep with its whining; in addition, it brings danger of sickness, death, and fire. This pest cannot be gotten rid of until the next Yule, when the Hunt passes by again.[37] Frau Gode's

Hunt, like her husband's, is also apt to snatch up the unwary or unwise person and carry him away, often leaving him dead or mad after the experience.

The Hunt is not solely for the purpose of terrifying mortals, however. Its passage is supposed to ensure the fertility of the fields. Reapers in some areas of Germany used to leave the last few stalks of the harvest for Frau Gode, sometimes decorating it with leaves and flowers. In other districts the same gifts and chants were offered to Wodan.[38] This association of Wodan and his wife with the harvest is echoed in a procession that took place in northern England at certain times of the year, but particularly in the autumn. This festival included a giant's dance featuring huge figures of Wodan and his wife Frigg as well as a folk play in which two swords were clashed around the neck of a boy without hurting him.[39] This last custom is reminiscent of the gods hurling weapons at Balder without harming him.

OTHER DEITIES ASSOCIATED WITH FRIGG

Nerthus

While she is not the same goddess as Frigg, the older Germanic deity Nerthus has some definite similarities and seems to have bequeathed some of her functions to Frigg. Most of what we know about Nerthus comes from the Roman historian Tacitus, writing in the first century CE. In his *Germania* (ch. 40) he identifies this goddess with the Roman Mother Earth and describes how she was carried through the land at certain times in an ox-drawn wagon to bring fertility to the fields and the people. During her procession all weapons and iron objects were put away and a holy peace was kept. Afterward, the goddess and the wagon were bathed in a lake by servants who were then drowned, and Nerthus retired to her island until her next journey.

Both Nerthus and her later German counterparts, Holda and Berchte, make an annual progression to bring fertility to the land. In each case the goddess travels in a wagon drawn by cattle, and certain tools—iron objects and weapons in Nerthus's case, implements of spinning in Holda's and Berchte's—are hidden and their use prohibited during the holy period. Also, Nerthus shares with Holda an affinity for lakes and bathing. Perhaps the drowning of her servants indicates a belief that the world of the goddess could be reached by passing through water.

Brigid

Although I personally dislike the practice of taking the gods of one culture and trying to equate them with the gods of another, the Celtic goddess Brigid shares so many similarities with Frigg and her German counterparts that she deserves a closer look. The Irish goddess Brigid, who was known as Ffraed in Wales and Bride in Scotland, later had to be made a saint because the people wouldn't give her up after they became Christian. Like Holda and Berchte, Brigid is a goddess of craftsmen, especially smiths, and of childbirth, prophecy, and poetry. On her feast day certain types of work were prohibited, typically spinning, milling, carting, or other work involving wheels. Washing, plowing, and smithwork were sometimes also restricted.[40]

Like Holda and Berchte, Brigid makes a procession through the country to ensure the health of the cattle and crops. The house was traditionally cleaned in her honor, and gifts of butter, bread, and porridge were left out for her in the cottages or at special healing wells. Brigid's Eve was often enlivened by wild processions of masked revelers called "biddies," similar to the festivities at Perchtenlauf.[41]

Brigid is strongly associated with midwifery and childbirth. Christian legends depict her as taking care of the newborn Christ, wrapping him in her cloak and providing him with milk. She was also said to have helped the Virgin Mary to slip unobserved into the temple for her purification after childbirth. To do this, Brigid drew the crowd's attention to herself by wearing a headdress of lighted candles, just like the Swedish Lucy. These images are obviously remnants of Heathen lore that were later grafted onto the Christian saint to make her acceptable to the Celtic people.

Brigid's Day is celebrated in the Celtic countries on February 1, the day before the Christian feast of Candlemas, but the beginning of February also seems to have some connection to Frigg and her German counterparts. The second month of the Icelandic year, Gói or Gómánuðr, roughly corresponds to February (February/March, to be exact). In Iceland it was celebrated by the mistress of the farmstead, who rose early in the morning and went outside clad only in her shift to welcome Góa to the farm, after which she gave a feast for the other wives in the neighborhood.[42] The season of Carnival, which is celebrated just before Lent in many European countries, also falls in February and was often associated with Holda and Berchte. An old German folk custom maintained that if women danced in the sun on Candlemas, their flax would thrive.[43]

SYMBOLS OF THE GODDESSES

Berchte, as has been stated, is a goddess of agriculture, and the plow is one of her symbols. She is said to have taught people to grow turnips,[44] another staple in the peasant winter diet. Both she and Holda are also involved with domestic animals, the traditional preserve of the earth goddess. They are especially associated with cattle and milk, but also with goats, sheep, and pigs. Holda's cart is sometimes described as being drawn by cows, and Frigg's by rams (this last is chiefly from Wagner's operas, but it does make sense that a goddess of spinning and weaving would be associated with sheep and wool, as well as flax). The Celtic Brigid is often accompanied by her favorite white cow.

This interest in farming and husbandry is all part of the sphere of the good housewife. Norse women often took charge of most of the activities of the farm when the men were away "viking," sometimes for years at a time. Certainly the care of most of the farm animals often fell to the women of the household, and indeed still does today. "Butter and egg money" has long been the inalienable property of the mistress of the farmstead.

When a culture begins to domesticate animals and to farm, it creates larger communities and more complex social relationships, which are the sorts of things Frigg takes great interest in. It also sets the stage for the development of more advanced arts and crafts. Without the sophisticated kinds of political, intellectual, social, and artistic developments that grow out of a more stable society, Odin and his warriors, skalds, and magicians would have no context in which to operate, and this is why, despite their temperamental differences, Odin and Frigg are a good match.

Georges Dumézil, influential French mythographer and comparative mythologist, introduced the theory of the three-part Indo-European societal structure, which he claims can be used as a model for understanding all Indo-European religions and societies. The first function was that of the priest or judge and represented the social class of kings. The second function was that of the warrior. The third was the provider, those who supplied the means to live, such as farmers and craftsmen, and represented the yeomen or peasants. The Norse gods and goddesses usually chosen to represent these functions are Odin and Tyr for the first, Thor for the second, and Frey and Freyja for the third.

There is much controversy over whether this system can be applied in all cases, and I won't go into the pros and cons of this theory here, but I would like to make the observation that Frigg, often assigned to the third function because of her interest in agriculture, crafts, and fertility, is also in many ways similar to Tyr. She presides over vows and is concerned with order, justice, and stability. She is also a queen. Seen in this light, she and Odin represent a marriage of the two sides of the first function and, as a couple, make the ideal ruling partners.

FRIGG AND FREYJA

Frigg is often confused with Freyja, or even thought to be the same goddess. Certainly the two share a number of traits, and undoubtedly their worship and attributes have been confused and melded together over the years. They are, however, two very different goddesses. Odin and Thor are both battle gods of sorts, but we don't go around saying they're the same.

In the *Prose Edda,* Freyja, the chief Vanir goddess, is said to be as well-born as Frigg, the highest-ranking Aesir goddess (Gylfaginning, ch. 35). In some ways the two can be seen as performing similar functions for each of their respective groups of deities, thus leading to some of the similarities between the two. The confusion may even reflect a merging of two different cults of worship. The ancient Romans compared both goddesses to their goddess of love, Venus, and the Christians carried on the tradition of confusing the two by assigning to the Holy Mother Mary many of their beneficent attributes while banishing all Heathen goddesses of any sort to the ranks of demons and labeling them lustful and evil.

Fertility, Healing, and Love

Frigg and Freyja share a connection with the rites most closely associated with women and traditionally performed by priestesses. Both are petitioned for fertility and healing and are called on in marriage and childbirth. Both possess magical hawk dresses that enable them to shape-shift and travel between the worlds, and Frigg is sometimes credited with possession of a jewel reminiscent of Freyja's Brisingamen, as is Gefjon, one of the goddesses closely associated with Frigg (did the dwarves make these necklaces for all the goddesses?).

However, despite these and many other similarities, the two goddesses have very different styles and personalities; each has a very different "feel" to her. The differences may not be clear when written down on paper, but if you invoke both goddesses in ritual, the distinction is striking and unmistakable. While they are both interested in many of the same activities, their reasons and their methods are very diverse.

For example, Frigg and Freyja are both called on in matters of love. But the kind of love Frigg represents is that of the long-term relationship, the kind of love that also has social and economic consequences. Freyja, on the other hand, represents sexual abandon and wildness, sex engaged in for fun or for magic, passionate love that takes no note of consequences, unconventional and unfettered love. In matters of healing, Frigg would govern areas where rest, quiet, and recuperation are needed, while Freyja would be more useful in cases where vitality and the strength to struggle against disease are required. In many cases, such as childbirth, for example, a little of both is needed. Freyja brings a kind of wildness, a freedom and restlessness, a passion, a desire for adventure, and an unsettling, disquieting, and yet revitalizing kind of feeling. Frigg brings feelings of safety and stability, quiet, peace, comfort, trust, changelessness, acceptance, security, and the kind of independence that is based on having adequate resources, knowledge, and skills. Mother versus Lover. We need both, and it helps to know who you're asking for what. If they share traits, perhaps it is because they share interests and collaborate, much as two women who are friends might do. But then Freyja rides off with the Valkyries to collect her share of the slain, while Frigg goes off to teach women how to spin and men how to plow.

Women's Work

I think women today tend to trivialize Frigg's functions in favor of the wilder and more uninhibited Freyja, a symbol of the powerful, independent, and sexually uninhibited woman. For women who are still trying to disentangle themselves from unfair societal restrictions, many of which stem from the medieval Christian social structure with its roots in Roman feudalism, a goddess devoted to marriage, children, relationships, and domestic skills is much less appealing. But we need to try to appreciate what these skills meant in the context of the society in which the figure of Frigg originated.

Women today feel restricted and undervalued when limited to the role of housewife, a role that is perhaps based on memories of television from the 1950s, visions of perky wives in starched dresses baking cookies for the hubby and kids and wailing over their laundry. This role is less vital and less satisfying today, when technology has made the task of running a household much less demanding than it used to be. (Yes, I know it's still hard, but we don't have to haul our own water, build our own fires, and slaughter our own livestock, among other things.) Many men, as well as women, feel just as limited by dull and pointless office jobs that are far less demanding than a person's role might have been on a Viking Age farm.

The mistress of a Norse household was first of all the manager of a vast and varied enterprise staffed by a large number of employees. Hiring and managing the household help was the wife's job up to our own time, when all but the wealthiest households quit using large numbers of servants. Providing fire, food, drink, clothing, and bedding, as well as incidentals like soap and candles, for all the inhabitants of a Norse farm was much more complicated than microwaving a few leftovers, and if the housewife didn't plan carefully through the winter and spring, the consequences of running out of something around, say, February, were very serious.

Brewing and Baking

The brewing of ale and mead was generally considered the province of the women, and in Norse society this was more significant than merely hosting a few drunken brawls. Ale was viewed as a spiritual substance, imbued with the power to unite both gods and humans, and without which the high feasts and rituals were impossible. Besides their use in worship and in the practice of medicine and magic, mead and ale were used to formalize councils; to seal important agreements and bargains, such as treaties, marriages, and the transfer of property; to celebrate festivals; to display hospitality and goodwill; and to honor all important life occasions. Indeed, contractual agreements depended on intoxicating beverages to be considered valid, and the sharing of drink was a key element in religious ritual.

The processes of both brewing and baking have something of the holy and mysterious about them, even today. One takes these seemingly inert ingredients—grain and milk, honey and water—and adds this magical substance known as yeast (in reality the living cells of a small fungus), and after a period of hours or months, the original ingredients have mysteriously changed, transformed into something else—the bread rises, the ale or mead ferments. In earlier times, when fermenting was left to the mercy of wild yeast from the air, this change must have seemed even more miraculous. Therefore, brewing was probably endowed with the formality of ritual, incorporating special ceremonies and practices. In the Telemark district of Norway, the people prepared their ale with great care for fear that any carelessness might keep the brew from becoming strong enough, which would be not just an inconvenience but a sign of ill luck and misfortune.[45]

Thus a woman's skill in brewing was more than just proof of her housewifely prowess; it was proof of her holiness, her luck, and her kinship with the gods. *Hálfs saga* gives an example of the significance of brewing. King Alrek's two wives, Geirhild and Signy, had an ale-brewing contest to determine which of them would be queen. Geirhild called on Odin, who spit in her ale to ferment it, and she proved the winner.[46] This shows another point of similarity between Odin and Frigg. Odin is considered the giver of the holy mead of inspiration, but Frigg guides the people who brew its earthly counterpart.

Milking and Butter- and Cheese-Making

The tasks of milking and making butter and cheese, another traditional province of women, are also tinged with mystery and magic. Butter was a highly regarded commodity in the past. In Norway old legal documents regarding estate settlements and taxation frequently mention butter among the assets; in fact, the value of the land itself was expressed in measures of butter (*lauper smør*). Because it could be produced in excess of a family's need, it was used as legal tender in trade, like money.[47] Butter was also valued by supernatural beings, particularly the *nisser,* elflike creatures similar to the Scottish brownies. Each household had its personal *nisse,* who helped with chores around the house and barn and generally looked after the family's interests. In return, every Yule the nisse expected to receive the annual gift of a bowl of rice porridge topped with a large piece of butter. If the butter was omitted, the nisse would avenge himself in some fairly serious manner.

Like ale and bread, the magical attributes of butter arose in the past from the uncertainty involved in making it. Despite the dairymaid's care, any number of disasters could occur during the process—the cow might fail to produce, the milk might be sour, and the butter might fail to churn despite all efforts. Unaware of scientific reasons like improper cream temperature or low fat content,[48] people in the past could only assume that either lack of luck or some sort of supernatural interference was to blame. Therefore, the dairy was surrounded by as much ritual as the brewery or the bakery.

The Magic of Spinning and Weaving

Although Norse women were skilled at a great number of crafts, the occupations most strongly symbolic of the housewife were spinning and weaving. Spinning on the distaff was a skill every girl was expected to learn. Through medieval and into early modern times, spinning was regarded as the perfect female occupation, one that required little training or capital and could be easily integrated into the other duties of the household, because it could be started and stopped frequently with no adverse effect on the product.[49] Spinning was considered a vital part of a woman's life and being. Women of wealth and power, criminals serving time in jail, prostitutes in between customers, even the mad and the maimed—all women were expected to spin, and indeed, it was considered their intrinsic, god-given right to do so.[50]

Spinning was so universal an occupation among European women that a number of goddess figures are associated with it, and one must be careful not to regard them all as patrons of spinning or to consider them all the same goddess. However, Frigg and her German counterparts, Holda and Berchte, seem more strongly connected with this occupation than most, and thus Frigg can be thought of as the patron of all working women.

Weaving, which follows spinning in the creation of cloth, was also the province of women in Norse culture and remained so well into the Middle Ages. It is very likely that weaving was once performed by two or three women together, judging from how the threads of the weft (those running crosswise) run in pieces of cloth from the Viking period.[51] We of the post–Industrial Age tend to take for granted the importance of textile production by European women. Women wove the cloth that provided all the clothing of the household, both for men and for women, a fairly critical job in a cold climate.

We are enthralled by the adventures of Viking merchants and explorers, but without cloth for tents, awnings, wagon covers, and the all-important sails for the famous Viking ships, those adventurers would not have made it very far. The Norse produced many beautiful forms of art, but paintings were not among among them. Instead, they used woven tapestries as wall hangings. Therefore, many of the great artists of that culture must have been the women who designed and wove them.

The cloth-making industry was a very important and lucrative one throughout the Middle Ages and up through modern times, and until the medieval guilds took over the prestigious art of weaving, it was an industry almost exclusively dominated by women. Cloth was a major export for a number of northern European countries and kept more than one kingdom's economy afloat. When King Charlemagne received a valuable chess set from the great caliph Harun al-Rashid, he could think of no richer gift to offer in return than his country's finest, a woolen cape dyed vermillion.[52] Only in modern times, when cloth is mass-produced by machines and the textile industry has been handed back to women workers—minus much of its prestige and pay—have we ceased to regard its manufacture as valuable.

Spinning and weaving, like brewing, have a magical side to them. The act of drop-spinning involves taking a bunch of loose fibers on a distaff in one hand and forming a thread by a combination of twisting and drawing out fibers in a continuous line with the other hand. The twisting process is aided by the turning of the spindle, around which the finished yarn is wound to prevent the thread from unraveling.

The spinning process is suggestive of the power that brings things into manifestation, the shaping might that defines the fate of all that exists. For this reason, spinning was associated with the Norns, the Norse incarnations of time and causality. Paul C. Bauschatz, author of *The Well and the Tree,* associates the name of one of them, Verdandi ("Becoming"), with various root words that all relate to the concept of "turning."[53] The spiral-like movement of spun thread reminds one of the cyclical nature of the Germanic worldview, in which life was seen as a continuously repeating pattern rather than a linear progression.

Weaving is also associated with the Norns and with magic. It is the process of forming a textile by interlocking two sets of threads, the passive, lengthwise warp with the active, crosswise weft, or woof. This process is dependent on the interconnectedness of the threads and hence is often seen as symbolic of the web of life, where lives and events overlap to create a pattern that is only observable by stepping back to view the finished product as a whole.

Linen, the cloth made from the fibers of the flax plant, which the goddess Holda is said to have given to humans, is one of the most difficult and challenging fabrics to spin and weave, and thus is an appropriate symbol for the goddess of handicrafts. The practice of harvesting and preparing flax and linen is to this day a ritualized process, fraught with tradition and secrecy. The fibers are removed from the tough and woody flax stalks and then laid out in the fields for about six weeks to absorb the dew. After a second drying, the fibers, which look remarkably like human hair, are cleaned and combed. They are difficult to work with because of their lack of elasticity, and the best results are obtained from "wet-spinning" and weaving in rooms heavy with humidity. In fact, Europeans used to weave linen in caves, one of Holda's favorite dwelling places.

Techniques for finishing the linen vary and are usually carefully kept secrets. In the past, the finished cloth was again laid out in the fields to be bleached in the sun, rain, and dew, and this may still be done in some places even today. Those bleaching fields are another favorite haunt of the spinning goddesses, and Holda's association with rain and snow may have some connection with the bleaching of linen out in the elements.

Flax and linen thus have a hint of mystery and magic about them. The tiny blue flowers produced by the flax plant are extremely fragile, lasting only a few hours, but the linen cloth the plants produce is one of the most durable materials on earth. The concept of turning a bunch of woody stalks into one of the most elegant and valued fabrics in the world reminds one of the old tales of spinning straw into gold. One of the most famous of these, the Grimms' tale of "Rumpelstiltskin," bears many resemblances to the legends of Lauma, a Lithuanian goddess of earth and weaving. Like Holda and Berchte, she can be found bathing on the beach and is said to steal children. She appears in the homes to help the girls weave and can create a fine piece of linen in record time. When she's done, Lauma will give the cloth to the girl if she can guess the goddess's name.[54]

As mentioned before, Frigg is said to have great powers of magic and the gift of foresight. Spinning and weaving can be seen as the key to her powers, and the spindle is the symbol of her might in the same way the spear symbolizes Odin's or the hammer symbolizes Thor's. Spinning is one of the great deeds of might that can attract the attention of the gods and other powerful wights. The magic of spinning lies in its shaping, manifesting action. To spin is to make order out of chaos, to create something from nothing. The drafting zone—the place between the loose fiber and the growing thread where the drawing out takes place—is the point of the eternal present, the place of that-which-is-becoming, the cutting edge of time where deeds are drawn from the unmanifest future and are joined to the skein of the past. This is the same present that exists within the holy stead, where the worlds overlap and exist as one for a time, the place where magic happens.

Weaving is also a work of magic and fate. The interconnectedness of all the threads, the overlaying of layer upon layer of action, the pattern that is undiscernible as you work on it at close range and only becomes clear when you step back and look at the work as a whole—all these mirror the workings of the universe and of ørlög. This word, used to describe the Norse concept of fate, literally means "primal layers." It is a concept of destiny that is based not on a preordained future but on the pattern of past actions. Each layer of past deeds creates a pattern that determines how each subsequent deed must evolve.

There is no such concept as being "born again" in Norse philosophy—it would be impossible and inconceivable to wipe the past clean and start over. This does not mean that you are bound to pursue one rigid course of action, like a robot, without the ability to change. You always have choices, but the deeds of the past limit and direct those choices, leaving some paths open to you while closing off others. Similarly, weaving builds on the patterns that have already been laid down, each thread and layer growing from what has gone before. You can add new colors or change the pattern somewhat as you go along, but you have to do it based on the web that has already been created.

Thus, Frigg's power to know all ørlög probably stems from her might in weaving and spinning. Weaving implies an ability to view the universe holistically, to see the interrelationship of past and future actions with the ever-becoming present. Frigg's reluctance to speak of what she knows may arise from the intrinsic difficulty of explaining such knowledge to anyone else. To see the pattern as a whole, to know in your gut where a thread will eventually lead or from what point in the past an event has grown, are ways of knowing that each person must discover and experience for herself.

The magic of spinning and weaving is the power to shape events, to bring ideas into manifestation. Although Frigg is never shown going into battle herself, as Odin and Freyja do, it is quite possible that she holds the power to magically shape events from a distance. Some believe that the women described by Tacitus as accompanying their men into battle were there not only as healers and to give moral support but also to aid the battle with their magical workings and prophecy.

Njáls saga (ch. 157) records a rather gruesome image of twelve women weaving intestines on a loom weighted with human heads, using a sword and arrow for beater and shuttle and chanting a description of a battle as they wove. These magical women were presumably Valkyries, and their actions indicate that their weaving was shaping the course of the coming conflict. In the *Orkneyinga saga* (ch. 11) the mother of Jarl Sigurd sews a raven banner to bring her son victory in battle. It was said that when the wind blew, the raven seemed to be flying. This sort of magic ties in not only with Frigg's power to shape events or fate but also with her warding and protecting nature.

At any rate, the homely crafts and domestic activities presided over by Frigg should not be belittled or discounted simply because society has lost respect for such duties in this day and age. The role of the mistress of the household in Norse culture was one of vital economic importance to both the family and to society as a whole, and domestic crafts were not only necessary for survival but were also filled with magical might. The interwoven social relationships between individuals were the core and the strength of Germanic society, and an individual could no more be separated from the roles of mother, father, daughter, brother, or spouse than a single thread could be removed from a fabric without spoiling it.

To recap a bit, Frigg is a goddess of weaving and spinning, which can be extended to include all crafts and skills, such as pottery, agriculture, smithcraft, carpentry, and, in the modern world, technology. As queen of the Gods, she represents authority and law, and displays as much interest in politics and world affairs as Odin does. As a mother goddess, she is the mother who teaches and rears, rather than the one who bears. She is Allmother to the gods, not because she is their blood mother, but because she is their mother in function, raising them and caring for them (one can picture Thor treating her with the respect and affection of a son and Frigg packing him a large lunch to take on his adventures). Frigg is the earth transformed by the labor of humankind, the tilled earth rather than the wild earth. She takes great interest in the doings of people and their labors and efforts to improve themselves and their world. On the other hand, those who do poor work and spoil her earth through greed and carelessness incur her wrath.

FRIGG AND RELATIONSHIPS

Frigg is a goddess to whom relationships are particularly significant. Many of her functions grow out of her relationships with others: daughter of Fjörgynn, wife of Odin, mother of Balder, stepmother of Thor, mother-in-law of Nanna, leader of the Aesir goddesses. Yet this does not mean she does not possess power and significance in her own right; rather, she rules over one of the more important areas of all our lives, those areas where we intersect the lives of others, socially, economically, politically, and personally. In an era when so many of these relationships seem to be falling apart, she is a goddess who merits some attention.

As Odin's wife, Frigg complements him both as his queen and his friend. While he is wild and dangerous, she is calm and comforting; whereas he is innovative and revolutionary, she stands for social order and convention. Odin brings to humanity esoteric knowledge, inspiration, and spiritual development; Frigg brings practical skills and the means of economic survival, and the kind of personal development that grows out of being able to express one's ideas in material terms. Odin is the shamanistic priest-king; Frigg is the beneficent constitutional monarch.

Frigg and Freyja share many functions and traits but are essentially different in character and spirit. Freyja has many of Odin's traits of wildness, unpredictability, and innovation, while Frigg is more similar to the god Tyr in her devotion to order, justice, truth, and honor. Frigg guides people's development as they act out their many roles as a part of society and of family, while Freyja stimulates their self-realization as individuals.

All in all, Frigg appears as a woman in her prime, stately and calm, very wise and patient and kind, the maker of homes and peace and security. She teaches all men and women the skills they need to survive and be happy and imparts her knowledge of healing and second sight to some. Frigg supports the harmonious interaction of men and women, parents and children, people and their rulers, nation and nation, humanity and the gods, people and the earth. She shows how to use earth's gifts properly and to the benefit of all.

8

Frigg

The Allmother and a Sample Goddess Ritual

 ## Lore

Little information exists about the worship of Frigg (ON Frigg, OHG Frija, OE Fricg, *Frijjō), but there is no reason to doubt that her cult was important. Her worship probably centered on family and clan and domestic concerns, and many of her rituals may have been conducted within the privacy and intimacy of each individual hall rather than at public holy sites. Also, many of her rites undoubtedly focused on women and hence may have been overlooked or discounted by later historians.

Artifacts found at pre–Viking Age offering sites in Scandinavia include rings and women's ornaments, cuttings of human hair, and remnants of flax and the tools used for processing it, which suggests that women left gifts to deities, most likely female ones, at these places.[1] There is evidence that Frigg was toasted at weddings and invoked for help in childbirth. Her aid also appears to have been sought in conceiving children and in baby-naming ceremonies, and it seems likely that she was petitioned for help in matters pertaining to the family and the running of the household. Her German counterparts, Holda and

Berchte, were called on in matters of spinning, weaving, and agriculture and were particularly honored at Yule.

Using what we know about the traditional worship of Frigg as a starting point, we can add to that information by examining myth and folklore and discover what sorts of worship are appropriate to her. Although we do not live today as pre-Christian Germanic people did, we can examine that culture and discover ways to fit the old folk customs into our modern world. Frigg is a complex goddess with a substantial number of aspects and functions, so rituals and workings to her cover a lot of ground.

Archetypal Wife and Mother

In the role of archetypal wife and mother, Frigg can be petitioned in matters dealing with marriage, children, and the family. She would be good to enlist in love workings, but only for those leading to committed, long-term relationships. All matters dealing with betrothals and weddings would be within her sphere of influence, both as a patron of marriage and as a goddess concerned with social and civil contracts. You might want to conduct such ceremonies on a Friday, Frigg's holy day, and you would definitely want to drink a *minne,* or toast, to her on these occasions. She would be a key figure in all aspects of the marriage ritual, especially the vows themselves, and in any working commemorating the bride's change of status from single woman to wife.

Marriage in early Germanic culture was characterized by detailed financial arrangements, involving dowries and bride gifts, designed to ensure the financial support of both partners and especially to provide for any children produced by the union. Therefore, Frigg might be invoked to witness any financial arrangements and investments made by a prospective couple, as well as any prenuptial agreements or marriage contracts setting forth who gets what in case of death or divorce. Divorce was relatively easy to obtain in Germanic society, and there was no particular moral stigma attached to it, as long as the children were provided for. Frigg could be called on to help end a marriage fairly and with minimal emotional stress and rancor.

Frigg is also strongly tied to motherhood and should therefore be invoked in rituals to aid conception. One such working that I have used is taken from the story of King Rerir, in which Frigg persuaded Odin to give a magic apple to help the king and his wife conceive a son (see pages 58–59). In this working, an apple or a nut is used in a ritual to Frigg and the dísir, serving as a sort of battery to store the power generated. The couple desiring a child can be physically present at the ritual, although it seems to work better if they are not. If they are absent, pictures or other emblems of them can be placed on the altar. After the apple or nut has been charged, the couple divides it and eats it together. Sometimes this takes a bit of time to work, in some cases several years, but it very often proves successful. Another fertility working might involve leaving gifts or talismans at or in a well or pool, because the souls of children were said to come from Frau Holda's watery home. Frigg can be appealed to in matters of birth control and family planning, as well as those dealing with fertility.

As both mother and healer, Frigg is good to call on throughout a pregnancy, both in matters related to the health of mother and child and in the preparations that need to be made for a new baby. The latter include not only the practical considerations of acquiring money, supplies, and space but also the psychological preparation of both partners to assume the roles of mother and father, particularly at the birth of their first child. The move from young couple to parents is a rite of passage every bit as traumatic as puberty or marriage. Even more than marriage, parenthood is a long-term commitment, and anyone with children can tell you how it turns your life upside down.

Frigg, as well as Freyja, was traditionally called on during childbirth by Norse women in the past and should be included in any birthing ceremonies today. Gifts of milk and fruit can be made to Frigg when the first contractions begin. In earlier times, Norse women would begin to weave a red, three-stranded cord at the onset of labor; this cord would later be used to tie off the baby's umbilical cord. Even today, when modern hospital practices forbid this, Scandinavian women will tie the cord around the child's wrist until its naming day.[2] The work of braiding itself is an act of holiness to Frigg, similar to weaving and spinning, and serves to draw her attention and blessings to the worker. The weaver could also concentrate her own will for her child's luck into the cord as she braids.

Frigg is also connected with naming and ørlög and should be included in the *vatni ausa,* or naming ritual. This takes place nine days after the birth and is what makes the child a true part of the family and gives him a soul and a destiny. Frigg might be petitioned early on in the process for guidance in selecting an appropriate name. Dreams, especially those about deceased family members, are considered important sources of guidance in such matters, so you might want to invoke Frigg's help in some sort of dreamwork during this period. The naming ritual itself consists of the father, or another designated person, taking the child from the mother, sprinkling him with water, and naming him with the name previously agreed upon by the parents. After the naming itself, it would be good to call on Frigg and the Norns, honor them with gifts, and ask their blessings on the child's path in life. (Remember all those angry fairies in folktales and what they do when they're slighted on festive occasions? Be sure to treat these goddesses accordingly.) Despite some similarities to Christian baptism, this ceremony was practiced in Germanic culture long before the coming of Christianity. Variants have existed in many cultures throughout history.

Frigg does not abandon her concern for children once they are born. She is even more involved in the raising of the family and the running of the household at that point, and she should be called on in all matters pertaining to these affairs. This may include things such as obtaining a good place to live; acquiring the financial stability needed to adequately run your household and being able to budget what you do have; and attaining and using the skills necessary to keep a house, including cooking, cleaning, sewing, gardening, household repairs, home security, automobile maintenance, and bookkeeping. She would be the one to invoke for house blessings and other such rituals.

One simple working is to call on Frigg while cooking and to

visualize health, joy, and goodwill going into your food as you stir it with a clockwise, spiraling motion. This is particularly effective at large family gatherings where you suspect some members might start bickering. One can also do this while making beer or mead, creating a truly ritual brew. If you are brewing for a particular festival or event, you can visualize qualities appropriate to that occasion flowing into your beverage.

Caring for Family

All matters related to caring for and teaching children are part of Frigg's domain. This may include everything from mastering the intricacies of diapering, bathing, and feeding to arranging for appropriate schooling and social activities for your children. Frigg is generally seen as a home-loving goddess, but the myths are also very clear about her ability and willingness to fare out into the affairs of the world when her interests are concerned. She can therefore be called on in matters involving school boards, child welfare agencies, legislative bodies, and other public entities as well as those involving one's private household.

The concept of family encompasses more than children; it also includes one's parents, grandparents, aunts, uncles, and other family elders. Frigg could therefore be appealed to in matters dealing with caring for the elderly, both their physical health and emotional well-being. Frigg and her German counterparts often appear in folk stories as teachers, especially of practical skills. In this aspect Frigg might be invoked in matters involving the education of adults as well as that of children. In addition to all the human members of the family, Frigg is also in charge of domestic animals and can be petitioned to help anything from the family pet to a stable of milking cows.

Craftmaking

Spinning, weaving, and other types of textile crafts are Frigg's special works, but she can be called on by practitioners of all sorts of crafts—both practical and artistic. Frigg favors those who can use their hands and get things done in the material world, and she should be invoked by artisans and workers of all types. This covers traditional crafts, such as woodworking and smithing, but may also include more modern crafts, such as motor vehicle and computer repair.

One way to harness Frigg's might while spinning is to focus a magical intent into the forming thread while you work. This can also be done with crafts such as knitting, crocheting, tatting, and others. For example, while knitting a baby jacket one can strongly visualize the health and happiness of the child who will wear it. Spinning a magical thread can be an end in itself, with the finished yarn buried or cast into water as an offering.

Another working to Frigg involves weaving or embroidering a scene that symbolizes an event or condition that you want to come about, such as you and your mate with children or yourself happy in a new job or a new house, or a more general goal, such as the protection of loved ones or spiritual growth. Each time you work on the piece, let yourself daydream about the end result you want. You might even consider pricking a finger and letting several drops of your blood fall on the work, as Sleeping Beauty's mother did when she was wishing for a daughter. After the work is done, it should be carefully kept, either hidden in a safe place or proudly displayed in your home, or perhaps given away if the working was done for someone else.

Hospitality

Frigg should be invoked in affairs involving hospitality and guest rituals and in all matters promoting friendliness and goodwill among people. She should be one of the deities called on at any big social undertaking or festival to ensure that frith—peace and harmony (see pages 154–55 for more on the meaning of frith)—is kept and that all the mundane concerns run smoothly.

Remember that Frigg values rest and celebration as well as work, provided each is done at its proper time. She will aid in stopping quarrels, especially among family members, and is good to invoke to help resolve all civil disputes. She presides over contracts and civil legal proceedings, especially those involving marriage, families, children, and property. In her role as queen, she is involved in political matters, especially those involving the selection of leaders and the promotion of domestic stability.

Promoting Prosperity and Learning

Frigg will help on all occasions where subtlety and manipulation are required to achieve one's goals. She can be invoked in rituals for prosperity, but hers is a comfortable prosperity, which is earned by one's own work, not a pile of easy riches or excessive indulgence. Many of the myths suggest that if you want something from the god Odin but are uncomfortable working with him, or perhaps don't quite trust him, you might do well to approach him through his wife, or at least to petition Frigg in addition to Odin. She has proved that she has influence with the Allfather and is often a more predictable patron than he is.

All coming-of-age rituals for girls and women may include Frigg in them as she is particularly concerned with women's lives. The image of Sleeping Beauty, who, on reaching puberty, pricked her finger on a spindle and fell into a magical deathlike sleep, could be incorporated into a woman-making rite. Rites and ceremonies preparing a woman for marriage, motherhood, and menopause can also benefit from petitioning Frigg's aid.

Frigg should be called on for help in learning to scry and perform other similar types of divination. As a goddess of brewers and of hospitality, she would be one of the key deities of the sumble, an ancient Germanic drinking ritual that involves passing a horn among the people and making oaths, telling tales, toasting gods and ancestors, and speaking other words of power. The horn was traditionally passed by the mistress of the household, which ties it to Frigg, but even more than that, sumbles tend to bind a group of people together in the kind of frith and harmony that are Frigg's hallmark.

Honoring Yule

The season of Yule is strongly associated with Frigg, as is the period between Yule and Easter, and many of the old Yule customs can still be performed in her honor. One practice is to make an effort to finish your work by the end of the old year, be it spinning or writing a term paper, and to keep the twelve holy days of the Yule period as a time of rest as much as possible.

I know this is often difficult in modern times, with jobs and other obligations, but one can still try to put aside as many of one's regular duties as possible and make Yule a special time devoted to festive activities and preparations. The first or last night of Yule may be dedicated to Frigg and special foods eaten in her honor. These items may include fish, especially herring, and dishes made from grains, particularly oats and barley, such as dumplings, pancakes, or porridge. In some areas the day after the end of Yule was "Berchte's Night," and indeed, a simple meal the day after the excesses of New Year's Eve is often welcome.

Frigg's Symbols

Frigg is associated with a number of symbolic objects. The spindle, in particular, as well as the distaff and the weaver's sword, are all Frigg's special emblems. Linen, flaxseed, and linseed oil are also strongly associated with her and can be used as symbols in making charms for her rituals. Linseed oil is often used as a finishing touch on runic wands and talismans, which highlights another connection between Frigg and her husband, Odin, the god of runes. Some of the stones and jewels that can be used in workings to Frigg are silver, rock crystal, jet, and onyx. Her colors include white, blue, and gray.

A number of runes are associated with Frigg. *Uruz* is one, because of its shaping and manifesting properties. *Raiðo,* the rune of right and order, also symbolizes the holy procession of the god or goddess in the ritual wagon. *Kenaz* is related to Frigg because of its connection to crafts and smithwork. *Gebo,* the rune of gifts and contractual alliances, including marriage, and *wunjo,* a rune of harmony, kinship, and the home, are very strongly associated with Frigg as a goddess of relationships and family. *Hagalaz,* although seemingly destructive, is essentially another rune of order and shaping, representing the underlying structure of the universe that wards off chaos; it also seems like a fitting symbol for Frigg's German counterparts, Holda and Berchte, in their wilder aspects. *Perþro* is traditionally associated with ørlög and divination, and thus represents Frigg's magical and soothsaying aspects. *Berkano,* the birch goddess rune, is a rune of fertility and protection and is also one of the chief birth runes, thus tying it to Frigg in her role as a goddess of childbirth. The watery images of *laguz* are reminiscent of Frigg's connections with water and wells; it is the rune of the passage to and from life, the rune of the vatni ausa, the naming ceremony. It, like perþro, is also tied to Frigg's ability to see ørlög; its alternate name, *laukaz,* means leek, an onionlike plant of fertility and protection. The last rune, *oþala,* is the rune of ancestral property, the wealth and strength of the clan and the protective enclosure that keeps the world of order and society safe from the chaos without.

Plants Sacred to Frigg

Many plants and other natural objects are connected with Frigg. The linden tree, whose wood warriors used to make shields, is associated with her, representing her protective function. The birch, a tree held sacred to goddesses in general, can be connected with Frigg because of its cleansing and healing properties and its association with fertility. Birch branches are used in saunas to this day to promote circulation by lightly slapping them against the skin. Birch trees are also often used for Maypoles or Midsummer poles and have been compared by many writers to fair young maidens; hence the tree's association with female deities. Birches always seem more like young women or girls to me, however, more appropriate for Freyja or Idun. Beech trees look more like elegant matrons, stately and silvery. The beech is sometimes linked with the rune perþro and Frigg's role as a goddess of divination and ørlög.[4]

The elder is another tree often connected with Frigg, especially in her German forms. It is a tree associated with healing, protection, death, and magic. The Old English (OE) name for it was *aeld* ("fire"), probably because its hollowed-out branches were used to start fires. They were also used for toys and musical pipes, giving the elder the nick-name "pipe-tree."[5] This tree was also associated with grief and death; it was sometimes buried in graves or carried in funeral processions to protect against evil spirits. Each elder was believed to have a guardian female spirit, called the *Hyldemoer* (Elder-Tree Mother), dwelling in its branches,[6] and many people still fear to cut down an elder tree without performing some sort of ritual asking the spirit's permission. The elder is also sometimes associated with Berchte's Night, the last night of Yule. If one stands in a magical circle holding elderberries gathered from the tree at Midsummer, one is protected from any evil wights that may still be abroad.[7]

A number of herbs are believed to be holy to Frigg, especially those used for healing and for women's reproductive health. Mugwort is useful for menstrual cramps and is also said to induce a mild trance state suitable for meditation and divination. A charm for dreaming can be made by sewing some mugwort into a small linen pillow and then sleeping on it. Mugwort got its name from its use in brewing; before the discovery of hops, it was used to flavor beer and ale. It is one of the nine holy herbs mentioned in the Anglo-Saxon Nygon Wyrta Galder ("Nine Herbs Charm").

Two other herbs from that charm—nettle and chamomile—may also be associated with Frigg because of their healing and tonic properties. Nettle stalks were used to make a cloth similar to linen before the introduction of flax. The Latin name for chamomile, *Matricaria,* means "Beloved Mother," and it was also sometimes called "Balder's Brow." The herb was considered useful for menstrual problems and children's ailments, particularly nightmares. Motherwort is another herb strongly associated with female disorders and hence related to Frigg. In addition, it is used for protection, to promote longevity, and as a cure for melancholy and nervous complaints. Yarrow was also taken to treat melancholy and was noted for its effectiveness in treating wounds. It was used in magic and divination, particularly in matters of love, and was so magically powerful that after the introduction of Christianity it was associated with the Christian devil.[8]

European mistletoe, which was best known as the plant that killed Frigg's son, Balder, was sometimes used to treat complaints associated with menopause.

Animals and Frigg

There is no animal specifically designated as Frigg's special symbol, but a number of creatures might be associated with her. As the archetypal housewife, she is connected to all domestic animals, especially farm animals, and the products obtained from them. These include geese, ducks, and chickens (eggs and bedding), sheep (wool, with its association to spinning), and cows and goats (milk, cheese, and butter). Frigg can travel between the worlds in the shape of a hawk, so this can be considered one of her animals. The German Frau Gode rides in the Wild Hunt and is generally accompanied by black hunting hounds, so horses and dogs might also be associated with Frigg. The hawk, the horse, and the hound are traditionally thought of as noble creatures and would be suitable symbols for Frigg in her role as queen.

 # Ritual

There are many types of rituals and many ways to do them, and your choices generally depend on your personal preferences and those of the gods and goddesses with whom you are working. Some basic elements that are present in most rituals are the following: the marking and hallowing of a holy space, a statement of some sort regarding the purpose of the ritual, calling on any deities or other powers whose presence is desired, an exchange of energy, parting with the powers, and closing the ritual space.

Hallowing creates a place and time that are set apart from the everyday world, a ritual space in which the worlds of gods and people overlap.

The **statement** is designed to set forth the purpose and intentions of the rite. It can be a few brief and simple sentences or a more elaborate performance, incorporating music and poetry. It centers and clarifies your thoughts, making sure that everyone participating in the ritual is in agreement and knows what they are doing. It also alerts the gods and goddesses to your presence and your desires.

Calling on the deities and other powers whose presence you desire can consist of anything from a very simple invocation to an elaborate ritual drama. The purpose is to attract the attention of the gods and goddesses and draw their might to the holy place, as well as to evoke an intellectual and emotional response in the minds and hearts of the human participants. The calls should reflect the purpose of the rite and the nature and preferences of the gods and goddesses being invoked.

The **exchange of energies** between humans and deities is the centerpiece of most rituals and can take many forms. In Germanic religion this blessing (or *blót*) usually consists of charging a container of drink with the might of the gods and goddesses, sharing it among the participants, and making a gift of the remainder to the deities. During the charging, all the emotional energy raised during the calls mingles with the might and presence of the gods and is focused into the vessel of drink. The sharing usually includes drinking and then sprinkling the liquid on the *hörg,* or altar, the holy space, and the participants. The remainder is usually poured out on the ground but can also be poured into water, cast into the air, or thrown into fire, depending on the nature of the rite and of the deities invoked. This exchange of gifts among gods and people is of the highest importance. It allows might to be exchanged among the worlds and serves as a bond of friendship and loyalty between gods and humans.

Parting with the powers you have called and **closing the holy place** can be combined. This concluding routine usually consists of a reversal of whatever acts were used to create the ritual time and space. The gods, goddesses, and other powers invited to the working are thanked and honored one last time, and the holy place that was marked off and made special is returned to its former state. This also has the effect of returning the consciousness of the participants to the everyday world.

I have not gone into great detail about ritual workings, because that is not the focus of this work, but I will include a very brief ritual to Frigg to serve as an outline for anyone who has never created or done a ritual before and would like to try working with some of the goddesses in this book.

Ritual (Blót) to Frigg

Hallowing
(Details about how to do this are included in chapter 4, "How to Do Trancework.")

- Chant *Ansuz—Laguz—Uruz* and light the Candle of Will.
- Chant *Woden—Wili—We* three times to center yourself and draw all the participants together.
- Perform the hammer hallowing.

Statement
- "We gather to greet the queen of Heaven and to share our gifts here on her hearth . . ."

Call to Frigg
Frigg, mighty mother,
Mistress of Fensalir,
Lady of the Aesir and the Asynjur,
Daughter of Fjörgynn,
Wife of Odin,
Mother of Balder and his blind brother.

We call you from Fensalir, the Hall of Mists,
From the high throne of Hlidskjalf, the magic mirror,
From the Lyfjaberg, the hill of healing!

Queen of High Heaven, weaver of clouds,
Prudent wife and wisest of counselors,
Knowing all fates, though speaking them never.

The keys of Asgard hang at your waist.
Unlock the doors to those bright halls,
High Hostess, greet the people of Midgard,
And loving counsel give your children.

Frigg, the queen, the star mother!
You fashion the clouds on the loom of heaven
And spin your thread on the wheel of time.

You bring order to the Nine Worlds,
And knowledge to men and women.
You are midwife to the earth;
By your skill you bring forth the fruit of her labor.

To all who seek, to all who aspire,
You give your candle to light the way
And teach your song to startle the stillness,
For those who have wisdom need never fear.

We call you from Fensalir, the Hall of Mists,
From the high throne of Hlidskjalf, the magic mirror,
From the Lyfjaberg, the hill of healing!

Great Mother, greet the people of Midgard,
And loving counsel give your children;

They who have called you
  Holda, Berchte, Frau Gode,
  Vrou-Elde, Ffraed, Brigid,
  Frijjo, Frija, Fricg, Frigida, Frigg,
Come!
Frigg, Mother, Come!
Frigg, Beloved, Come!

BLESSING

- During the final part of the above invocation, raise your hands (or spindle or other holy symbol, if you are using one) and then lower them over, or into, the vessel of drink. Visualize a stream of blessing and power flowing from the goddess and the participants into the liquid.

- Raise the horn or cup; make the symbol of a spiral over it and say, "Frigg, make holy this gift of our skill and our love."

- Pass the drink clockwise around the circle, letting all the participants take turns sharing it. If you are alone, drink part of it yourself.

- When you're finished, take a tree twig, preferably an evergreen, and sprinkle your hörg and all the participants. Sprinkle a little in each of the four quarters, saying: "Hail to the North!" and "Hail to the East!" and so on.

- Pour the remainder in a blessing bowl. Pour this libation out upon the ground, preferably at the base of a tree, saying, "Hail, Frigg, queen of Asgard. Accept this gift of our skill and our love." (If you are performing the blót indoors, keep the bowl on the hörg and pour it out on the ground immediately after the rite, or at the earliest convenient opportunity.)

CLOSING

- "Hail Frigg, queen of Asgard and mightiest of mothers!"
- Chant *Woden—Wili—We* three times.
- Chant *Ansuz—Laguz—Uruz; Alu* and blow out the Candle of Will.

◆

As mentioned earlier, after the ritual proper it is a good idea to quickly record your experiences and impressions for future use. It is also appropriate to have a small celebration or feast, which can include some suitable food and drink as well as any appropriate songs, stories, and other entertainment. After all, gods and goddesses, like human guests, like to be made welcome when they go visiting.

9

EiR

The Doctor

 LoRe

Eir (ON Eir) is called *honer loeknir beztr* ("the best of leeches"), the finest doctor, in the *Prose Edda* (Gylfaginning, ch. 35). In early Norse culture medicine was practiced more or less exclusively by women, which explains why Eir is a goddess of healing and not a god. The etymology of her name is not completely clear, but it probably means something like "gracious," "kindly," or "helpful." The Norse word *eir* ("copper") is not technically related to this goddess's name. Still, it is interesting to note the connection copper has, even today, with the cure of certain ailments, such as the wearing of copper bracelets to treat arthritis.

Eir is listed among the Asynjur and may be regarded as one of Frigg's attendants; thus the two can be assumed to share many qualities and functions. This is borne out by the fact that Frigg was also connected with healing, particularly childbirth. Eir also appears in the train of another goddess—Menglod. In the only surviving tale that Eir appears in, the Svipdagsmál in the *Elder Edda* (sts. 51–56), the hero Svipdag has come to seek Menglod's hand in marriage. Her giant warder, Fjolsvith (which is also one of Odin's many names), engages him in one of those question-and-answer sessions so dear to the Norse heart. In the process, he directs his attention to a nearby mountain—the Lyfjaberg, or

"Hill of Healing"—where Menglod sits happily with her nine maidens. Among these maidens, whose names all mean things like "Shelter," "Pleasant," and "Peaceful," is Eir. The figure of Menglod ("Necklace Glad") is sometimes identified with Frigg, but more often with Freyja. Freyja, like Frigg, was also connected with healing and childbirth. Also, the wooing and subsequent marriage of Menglod to the hero, as well as her situation on a fire-ringed mountain, is similar to the Valkyrie Sigrdrífa in the Sigrdrífumál (or Brunhild in the *Niebelungenlied*).

To arrive at a single deity solely in charge of childbirth and healing is thus very difficult. This is one of the areas where the powers of Frigg and Freyja intersect. They were both called on by women in labor, and often at the same time, as in the Oddrúnargrátr (st. 8). This kind of juxtaposition could be explained by the premise that the two goddesses were worshipped in different areas of the North until their functions gradually merged and became blurred. This duality might also represent different kinds of healing.

For all the similarities and confusion between Frigg and Freyja (see pages 74–84), in practice (that is, invoking these goddesses and seeing what happens) the feel or "flavor" of each is unmistakable and very, very different. Freyja, among other things, is full of movement, energy, and lusty life—the force of life itself, certainly a desirable thing for a healing. Frigg, on the other hand, brings peace, soothing, calmness—also good at the sickbed. Instead of worrying about which goddess is the "official" healer, it is more useful to decide what kind of healing you want for a given occasion—vibrant energy or soothing peace (or both, as in childbirth). For example, one might picture Freyja as a physical therapist inciting you to exercise and Frigg as the mother encouraging you to rest. Freyja would also seem more appropriate for invasive techniques like surgery and drug therapy, while Frigg is probably more interested in holistic types of medicine, such as herbalism, massage, and preventive practices. It is significant that Eir, the goddess of healing, serves both of them, although her main connection and energy seem to be related to Frigg and the Asynjur.

Medical science in Heathen times was part priestly, part magical, and part common sense. In the *Heimskringla* (ch. 234), Snorri gives an example of medical treatment in his account of the death of Thormod Kolbrunarskald after the battle of Stiklestad in 1030. In this tale the wounded were taken to a barn after the fighting, where a woman heated water and dressed their wounds. She then made a porridge of leeks and herbs and fed it to the wounded. If the smell of onions came from a man's belly wound, it meant his intestines had been pierced and he was dying. This use of a test meal for diagnosis is still used today, albeit not with leek porridge. Tacitus, in his *Germania* (ch. 6), describes how the German tribes took their womenfolk to the battle with them. There the women not only shrieked and shouted to frighten the enemy and encourage their own warriors, but they also performed magical rites of warding and divination. They also functioned as physicians, and they were said to be unafraid to count and compare the gashes.[1] This presence of women on the battlefield also ties in with Freyja and the Valkyries.

On a more peaceful note, healing goddesses also took particular interest in the well-being of women, who especially needed medical help during childbirth. The Lyfjaberg of Menglod was a holy place devoted to sick women; the Svipdagsmál states that if a woman climbed it, she would be cured no matter how long she had been sick. It goes on to say that these goddesses would aid all who gave offerings on the holy altars and would protect mortals from danger (st. 56).

This tie between ritual and healing can also be seen in the relationship of healers to seers and sorcerers. Great pestilences and serious illnesses required sacrifices to the gods as well as more practical treatment. By the Middle Ages, this ritual function had passed to the Christian priests, but some of the old folkways continued to be practiced by peasant wisewomen and wisemen who, as the knowledge became diffused and muddled over time, began to misuse the old remedies and brought on themselves the charge of witchcraft.

The healer Eir also has links to Frigg in the latter's role as ruler and mistress of the household. In ancient times queens, as well as kings, were often believed to have the power to cure certain illnesses by their touch. This connection between the lady of the estate and the medical treatment of the rest of the inhabitants continued through the Middle Ages and up to the present. The lady of the manor generally felt responsible for the health of the tenants, as did the wife of many a farmer or rancher. Even today it is usually Mom to whom you run for the aspirin and sympathy. It is ironic that women struggling to become doctors in the recent past and present have been told that medicine is "man's work."

Folk Remedies

Some examples of folk remedies that combined magic with medicine included measuring the patient, hanging the measuring thread or string somewhere for a specific time, and then checking to see if the measurement had changed; the result indicated the patient's fate.[2] Another practice was to stroke the affected part of the body with one's hand, a sleeve, or the back of a knife. Sometimes a thread or string was tied around the afflicted area, often with a medicinal poultice underneath it.[3] Some cures involved wrapping the patient in fresh, clean flax or laying her in a field of flax.[4] Flax and linen are, of course, also associated with Frigg.

The elder tree was incorporated into a number of healing customs. In Scandinavia an elder twig held in the mouth was believed to be a remedy for toothache. Some healing practices involved bathing the patient and drawing the disease into the water then emptying it onto an elder bush. Sometimes the illess was transferred to an egg or another object, which was then wrapped in linen and buried.[5]

The use of fire to cure certain ailments was also common. The practice of driving beasts and people through festival fires to ensure their health and well-being was common throughout western Europe. An old cure for fever, reminiscent of Hansel and Gretel, involved pushing a sick child in and out of a baking oven (not while the oven was lit, presumably). Another custom was to lay a child by the hearth fire to invoke the cure of the goddess and the night wives (female supernatural entities believed to haunt the night).[6] This brings to mind tales of the White Lady, who was said to sit by the fire at night and rock the babies of her chosen household.

The image of a motherly goddess of the hearth is found in other

European legends as well. For example, a Greek myth tells of a queen who is visited by a strange woman who offers to wet-nurse the queen's newborn son. One night the mother wakes up and wanders into the main hall to find that the woman has placed the baby in the hearth fire. When the mother understandably screams, the stranger, now recognizable as the goddess Demeter, snatches the child out of the fire and gives him to her, chiding the mother that the treatment had almost made the child invulnerable but that the mother's meddling has ruined it. Demeter was the Greek goddess of the fields and agriculture and, like Frigg, lost her favorite child to the deity of the Underworld.

It is also interesting to note the way in which certain diseases were personified, especially the dreaded plague. Usually depicted as a woman, she often bears a strong resemblance to Hel, the goddess of death. In certain areas of Germany and Central Europe she was called Kuga, and people had to be careful to avoid leaving unwashed dishes in the house overnight or Kuga would feel obliged to stop and clean them as she passed through.[7] This figure is reminiscent of the Germanic versions of Frigg—Berchte and Holda—who made it their business to inspect the housekeeping on Twelfth Night. But then, it is not surprising that death and healing should go hand in hand.

Eir piqued my curiosity because my meditations on her came in a spontaneous, rather than a structured, fashion, and I ran into some very interesting coincidences connected with her. In a way, she was the goddess that started it all for me.

It began one spring when I had become suddenly and violently ill—nausea, diarrhea, fever. I had assumed it was some sort of flu and gone to bed, resigning myself to the inevitable. Because a violent series of chills and shaking prevented me from getting to sleep, however, I decided to use some of this magic I had been studying—what good is it if you can't use it when you need it? I made a tea of sage, chamomile, elder, and peppermint, because this combination seemed appropriate somehow, according to my scanty knowledge of herbs. The previous summer I had listened to a workshop given by a woman who used a healing technique based on the chakras—energy, in the form of light, was drawn through each center of the body, beginning with the area just above the head and ending with the area just below where one stood or sat. At the time, I had just begun doing this Heathen stuff (lots of reading but not much practice) and I didn't know any appropriate healing techniques of my own, so I decided to adapt this. I took my tea and charged it, drawing energy down through the centers of my body and into the tea, and called on Eir, who I knew was the Norse goddess of healing. The chills and shaking stopped even before I finished; the knots in my stomach loosened. I drank the tea and tried to sleep, thinking how nice it would be if I had a dream about this goddess, Eir . . .

Trance

A woman is beside me. She has light-brown hair, done up in a soft, intricate knot. She is of medium height—sharp featured, sharp boned, square shouldered, angular. Her eyes are sharp, deep-set, and gray; she is calm and serious. Stroking me, laying her hands on my stomach, she begins doing the energy raising for me. She lies down, her body on top of mine, belly to belly, and breathes into my mouth. I sleep . . .

Well, I was pretty excited; I'd had a genuine visitation! Now before I go on, I want to make it clear that I'm a pretty suspicious, cynical type not given to believing everyone who thinks they've been walking between the worlds, not even me (especially not me). On the other hand, I do believe that such things are possible. I just want to make sure I'm getting the genuine article and not simply fooling myself. So I like to approach such visions of mine with a healthy degree of skepticism.

The telling point in this "dream" was when Eir lay on top of me and breathed in my mouth. I've read a few texts about shamanism, so I know this is a shamanistic healing technique used in many cultures. Only I didn't know it then. What's more, this kind of action was something I would never have pictured a dignified goddess such as Eir doing.

When a trance veers off in a direction very different from what I expect, I begin to think there may be something to it.

Oh, yes, I also got well. Turned out I didn't have the flu. I had salmonella poisoning, a type of food poisoning that the doctor assured me can be fatal if not properly treated. Fortunately, goddesses, unlike university health centers, are open on the weekend.

Years later I was giving blood to the Red Cross, a practice that used to make me very squeamish, I blush to admit. In fact, that's one of the reasons I was doing it, as an act of will. Because I'm a small person with small veins, it took quite awhile for the phlebotomists to get my pint out, and because I found the act not only tedious but also nerve-racking, I started using the time to daydream about gods and things, notably Tyr, from whom I thought I might borrow a little valor. I was very tired that afternoon, and gradually this daydreaming grew deeper until it became a sort of hypnogogic dream state . . .

I see Eir rushing from her room. It is made of rough wood with open beams. Bundles of herbs and flowers hang drying from them, and bottles and potions are lying all over the room. Her small, narrow bed is made with very white, clean sheets and a homemade quilt. She is running because this is the day Tyr is binding the wolf, and she knows there will be trouble. She has run to her room to get her medicines and now hurries back to the assembly of the gods. From the hill in the distance she hears their cries and shouts. She arrives to find that Tyr has lost his hand. All is turmoil as the wolf is led away bound, and the gods shout and talk excitedly to one another. Eir and Frigg support Tyr by the shoulders, helping him back to Eir's room. Eir treats him, trying to stop the bleeding. Alone with her now, he shows the pain and sorrow he would not yield to before the others. Later that night he is asleep, or unconscious, lying on Eir's small bed. She takes off her clothes and lies on top of him, her naked body against his. She breathes into his mouth. His sleep becomes easier . . .

I get the feeling that whenever Tyr can take a moment for himself, he seeks out this quiet, strong woman whose courage and devotion to duty match his own.

I found this interesting because I had never pictured Tyr with a mate or lover, or even "just a good friend," nor read of his being connected with a goddess, although there is a verse in the Lokasenna (st. 40) indicating that Tyr had a wife. Several weeks later I received an issue of a Heathen magazine in which there was an article describing a tranceworking that also dealt with Tyr's loss of his hand. In this trance the author had had a vision of Tyr lying on a bed in a candlelit room while a woman knelt at his side, her upper body lying across his, weeping.[8]

Reading this certainly excited me. Although Ariel, the author of the article, felt that the woman present in the room with Tyr was the goddess-figure Night, and the description of her differed somewhat from mine, it did seem striking that we both had had a vision of Tyr's loss that included his being cared for by a woman in blue garments, a woman who obviously had strong feelings for him.

Years later I came across some references describing several carved stones found at Housesteads, a Roman fort on Hadrian's wall (a Roman fortification in northern England). The inscriptions are dedicated to Mars Thincsus ("Mars of the Thing") and the two Alaisiagae, or Alaisiagis. Mars of the Thing is usually assumed to refer to Tyr in his aspect as the god of the Thing, or legal assembly. A stone relief shows a god, presumably Mars/Tyr, with two female figures. An altar found later also had an inscription to the Alaisiagae, this time referring to them as goddesses and giving their names as Baudihillie and Friagabi ("Battle Ruler" and "Freedom Giver").[9]

Echoes of Eir

These names and the presence of the female deities with a battle god would seem to suggest that these are Valkyrie figures, although the inscription stresses the god's lawgiving function. The name *Alaisiagae* seems related to the term *alagabie* ("lavish givers"), usually applied to the dísir. Jan de Vries, Dutch scholar of Germanic linguistics and mythology, goes on to connect this term to the Frisian word for lawspeaker, *asega,* and with the verb *aisjan,* which he relates to the word *eisa* or *eira,* arriving at the conclusion that the goddess pair might be related, albeit at some distance, to the Norse Eir.[10] Eir herself appears in a list of beings referred to as "Odin's maids" (Skáldskaparmál, ch. 75). Many of the other names in the list sound like Valkyries, although they are also called norns and are said to shape human destiny.[11]

This is not to imply that all of this proves that Tyr and Eir were definitely connected in Old Norse worship, although certainly a warrior god and a healing deity would have some overlapping interests. In addition, Eir's associate, Frigg, shares a number of qualities with Tyr, particularly their support of law and social order. Interestingly, something that started out as an independent dream or vision was mirrored in the vision of another person with whom I'd had no contact and later echoed in some actual inscriptions.

Eir, then, is primarily a goddess of healing and physical health. She is involved not only with all aspects of healing disease and injury but also with nutrition, exercise, and preventive medicine and health maintenance. Her scope encompasses mental and emotional well-being as well as bodily health. She is also a goddess of magic and shamanism, particularly those practices related to healing.

Eir and Frigg share this interest in healing, particularly women's health concerns and the process of conception and childbirth. They fulfill the role of the mother as nurturer and nurse. Although primarily mentioned in relation to human health, Eir is also presumably concerned with the health of the community's animal companions. Frigg too has a strong connection to domestic animals and herself appears in the "Second Merseburg Charm" as one of the deities attempting to heal Balder's horse. Eir also has ties to Freyja, both in her connection to childbirth and in her role as the healer and wisewoman present on the battlefield.

 ## Ritual

Rituals to Eir would obviously be concerned with healing, which would include the maintenance of good health in general as well as healing specific wounds or diseases. In cases of pregnancy and childbirth one would want to call on Freyja and Frigg as well as Eir. Eir seems connected to soothing colors, particularly blues and grays, greens, and also white. Copper might be used as a symbol, worn as jewelry or magically charged as an amulet or charm. People with knowledge of herbology could use appropriate herbs as symbols or as part of a charm, or even drink them in a tea or wine. Eir can be invoked in conjunction with most other healing techniques or any type of magic one would ordinarily use to promote health. In rituals to Eir, herbal teas, milk, or fruit juices often seem more desirable than alcoholic beverages for toasts and libations, particularly when one is actually ill. However, this goddess also seems to like cider and sherry and the occasional dose of medicinal whiskey.

Any healing magic should also be accompanied by a pledge to take specific practical steps in the physical world to improve one's health; praying for Eir to help you with your cholesterol level while scarfing down as many cheeseburgers as you can is not going to work. Eir, like Frigg, is a practical goddess who likes her petitioners to be willing to do some of the work themselves and to be able to take care of themselves in the everyday world. Rituals to Eir are often accompanied by a strong desire to be nice to yourself; yield to this. Make yourself the special, soothing, sickbed foods Mother used to give you (or those you wish Mother had given you); sleep late; take it easy; and give your body and soul a chance to be well and happy.

Call to Eir

Hail Eir—best of leeches—
the peaceful, the kindly . . .
partner of Frigg, the mother;
comrade of Menglod, the healer;
friend of Tyr, the one-handed god.

Solace of the sick,
Binder of bloody wounds,

Midwife to the mother,
Mother to the child,
        Herb keeper—tea brewer—
        Smoother of cool white sheets,
                the fever's bane.

Come to us,   gray-eyed goddess;
Bring healing and health,
        succor and strength,
        love and long life.

Eir—Healer—Come!

10

Saga

The Storyteller

 ## Lore

Saga (ON Sága) is another of the Norse goddesses who are numbered among the Asynjur. Snorri (Gylfaginning, ch. 35) lists her as the second goddess and states that she lives in a great dwelling called Sokkvabekk. In the Grímnismál (st. 7) we learn that Sokkvabekk is the fourth hall in Asgard, surrounded by cool waves, and that every day Odin and Saga drink there gladly together from cups of gold.

Although we are not told many details about Saga, there is still much that can be inferred from the sparse information available. Her name, while technically not the same word as the feminine Icelandic noun *saga,* undoubtedly comes from the same root, *segja,* meaning "to say or tell." The Old Norse word *saga* means "story," "tale," or "history," and in modern German and English it still means "legend" or "myth." More specifically, we use it to refer to heroic narratives written in the twelfth or thirteenth centuries that chronicle the feats of historical or legendary figures in Scandinavian culture or modern narratives written in the same style.

A saga is more than mere history—it blends fact with legend, narrative with poetry. The pre-Christian Norse made no distinction between factual, historical works and fictional, literary ones.[1] Instead, people sought to record all aspects of reality, combining factual, artistic, and spiritual truths into an organic whole. They had no concept of fiction but regarded all tales as true on a certain level. To them, legends were as real as documented occurrences, and therefore they did not distinguish between the two in their sagas. A saga records the history of a people's soul rather than mere events and thus is a link between the ancestors and the present and future generations.

A Personification of Legends

The goddess Saga, then, can be seen as a personification of these stories, and indeed she is not the only feminine figure to be used to personify a legend. The Greek muse Klio personified history, although what Saga represents would probably encompass several of the muses' functions. In Germany, when people took turns telling stories, they said the Märlein went around from house to house. This game of passing around the telling of myths or fables was also practiced by the ancient Greeks and Romans.[2] In Norway parents still tell their children *eventyr* ("fairy tales," from the ON *ævintyr* and related to the English *adventure*).

The poets of the thirteenth century captured the spirit of adventure in their verse. In their Frau Aventiure tales, Dame Aventiure wandered the countryside on foot, knocking at the doors of the minstrels and demanding that they let her in.[3] Peter Suchenwirt, late-fourteenth-century Austrian poet, describes a vision of Dame Aventiure. In it, she appears in a forest grove and says she has traveled throughout the land, visiting kings and lords as Frau Ehre's messenger, and now has come to make her report. Then, putting a gold ring on her finger, she disappears.[4] *Ehre* is the German word meaning "honor," "reputation," or "glory," and, like Saga, it is a feminine noun. Frau Ehre can be compared to Frigg, the queen of Heaven, who functions as a dispenser of glory much as an earthly queen would and who, as Lady of the Asynjur, is Saga's leader. Also, spinning and storytelling, the special functions of these two goddesses, have long been connected in the lore of the dísir and wisewomen of Germanic culture.

Saga has often been compared to Frigg, many seeing her as merely another name or guise for Frigg herself and not a separate goddess at all. Some sources claim that Saga is Frigg because Odin, Frigg's husband, drinks with Saga daily in her hall. Given Odin's reputation with women, I find this reasoning less than persuasive. But what is the relationship between Odin and Saga? Odin, in his function as poet and giver of divine inspiration, represents here all writers and poets who must return to the primal legends and the collective soul of their people to derive that inspiration that is the mark of truly great poetry.

The name of Saga's hall, Sokkvabekk, means "Sinking Brook," and the *Elder Edda* goes on to speak of the cool waves that flow there. In the Helgakviða Hundingsbana I (st. 39), Sinfjötli claims to have fathered nine wolf cubs in a place called Sogunes. *Sogunes,* or *Sagunes,* means "Saga's ness" or "Saga's cape" (as in a seacoast). The image of wolves, one of Odin's animals, and the appearance of the Odinic hero Sinfjötli reinforces the link between Saga and Odin. The fact that the place is obviously near the ocean supports the connection between Saga and water, and the use of Saga in a place-name gives her existence as a separate goddess more credence.

Vague as the mythical references to Saga are, she has managed to leave an impression on the modern Norse mind, as shown by a line from the Norwegian national anthem, "Ja, vi elsker dette landet" ("Yes, we love this land"):

> *Og den saganatt som senker,*
> *drømmer på vår jorð.*
> *(And the night of Saga sinking*
> *dreams upon our land.)*

Granted, they may have been thinking of saga, the tale, rather than Saga the goddess, but the images of sinking and dreams are highly reminiscent of Saga's realm of memories, the Sinking Brook.

Viewed symbolically, Saga's hall represents the stream of the unconscious, a typical meaning assigned to water in both myth and psychology. Again, Saga's dwelling is the source of our inspiration, our songs and stories that ring true and have the seeds of greatness in them. Odin, wise as always, knows he needs to periodically drink from this well of collective memory to refuel his energies. In return, the father of heroic deeds supports, favors, and protects history and the past, and through the poet's song remembers and glorifies it. The cup from which they drink is both the cup of poetic inspiration and the cup of immortality.

The waters of Saga's hall can also represent the Well of Urd, where the spiritual might of the past resides. The Germanic concept of time is dominated by the past, which is seen as an ever-growing accumulation of experience that shapes and nurtures the present and into which all actions are constantly being interwoven. Saga's power is strongly connected to the workings of ørlög, the primal events laid down from time's beginning that shape the patterns of present events.

Saga is connected with those aspects of ørlög represented by Mimir's Well, which can be considered part of the Well of Urd. Mimir is a jotun, or giant, whose name means "memory" and whose well contains everything that has ever been in all the worlds. By drinking daily from the well, Mimir partakes of the ever-growing ancestral wisdom of the entire cosmos, and it is this might for which Odin was willing to give up an eye. Odin's daily drinking with Saga could well be representative of his continuing affiliation with the powers of the unconscious and of the past.

Saga is also associated with the sumble, a holy ritual drinking feast. This is one of the oldest and mightiest of Germanic ritual works, and remnants of it are even found in modern secular practices, such as making toasts. The core elements of sumble involve passing a vessel, usually a horn, of ritual drink and speaking words of meaning and power, notably toasts, boasts, oaths, and short narratives about great deeds of the past.

The horn symbolizes the Well of Urd and the spiritual power of the past. During the sumble, the worlds of people and gods become one in a timeless place where the events of the past are interwoven with the events yet to be done. By speaking over the holy horn, the people are placing their words into the Well of Urd and helping to shape what is becoming.

Saga's links to the deeds of the past, to ritual drinking, and to song and storytelling all connect her to the sumble ritual. Moreover, the traditional bearer of the sumble horn was the mistress of the house. For example, in *Beowulf* the queen, Wealtheow, carries the horn around the hall. Frigg and Saga both share in this aspect of sumble, in which the hostess of a feast binds together a diverse group of people in goodwill and fellowship.

 ## Trance

I see a woman with dark hair—black, perhaps—pale skin, and blue eyes, tall and Junoesque, a mature woman in her late thirties or early forties. Her hair is elaborately done up, with interlacing braids and scarves and jewels scattered throughout. She wears much jewelry, and I notice in particular her earrings—big gold hoops. Her clothes are in various shades of blue. She is leonine, stately, dramatic. Her house lies by the sea, on rocks—not a high cliff, but overlooking the ocean, with a very rocky shoreline below. The house is stone and squarish in shape—but finished sculpted stone, not just rocks. It is fine and grand yet austere, with a terrace that overlooks the sea. She sits there with Odin, and they drink out of gold goblets and talk together—of poetry, of song, and of history, comparing what they know.

All the deeds of men and women on earth, at the minute they are carried out, appear carved into the walls of Saga's stone house, and somehow the walls never run out of room, despite how many new deeds are added to them. No matter how cleverly and carefully people may cover their tracks or trick history into falsehood, no matter what the world knows and does not know of deeds, the true deeds and actions of everyone are recorded in Saga's dwelling for all time, to the doer's everlasting shame or glory—and the walls sing to her, in a chorus of bell-like tones.

Saga often walks on the shore, out on the little rocky jetties, and looks at the sea, especially at dusk. The wind blows her scarves and clothes, which billow out behind her. She sings to herself then, in languages no one else knows or remembers . . .

This vision of Saga as the receptacle of human events and endeavors reinforces the image of her as the stream of unconscious memories of humanity. She represents history as it really happened, not as it was told or recorded. The telling of history is the province of Bragi and Odin, of the poet, and the telling can be exaggerated or falsified, but Saga is history, the story itself, the truth that cannot be changed or hidden. All poets, singers, bards, and scholars—or creators of any kind—need to know Saga, the ancient well of unconscious images and memories, if they wish to create truly from the heart and soul.

Ritual

Rituals to Saga can be done for a variety of reasons, many of them complex. For poets and authors, historians, storytellers, singers, and actors, Saga may be viewed as a patron, mentor, or muse and contacted frequently as a source of inspiration and wisdom and a model of skill.

More than that, however, she represents the deep-seated unconscious or collective memory of the folk, the time of sacred history and original action from which come the myths and paradigms that serve as models for all aspects of life. Anyone, whether artistic or not, can benefit by periodically returning to this source of inspiration to be renewed and reinvigorated. Saga can also be petitioned to redress wrongs and grievances. She should not be seen, however, as a participant in petty vengeance, for she functions in the realm of the eternal and not the mundane. She should be seen as a means to invoke the forces of ørlög, or fate (karma, if you will); her judgments are active in the timeless realms and not in this world. An unscrupulous but successful ruler, who is eventually exposed as corrupt years later in history texts, is an example of something Saga might bring to light.

Saga is associated with images of water or the sea, so blues, greens, grays, or whites might be appropriate colors to use in ritual, as well as shells and water-smoothed stones. She always seems a little flamboyant and flashy to me, so gold or jewels might make pleasing symbols, either as altar decorations or personal ornaments. If one is a skilled performer, an appropriate song or story could be enacted, especially pieces relating legendary or historical events. Group rituals to Saga might include a sumble in which all the participants share a piece with the others in Saga's honor. Silent meditation can be used in workings to Saga, usually following the invocation, with the aim of contacting the collective unconsciousness where Saga dwells to receive wisdom, inspiration, and renewal.

Call to Saga

Hail Saga,   mistress of memory,
    Keeper of the timeless records,
    Master storyteller,
    Speaker of true tales,
    Guardian of tradition, of fame, of honor . . .

Mistress of Sokkvabekk, the Sinking Brook,
House of the singing walls beside the stream of life.

Benchmate of Odin,   mead-glad matron,
Gold-decked lioness,   singer of songs,
Friend of the poet, the minstrel, the sage—
Judge of rulers, of priests, of warriors—
Keeper of the bright mirror and the dark.

Lead us once more to the ancient waters;
Drink with us in gladness and sing the old songs;
May our deeds and works honor your halls,
    and ring true in the telling.

Saga of Memory—Muse—Dame Aventiure—Frau Ehre—
    the Märlein—Saga—Come!

11

Gna

The Messenger

 LORE

Snorri (Gylfaginning, ch. 35) lists Gna (ON Gná) as the fourteenth Aesir goddess (*ásynja*) and identifies her as Frigg's attendant. Her name is related to the verb *gnæfa,* meaning "to tower up high" or "to project." Gna is Frigg's special messenger, able to travel with great speed through air and water and between the worlds. She sees all that goes on and reports it back to Frigg. Gna accomplishes these missions by means of her marvelous steed, Hofvarpnir ("Hoof Thrower"). Some nineteenth-century writers, who were given to seeing all the old deities as nature symbols, present Gna as a personification of the gentle breezes sent by Frigg, the sky goddess, to bring good weather to Midgard.[1]

Grimm compares Gna to the personification of Rumor in classical mythology—that divine messenger sent out through the air to listen to all that goes on and bring the tidings back to the high gods, who need to know everything.[2] The Latin equivalent, Fama, taken from a feminine noun meaning "talk, rumor, report," was also personified by many classical authors. Virgil describes her as a being who was small at first, but quickly grew to enormous size, with countless feathers, eyes, ears, and mouths. Fama is often portrayed with wings or feathers, or in flight like a bird.[3] Here one is reminded of Odin's ravens, who fly through the worlds and report back to the Allfather.

Gna's function is very similar to that of Huginn and Muninn: she also gathers news and reports it to Frigg. Ovid gave his Fama a home with many approaches; this is reminiscent of the house in which Loki is said to have hidden after exchanging insults with the other gods at Aegir's feast, a building with doors on all sides.

Guerber confuses Gna with the wish maiden Hljod in the story of the childless King Rerir. The king received a magic apple from the god Odin, enabling his wife to conceive (see pages 58–59). Guerber also enlarges Frigg's role as Odin's advisor and makes her the actual giver of the apple.[4] Guerber does not list a citation for this version of the tale, so it is difficult to tell where she got it or how authentic it is. However, because of Frigg's connection with conception and childbirth, she might certainly come to be seen as the dispenser of the apple of fertility, and, indeed, it is altogether possible that Odin got this apple from his wife. With Frigg as the apple-giver, the next logical move is to recast Odin's wish maiden as Frigg's own messenger, Gna. Despite the unclear origins of this version of the story, it does show how similar the relationship of Frigg with Gna is to that of Odin with his wish maidens, or Valkyries. Like Odin's womanly attendants, Gna carries Frigg's messages and works her will, sharing in Frigg's powers.

Gna's Shamanic Traits

Gna also exhibits a number of shamanic characteristics. She has a magical steed that travels between the worlds and through the elements, a familiar symbol in Northern shamanism. In this she is similar to both Skirnir, the messenger in the Skírnismál who rides Frey's steed to Jotunheim to court the giantess Gerd for him, and Hermod, who rides Sleipnir to Helheim at the request of Frigg to try to ransom Balder. In all these cases a lesser-known god or goddess rides a magical horse to another world to act there for another, more powerful deity. Like the shaman, Gna journeys to these other worlds to find out information and to perform magical acts for her people, in this case Frigg and the Aesir.

In one story associated with Gna (Gylfaginning, ch. 35), she is riding through the worlds one day when some of the Vanir look up and see her in the sky. One of them exclaims, "What flies there through the air?" Gna answers:

> *I don't fly,*   *but fare away*
> *swiftly over the clouds*
> *On Hofvarpnir,*   *sired by Hamskerpir*
> *out of Gardrofa.*
> GYLFAGINNING, CH. 35

Here Gna is clearly shown traveling to other worlds, in this case Vanaheim. It is also interesting that the Vanir don't recognize Gna. Perhaps she was flying too high or too fast, or the Vanir are so isolated from the rest of the worlds that they are unfamiliar with the members of the Aesir. Another possibility is that Gna is a shape-shifter and was not appearing in her usual form in this story. The final point to note is the element of humor that Gna exhibits. The names of her horse's sire and dam mean "Hide Hardener" and "Fence Breaker," respectively. Gna seems to be slightly mocking the Old Norse custom of formally reciting one's parentage when introducing oneself to strangers. Instead of admitting who she is, Gna teases the Vanir with a riddle about her mode of travel and gives the whimsical lineage of her horse instead of her own.

Gna seems so tied to the concept of movement that when I came to do a tranceworking on her I decided I should use a more active form of invocation than usual. I had been reading some books on shamanism at the time and was inspired to borrow some ideas for going into trance. I used a pair of old rattles and jogged in place, shaking them in rhythm while chanting this little song (se fig. 11.1), taken from Gna's speech to the Vanir:

> *I fare forth*   *through the air,*
> *I gallop and glide;*
> *On Hofvarpnir,*   *Hoof Thrower,*
> *swiftly I ride.*

I fare forth   through the air,
I gallop and glide;
On Hofvarpnir,   Hoof Thrower,
gently I ride.

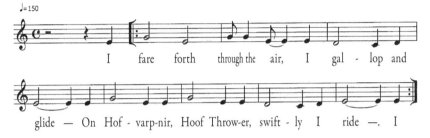

Figure 11.1. The sound of this chant is represented in these musical bars.

This chant can go on and on, with the same or different adjectives used before the phrase *I ride* in the last line. As I first did this I became extremely, hysterically giggly, and a feeling of great elation came over me. I later stopped running and lay down to go further into trance.

 ## Trance

I see a small, very tiny woman, or girl rather, no older than her teens, with masses of very wavy black, or dark brown, hair that flies out wildly all around her. She brings a feeling of great, almost hysterical, elation, plus wild giggling and mirth and almost constant motion. She has light skin and blue, or perhaps green, eyes, which sparkle greatly. She is never at rest and never stops laughing as she rushes in and out of the rooms in Frigg's hall. She spends much of her time riding around on an enormous bay horse whose back is incredibly wide, especially in comparison to Gna's tininess. She laughs uproariously as she rides. When questioned by the Vanir about who she is, her answer, in which she includes the lineage of her horse, is meant by her as a great joke—she laughs madly as she shouts out to them; she finds the fact that they are taking her seriously extremely funny. She reminds me of Gilbert and Sullivan's "Three Little Maids from School," who sing, "Everything is a source of fun"—and somehow, in the midst of all this hilarity, she manages to carry out Frigg's errands correctly—but not solemnly!

Gna seems to do everything in extremes. Unlike most of Frigg's attendants, she is not quiet or gentle or sensible or comforting. There is a feeling of wildness and almost manic joy and hilarity about her, a much sharper and stronger feeling than I've experienced with any of the other Asynjur. Gna is also more difficult to describe in human terms; her functions, what she might be expected to contribute to Midgard, are unclear.

As Frigg's messenger and the worker of her will, as shamanic traveler between worlds, Gna seems to represent Frigg's magical self. The German versions of Frigg—Holda and Berchte—both have a darker, wild form. Frigg herself never directly appears in this role, but Gna could be seen as embodying Frigg's wilder, freer side. Gna is not tied down to responsibilities, and roams freely through the worlds, heedless of convention or decorum.

Gna is a powerful, potentially unreliable, or even dangerous force, held in check and controlled by the powerful sky goddess, yet a force necessary to fuel Frigg's will and give her magical acts the necessary impetus to propel them into fruition. And if Gna carries Frigg's will out to the worlds, she is also able to carry our will back to Frigg and the Aesir. Gna is a representative of Frigg's darker and powerful magical side, the strange, wild, unpredictable messenger of the sky queen.

Ritual

Rituals to Gna can be performed to enlist her aid to carry messages to and from Frigg, the Allmother, and to ask Gna to encourage Frigg to grant wishes or offer help for an appropriate project. Gna, in her role as messenger, can also be petitioned to speed, protect, and encourage any messages (which could include letters, phone calls, telegrams, and personal visits). By the same token, people working in professions involving any sort of communication can call on her to help and protect them in their work. Because of her shamanic characteristics, Gna can also be invoked to aid in any magical workings involving journeys to the other worlds and communications with the beings that dwell there.

Gna seems to be associated with light but strong colors, such as bright yellows, oranges, greens, or blues. Symbols of the messages to be sent (a letter, for example) and the persons or beings to be contacted could be placed on the altar if the ritual is for a specific communication. A symbol of Hofvarpnir, Gna's horse, would also be an appropriate decoration. The use of percussive instruments and dancing in the ritual is very effective for Gna, who seems to inspire an atmosphere of greater improvisation and informality than some of the other goddesses. If one doesn't want to experiment with the chanting invocation mentioned above, a more traditional style of invocation can always be used.

Call to Gna

Gna—far-traveler—
  swift messenger of Frigg,
    rider of Hofvarpnir—

You who soar through the high towers of the sky,
You who speed through the dark currents of the sea,
You who are the eyes and ears of heaven,
    the voice of the goddess.

Loud of laughter,   light of limb,
    swifter than light or thought—

You carry the seed to the womb,
    the word to the heart,
      the greeting of kinship and the riot of rumor.

Come to us, wild one,
Carry fame and fancy,
Carry mystery and joining,
Carry our minds and our hearts—

Gna—Messenger—Come!

12

Gefjon

The Worker

 LORE

Unlike some of the Asynjur, Gefjon (ON Gefjon; also called Gefjun) has a clearly established identity of her own and appears in skaldic poetry, art, and legend as an independent figure, although she has also been associated and confused with both Frigg and Freyja. Her name means the "giver" and derives from the ON verb *gefa,* meaning "to give" (with the further connotation "to give in marriage"). The name *Gefjon* has also been linked to the OE *geofon* ("ocean, sea"). Gefjon is associated with the Danish island of Sjelland (Zealand), thought by some to be the center of worship of the goddess Nerthus, mentioned by Tacitus.[1] However, there is little evidence to suggest that Gefjon was thought of as a sea goddess; rather, she is more strongly connected to agriculture and the land.

The OE word for "gift," *giefu,* is also the name of an Anglo-Saxon rune, *gyfu* (Gmc. *gebō*), which means "gift, generosity, hospitality." In early Germanic culture, the concepts of gift and giving had a deeper, more magical meaning than contemporary society gives them. More than the mere exchange of physical property, a gift symbolized a blending of the minds and lives of both giver and receiver, a magical state of communion and inspiration that was heightened when it included exchanges between humans and gods. Giving cemented the bonds of human society, creating reciprocal ties of interdependence, quelling feuds and quarrels without bloodshed, and enabling independent persons and kinship groups to function together for the greater good. Gifts were required to seal business dealings, solemnify marriages, and ratify peace treaties and were necessary to make binding almost any agreement or ceremony.

The Tenet of Hospitality

Hospitality, which was considered a moral obligation by Northern peoples, included help that friendless travelers could depend on to sustain them on journeys. Without this concept of generosity travel, trade, and communication in general would have been hindered, if not impossible, in older times. Between host and guest existed a sacred bond of reciprocal aid and peace; to do violence to host or guest was a terrible crime, violating laws both human and divine. Sagas and legends are full of occasions where enemies were forced to meet amicably because they were all guests of a host who was anxious to keep bloodshed from violating his hall. The *gebo* rune also symbolizes ritual and sacrifice, the divine exchange of gifts between humans and the gods creating a relationship of kinship and mutual interdependence.

The host-guest relationship and the concept of giving shows up in the major extant myth pertaining to Gefjon. This story is told twice by Snorri, in the beginning of the Gylfaginning (ch. 1) in the *Prose Edda* and in the *Ynglinga saga* (ch. 5) of the *Heimskringla*. The skaldic poet Bragi Boddason the Old also wrote several stanzas about the event, showing that the story must have been fairly widely known. In the Eddic version, Gylfi, the king of Sweden, is greatly entertained by a traveling woman who stays at his hall, and, in return for her merrymaking, he gives her a plot of land as large as she and four oxen can plow in a day and a night. The woman, who is in reality the goddess Gefjon, brings from Jotunheim her four sons, fathered by a giant. She changes them into oxen and with their aid plows up a huge tract of land. The goddess then proceeds to drag her prize away across the ocean, where it becomes an island along the coast of Denmark. This island is said to be Sjælland, the largest of Denmark's islands and the site of the city of Copenhagen. There is a lake in southeast Sweden, Lake Malaren (Malar), whose indentations are said to correspond exactly to the headlands of the Danish island. The version of the tale in the *Heimskringla* is basically the same, with two slight variations. Here Odin sends Gefjon to Gylfi in quest of land, and the goddess goes to Jotunheim to conceive her four sons after accepting Gylfi's gift.

The story of a person who makes a seemingly insignificant promise and is later forced to give more than he bargained for is a common theme in northern European folk literature and myths. Modern readers may often fail to see why someone would allow herself to be tricked so, but this is because we no longer see the idea of giving one's word or a gift to be holy. To break such a bargain once made would cause a rift in the stability of society itself, and, on a spiritual level, it would cause unpleasant repercussions in the oathbreaker's ørlög. Gefjon is often regarded as a patron of Denmark because she gave the island she won from Gylfi to increase that country's holdings; there is a statue of her and her oxen in Copenhagen. However, she also has ties with Sweden because she accepted the king's gift of land in exchange for her entertainment.

The *Ynglinga saga* tells that after winning her island, Gefjon married the legendary Danish hero Skjold (Scyld), king of Leire and son of Odin, and with him founded the royal Danish race, called the Scyldings in his honor. (This is the same Scyld Scefing who shows up at the beginning of *Beowulf* as that hero's father.) Gefjon is known to have had a sanctuary or place of sacrifice at Leire, and there are a number of other place-names in Denmark that could have been derived from her name.

Gefjon's Ties to Agriculture

Because of the Gylfi myth, Gefjon is seen to have a strong connection with agriculture and especially with plowing. Carvings from the Viking Age have been found showing a female, assumed to be Gefjon, with her plow and four oxen. Her connection with oxen or bulls also suggests a fertility deity, although in her case dealing specifically with fertility of the soil. She may have been associated with plow-blessing rituals, such as the old Anglo-Saxon charm to make the land fertile, a thinly Christianized spell performed when plowing the first furrow of the season, which includes the following invocation:

> *Erce, Erce, Erce, Erce, Earth Mother,*
> *Be fruitful now in God's embrace,*
> *Be filled with food for the use of men.*

The plow was blessed and rubbed with various herbs and all the types of seeds that would be planted during that year's sowing. Next, the plow was taken out into the fields and and used to turn the first ritual furrow, into which a cake made from every kind of grain grown in that region would be planted. This was done presumably to let the powers that be see the expected goal.

In Germany people held plow processions, accompanied by dancing and bonfires, to promote the health of the crops. In some places the young men yoked all the dancing maidens to the plow and had them draw their piper, who sat on the plow still piping away, into a lake or river. In other areas they set the plow on fire and drew it through the fields, a practice similar to the use of burning sunwheels at Midsummer. Still other regions practiced the custom of allowing young men to accost unmarried women and make them either pay a ransom or be yoked to the plow.[2] This also ties in with Gefjon's relationship to maidens, which will be discussed later.

Ties to Fertility

De Vries speculates that Gefjon and Thor may have been worshipped together in Denmark as gods of fertility, due to the presence of some of Thor's place-names close by thought to be connected with Gefjon.[3] However, these same place-names could also be related to Freyja, one of whose bynames, *Gefn*, comes from the same root as *Gefjon*. The etymology of both names brings to mind Latin inscriptions found in parts of Germany that are addressed to female fertility spirits called Gabiae, Alagabiae, and Dea Garmangabis.[4] These spirits are similar in function to the dísir, female fertility deities associated with Freyja.

Another point of similarity between Freyja and Gefjon is that both are said to possess a necklace or jewel that they received from a lover. In the Lokasenna (st. 20), Loki accuses Gefjon of obtaining a *sigli* (a "throat jewel") as a result of throwing her leg over a young lover. This contradicts the common assumption that Gefjon is a virgin, which stems from Snorri's description of her as a *mær* ("maiden") in the Gylfaginning (ch. 35). He also states that all women who die maidens attend her in the afterlife. Gefjon's four giant sons and her fertility functions certainly seem to give the lie to this picture.

The only other evidence of this connection to virginity is in the Völsa þáttr section of *Oláfs saga hins helga* in the *Flatejarbók,* where a girl who opposes the phallic cult worshipped by her family invokes Gefjon, but this could be merely evidence that Gefjon was seen as an alternative fertility deity.[5] The word *mær* does not necessarily indicate a virgin but rather any young maiden; it can even be translated as "daughter" or "wife."[6] Everything else known about Gefjon suggests anything but a chaste maiden, and even if she is in charge of dead virgins, it doesn't necessarily mean she was one herself. Young women between puberty and marriage can be said to symbolize potential,[7] and Gefjon's association with them could be part of her fertility function.

Gefjon has connections with Frigg as well as with Freyja. Snorri lists her as the fourth of the Asynjur, and, in the Lokasenna (st. 21), Odin claims that Gefjon knows the fates of people as well as he does; this echoes another verse where nearly the same thing is said of Frigg. The *Hymskringla* version of the Gylfi myth also shows Gefjon connected to Odin, going east in search of land for him. The picture of Gefjon and her plow is reminiscent of Berchte, who was often pictured traveling throughout the countryside with her plow and who was thought to ensure the fertility of the crops.

There is also some evidence that Gefjon was invoked when oaths were taken, with the phrase *"Sver ek vid Gefjon* [I swear by Gefjon]."[8] This is a function similar to that of another of Frigg's goddesses, Var, who hears marriage vows. Tyr, the god of justice, is also called on to witness oaths, as are Thor and Ull. This role stems from the whole concept of the gift as a binding element in a promise and agreement.

Despite similarities and connections with other goddesses, it is apparent that Gefjon was at some point worshipped as a goddess in her own right, particularly in Denmark. Her main role seems to be that of a deity of the fertility of the land and a patron of farming. Farming was a major occupation in Viking times, practiced by all to some extent, despite any other occupations and activities they engaged in. Even rulers and other members of the upper classes took part in day-to-day farming activities, and it is not unusual in legends and sagas to find a queen out in the butter house.

Farming was the basis of survival and required hard work, flexibility, good timing, skill, and luck. In the Rígsþula (st. 22) there is a list of some of the activities of farming, including taming oxen, tempering plowshares, making carts, building wooden houses and barns, plowing, reaping, and threshing. The Scandinavian growing season was only about five months long or less, and during the peak periods of work all the people devoted long days, from dawn to sunset, to the feverish activity required by the season. After the sowing in mid-April, many men went off trading, exploring, or viking; in their absence the women of the house were in complete control of the farm and all related business activities. During autumn, when all hands were again needed, the men returned for the reaping and harvest, followed by a long and hopefully pleasant winter in a comfortable hall. A goddess who ruled over such activity would have to be strong, vigorous, diligent, independent, and hardy.

 ## Trance

I see a strong woman. She is the goddess of women who are alone. She works hard, and plays hard. A woman in her thirties, in her prime, she has much

strength and vigor, with a strong face and a tall, large-boned body. Her hair is reddish blond, or ash blond, and she wears it tied carelessly back, with wisps escaping from the scarf she ties around it. Her arms are bare and her sleeves are rolled up high, above the shoulders. Her arms are sunburned and bronze. She is a farm woman. She is fond of heavy drinking in the "old mead-hall, where warriors sit blithely together" (from the OE rune poem mentioned below). Excelling in merrymaking, she is the life of the party, one of the guys. She is very proud of her four giant sons and, like Queen Boadicea of the Celts, might also exclaim of them, "These are my jewels!"

She is a goddess of agriculture and work and takes special care of working women and men. Her symbol is the plow. She can handle the elements of chaos and subdue them with her strong arms; she is not afraid of "dirty work." They call her goddess of maidens, though she is not one, because she cares for women. She teaches them to know how to deal with men, to know themselves, to take care of themselves, and to become women, not girls.

The picture of Gefjon I saw in my trances was pretty much the same as that obtained from research. Her outstanding characteristics are strength, hardiness, and overwhelming vigor or life force, the strength and energy palpably emanating from her body. One can picture her picking up oxen with her bare hands, arm-wrestling warriors in the mead hall, and generally overcoming all obstacles with ease. Although she seems strongly interested in women and their work, she also appears at ease with men in a man's environment. She not only can compete with men, but she genuinely seems to like them and enjoy their company and amusements. The mead-hall scenes and vigorous carousing caused me to think of the Old English rune *perþro,* whose rune poem conjures up the image of warriors drinking together in the hall.

I find it interesting that Gefjon has been thought of as the patron of maidens and the one to whom they would go after they died. If the historical evidence were not enough to convince me that Gefjon herself is no virgin, the trances did the job, because a less maidenly character cannot be imagined. However, it seems much more sensible to put a bunch of inexperienced young girls in the care of a woman of the world, rather than sending them to an equally inexperienced maiden goddess. One could also apply the old classical concept of a virgin as simply an unmarried or unattached woman, with chastity not necessarily being a part of her character.

Gefjon, in her independence and confidence, seems like an excellent image for women working and living on their own. Especially today, when so many more women live alone, struggle with single parenthood, or work at various occupations, Gefjon is a noble example. Not only did she do her work well, she negotiated a premium wage for it. Although historically connected with farming, she can also be invoked for help in any kind of honest work by people of either sex. For women, she is especially ready to lend her strength and cunning. She would perhaps be a good deity to call on when looking for a job or when seeking decent wages or a raise. And although fewer of us today do our own farming, we all still eat, so Gefjon's role as goddess of agriculture is still important to all of us. Rites to her during key points in the growing season, especially just before plowing time, would be appropriate. Gefjon would also be good to call on in rituals involving young women, such as rites of passage at puberty. She might also be involved in workings to protect women and girls from premature or unwanted involvement with men.[9]

 Ritual

An altar for Gefjon could be covered with a cloth of grain-yellow or any color indicative of crops or growing things. Grains, fruits, breads, and other gifts of the earth are useful decorations. Farming implements, such as scythes and trowels, could also be used as ornaments. The plow, of course, is her main symbol, but unless you're lucky enough to be doing your ritual in a barn or in a real field, that's a little cumbersome for the average altar. If your ritual involves your work, you might include symbols of your career or occupation, or any particular project with which you might want help. Because Gefjon is such a hardworking goddess, be prepared to pledge what steps you plan to take to ensure your success in the work you're asking help with, and then be prepared to work your hardest to carry out your goals, with the aid of luck added by the goddess.

Call to Gefjon

Greetings Gefjon, goddess of maidens;
The doom laid down for all you see,
Even as Odin the wise.

Gefjon in gladness drew from Gylfi
Dark earth to add to Denmark.
The stout oxen steamed with sweat;
Eight eyes like moons beamed out
From four fearless beasts of the furrow.
Off they hauled the handsome island,
Picked as prize from Sweden.[10]

Hail, laughing one, joy of the men of the mead hall!
Hail, Gefjon of the white leg,
Whose favor wins fine-fashioned gold
     and fair fruitful fields!
Hail the giant's four sons, bearers of the plow!

Hail, goddess of lone women,
     Lady of cunning and courage and sweat.
The jewel you wear is your own strong heart.
Grant us equal courage and strength and joy.
Bless our plows as we break the green bones of Jord
     and call forth shining fruits.

Bless our sea and our land, fair Mistress of Sjælland
     and Maker of Malar.

Hail, Gefjon! Come!

13

Snotra

The Prudent One

 ## Lore

Snotra (ON Snotra) is one of those goddesses who seems to have been chiefly the personification of a moral idea, a mere shadow of her mistress, Frigg. Listed by Snorri as the thirteenth Aesir goddess (Gylfaginning, ch. 35), she is said to be wise and prudent. Her name comes from the ON word *snotr* ("wise, prudent"), which can be used to describe any man or woman who is wise, sensible, and temperate.

The meanings attached to the word *snotr* and the qualities of the goddess Snotra are all in the same vein. She is a goddess of virtue, a worthy woman, prudent and of gentle bearing, wise, well behaved, neat, clever, judicious, moderate in manner, and a pillar of self-discipline. One of the few places in the old literature where her name turns up is in the Rígsþula of the *Elder Edda* (st. 25). In this story, which tells of how the god Rig sired the different classes of people, one of the daughters of the yeoman Karl is named Snot. Snotra, then, does not represent the ruler, the hero, the skald, or the shaman but rather embodies the ideal traits of the average person.

Exemplifying Ethical Guidelines
The virtues that Snotra exemplifies should not be confused with later Christianized concepts of meekness, chastity, and piety, the hallmarks

of the pallid sort of heroine who reached her peak in the Victorian novel. The virtues held in high regard by the Heathen Norse were qualities like honor, courage, loyalty, truth, hospitality, self-reliance, industriousness, perseverance, and discipline. If these traits sound familiar, it's because they continued to be held as desirable personal attributes by the Germanic people even after the Christianization of Europe and have been passed down to our own society, even though they're not much practiced of late. Many of the ethical qualities assumed to have grown out of the Christian religion were actually already honored centuries earlier among the Heathen Europeans and were simply co-opted by the church as a means of easing the integration into the new faith.

Honor is more than a virtue; it is an intrinsic part of a person's being. It is an inner consciousness of nobility, the knowledge that you are what you should be and that your actions are true and right. Honor is based not only on acts in the present but also includes everything a person did in the past. Honor encompasses all the other virtues, and they, in turn, are necessary to preserve honor from harm. A person whose honor is failing usually demonstrates this by starting to slip in other areas, such as becoming cowardly or stingy. Along with honor comes luck. Luck means more than a favorable turn of the dice; it means an inner power that extends itself into the physical world so that all your endeavors are successful. Luck is the outer manifestation of honor; when your inner self is true and right, you prosper in everything you do.

In order to maintain your honor, you need courage. Courage was one of the most highly admired qualities among early Heathens and is still important today in our complex and confusing world. It means not only physical bravery but also the willingness to stand up for what you believe is right, even when you risk trouble and unpleasantness in doing so. Lack of fear is not necessarily the key to courage but rather the ability to pursue your goals. Courage may also include being able to withstand physical hardships and discomfort.

Loyalty is the visible manifestation of honor in action. It means being true to yourself, your kin, your friends, and your gods. Loyalty includes being open, honest, and reliable, and being willing to cheer your fellows in good times and to defend them in times of trouble. Those with no ties of honor or loyalty to anyone have forfeited their humanity; they exist beyond the boundaries of society in the realms of chaos.

Closely tied to loyalty is the virtue of truth. *Truth* here refers to personal honesty and to keeping your word. It means essential truth and rightness, rather than unrelenting literal truth. Indeed, sometimes truth is better served with subtlety and cunning instead of dogged bluntness, particularly when dealing with your enemies. To your friends and kin, though, you should open your heart and mind and say and do what you really feel. Above all, you should present yourself truthfully in deeds, both past and future, indulging in neither unfounded bragging nor exaggerated modesty.

Hospitality was a necessity in earlier times, when a traveler had no recourse to motels or restaurants. But more than that, it is the glue that holds human society together and as such is even more important today when society is so fragmented and alienated. Generosity is also a reflection of honor; stinginess is a sure sign of failing luck and will. The act of giving forms a bond between giver and receiver, so hospitality fulfills spiritual and emotional needs as well as physical ones. To be miserly sends a message to the universe and yourself that you are lacking in power and unable to provide for yourself or others. Generosity proclaims that you are strong and honorable, that you trust enough in your future luck and prosperity to distribute what you have now to others. In addition to giving material gifts, hospitality means treating both guests and hosts with thoughtfulness, courtesy, and respect and, most important of all, keeping peace between all parties during any visit or festivity.

Self-Reliance and Industriousness

Closely tied to hospitality is the virtue of self-reliance. Hospitality only works if all participants are honorable people who are generally capable of supporting themselves; to use the virtue of generosity to induce others to support your own laziness is as bad as being stingy.

Self-reliance also implies taking responsibility for your own actions and choices and not always looking for someone or something to blame.

With these responsibilities comes the boon of freedom, of being your own master and pursuing your own goals and desires.

Industriousness grows out of self-reliance: you can't take care of yourself if you don't do any work. This does not mean cheerless drudgery but rather taking joy in doing and striving. It means aiming for excellence instead of mediocrity. Excellence does not happen by itself; we have to work hard to achieve worthy goals, but the joy of success is greater when you know you have earned it. Work is also tied to freedom, oddly enough. To be able to do things, make things, achieve things, rather than depending on someone else to provide them for you, gives you a sense of pride and independence that few things can shake. It brings the realization that you can exercise control over your environment and your life.

Perseverance is a matter of self-reliance and industriousness maintained over the long haul. It means being able to work for a long-term goal through hard times, trouble, and inconvenience. It means being able to delay immediate gratification to achieve a worthy goal and not getting bored every time a new endeavor loses the first flush of excitement and becomes routine. Endurance is part of this virtue—being able to live through failure, hardship, and bad luck and continue on your path without giving in to despair or self-pity.

Self-Discipline

Self-discipline means demanding excellence from yourself first, and then from others. It is part of the process of self-actualization, which has become so popular in modern psychology. It means constantly striving to improve and perfect yourself. Discipline involves living life actively instead of letting fate control you.

The valued personality traits of moderation, self-control, and evenness of temper are also part of this virtue. Throughout the Hávamál, that collection of wise counsels in the *Elder Edda,* the wise person is warned to eat and drink moderately, hold her tongue, and keep her temper in trying situations. This kind of self-discipline is exemplified by Queen Sigrid of Sweden, who was courted by the Christian king Olaf

Tryggvason. When she refused to convert but rather suggested that each should worship as he or she felt best, Olaf struck her in the face with his glove and called her a bitch. Although they were in her own hall at the time and she could have called on all her men to avenge her honor, she merely said, with great control, "That may well be your death." And indeed, Olaf did eventually meet his death due to an alliance forged by Sigrid, who waited until the time was right to restore her honor.[1]

The Norse scorned uncontrolled outbursts of temper; expressions of anger were appropriate only if they were the product of will and decision. Though Vikings are popularly presented as being somewhat similar to a rowdy group of undergraduates, only more bloodthirsty, in reality the Norse people fully appreciated the horror of a blood feud and sought to avoid such quarrels as best they could. It is still important today to avoid needless and unproductive conflict. You are not responsible for your emotions, but you are for your actions. A goddess who can inspire people to keep control of themselves and weigh events with objectivity before acting is definitely an asset.

Practical Skills

Snotra is also called wise because she is said to have mastered every kind of knowledge. To modern people, knowledge and study refer to activities like doing algebra or writing a thesis. But in Viking times the kinds of things an accomplished person was expected to know were, for the most part, practical skills. Because Snotra is a goddess and not a god, she presumably originally presided over those studies appropriate to a woman. Here Snotra echoes the housewifely skills of Frigg and the German goddesses associated with her.

In early Germanic society a woman was responsible for pretty much everything that went on within the house and its immediate vicinity. This included cleaning, which was related to the health of the household, since so much disease in early times arose from dirty living conditions. Cooking was another necessary skill, especially in a time when everything had to be prepared from scratch. For a Viking housewife, being in charge of the kitchen also meant being responsible for all the stores of grain, salted meat, and other foodstuffs. This was a fairly critical responsibility at a time when one's budgeting abilities determined whether the winter food supplies would last until the new crops came in. Its importance is reflected in the use of the keys of the house as the symbol for the authority of the mistress of the farmstead. Cooking also encompassed the semi-spiritual activities of baking and brewing.

Besides preparing food, women also obtained much of it. Although men usually tended the large fields of crops, women typically managed the smaller but vital kitchen gardens of vegetables and herbs necessary to a healthy and enjoyable diet. Women and children also were the ones who gathered foodstuffs such as nuts, berries, and mushrooms. Domestic animals as well as the products obtained from them were under the control of the women. These included the cattle, sheep, and goats, in particular, but also poultry, pigs, and bees.

A skilled housewife had to know how to preserve food once she got it. Milk was churned into butter and turned into cheese; meat and fish were dried or salted; fruit was made into preserves, jelly, and cider; grain was used to make bread and ale; and honey was brewed into mead. Storing food to last through the winter was vital to the survival of the family, as was ensuring that the house had adequate supplies of water and fuel.

Clothmaking was the major occupation of women and cloth contributed not only to the family's comfort and survival but was also a big market item for many a household's economy. Preparing flax and wool, spinning, weaving, dyeing, and sewing were all skills every girl and woman were expected to know. These textile products were not only functional but also offered an outlet for artistic expression in the form of woven wall hangings and dyed and embroidered fabrics.

Child care was another major responsibility and included both physical care and schooling. Knowledge of medicine and midwifery was another needed skill. A wife had to be a good supervisor, because it was her job to keep all the girls and women of the household busy and productive. Women would also be involved in arranging marriages for their family members, especially in the preliminary stages.

During the summer, when the women, children, and old men were often left alone on the farm, the wife became the head of the household. She had to know how to barter with visiting traders; to protect the crops from predators and disease; and to hide the people, cattle, and treasures if raiders attacked the farmstead. A skilled woman might know something about runes, because many a runestone was erected for the dead by wives, mothers, and sisters, and there are at least a couple of runic inscriptions indicating that they were made by female rune carvers.[2] All adults—both women and men—were also expected to be able to sing, dance, and tell a tale or make a verse to be considered really accomplished.

Trance

I see a quiet young woman in her twenties with honey-blond or light-brown hair and gray eyes. Her hair is very frizzy, curling in small ringlets around her face like a halo. She has long braids, or one long braid, which she twists meditatively and chews or sniffs on the ends. She is clad in light, austere clothes made of thin material—lightness of both color and texture.

I see her sitting in Frigg's garden, dressed as an English countrywoman of the seventeenth or eighteenth century, wearing a broad-brimmed straw hat tied with a wide ribbon. She is painting in watercolor. She offers me a small snack, some sort of nut sweetmeat, feeding it to me with her fingers. She has a lovely, low voice and is very intimate and informal without being sloppy or vulgar. "It's fun to be out doing things, to just relax and take your time, to learn to do something very well and share it with others," she tells me.

Snotra is spunky, with more humor than one might at first suspect—very quiet but with a sort of impish, all-knowing smile. She cannot be induced to lose her temper under any circumstances. Much given to daydreaming, she knows more than she tells. She often assists people and other gods with various projects and likes to be an advisor or helper. I often see her in the company of other goddesses in Frigg's court. Such a solemn, quiet little thing—but with that undertone of wry, dry, deadpan humor. She sits on a high stool, staring dreamily into space, her hand holding a quill poised over a long sheet of fine vellum on a desk, sniffing the ends of her hair.

That last image of Snotra with a quill is obviously an anachronism, no doubt influenced by my own involvement with writing, research, and other similar pursuits. Nonmagical writing and reading did not become common in the Norse countries until the medieval era. However, if we consider Snotra to be expert at every kind of study appropriate to a well-born woman, it is easy to see how literary accomplishments would be added to practical skills as the education of both men and women was broadened. After reading and writing became more common, at least among the upper classes, a goddess like Snotra might gradually come to also represent the guardian of scholars poring over curly-edged manuscripts.

In our own world, this nontraditional aspect of Snotra's skill has even greater importance. The truth must be faced—these are no longer preliterary Viking times. The world we know today depends a great deal on the written word. Therefore, in modern times Snotra can be assumed to have expanded her interests to include reading, writing, and other scholarly pursuits, as well as all the new skills required by our growing technology. However, Snotra's real forte remains street smarts and common sense. It is important to be able to function in the modern world and to take advantage of what technology and science have to offer, but it is also vital for us to take care of ourselves on a very basic level, to grow and make our own food and drink, to create things with our own hands, to be able to survive on a backpacking trip and to care for our own children. And, of course, the ability to know our limit, hold our tongue, and keep our temper are timeless. In short, Snotra governs the ethical qualities and personality traits that promote productivity and cooperation among people. She empowers them to be able to take care of themselves and teaches the kind of practical wisdom and understanding that allow people to survive and succeed in the mundane world.

 ## Ritual

A ritual to Snotra, then, could be performed for virtue in general—for evenness of temper, moderation of lifestyle, wisdom of action, diligence to duty—or for aid and inspiration, motivation, and stamina in any kind of study, from baking to biophysics. Snotra might also be called on to promote manners and appropriate behavior for any occasion, especially if you have reason to believe people are likely to get too rowdy or start bickering with each other.

The altar cloth or candles could be of light colors of gray, blue, dull gold, beige, or off-white—probably any muted, tasteful shade. Symbolic pieces could include emblems of the traditional housewifely skills, such as the distaff or needle; traditional objects representing scholarly pursuits, such as the quill or brush; or symbols of your own particular studies or enterprises—a pocket calculator, a spreadsheet, a thesaurus, batiking equipment, or whatever. Another nice touch might be finished examples of any kinds of crafts or skills you practice or of your work—successful term papers, debugged computer programs, perfect pastries, triumphantly symmetrical pottery, and the like. These emblems of past success are not only links between you and the goddess who admires such work but also function as proof to yourself that you have indeed been successful in past endeavors and thus can expect to be so in future ones.

Other aspects of the ritual might include a pledge to modify your behavior in some positive way designed to be pleasing to Snotra. For example, you could decide to keep your room neat, to refrain from getting drunk, or to avoid losing your temper and starting fights for a week or so. All these actions serve as a sacrifice pleasing to a goddess like Snotra and work as a link to her, putting you on the same wavelength, so to speak, so that you will be that much more receptive to her energies.

Call to Snotra

Hail Snotra—worthy woman!
Wise one,   clever one,
Daughter of the freeholder—

Gentle, prudent maiden,
Skillful woman of sense,
Calm, judicious counselor,
      a joy and comfort to the wise!

You who fare to the feast, cleanly clad,
      there to eat and drink the ale wisely with friends;
You who speak little and listen much,
      and quarrel never with drunkards or fools.
You who fare to the Thing and offer counsel,
      weighing words, each against the other;
You who shape the peace and pledge the fee,
      and hold holy the peace-stead.

Hardy helper,   quiet counselor,
Goddess of the needle and the quill,
      of the workers and the craft-wise,
      of scholars and students all—
the painstaking, fine-wrought arts you love.

Grant us your calm and craft,
      your diligence and drive,
      your skill and silence,
      your well-deserved peace.

Snotra—Worthy One—Hail!

14

Lofn

The Champion

 ## Lore

Lofn (ON Lofn, "comforter, mild one") appears in Snorri's list (Gylfaginning, ch. 35) as the eighth Aesir goddess and as yet another messenger and attendant of Frigg. Her name is associated with the ON verb *lofa* ("to praise"; "to allow, permit"). Her major function is to remove obstacles from the paths of lovers and to win permission from Odin and Frigg for people to marry, both women and men, even if the marriage has been forbidden. According to Snorri, such permission was called "leave," after the goddess. Lofn's name was also used to denote love and anything that is beloved.

Besides this slender evidence, nothing more is told of Lofn; there are no stories of her among the Norse myths. Again we see a goddess closely associated with Frigg, in this case partaking of her functions as a goddess of marriage. In early Norse society and later in medieval Europe, most marriages were contracted by agreement between the families of the individuals involved, and love had to come later, if at all. This was a typical practice among farming communities, where the family formed an economic as well as a social unit. Marriage was chiefly a financial and political transaction, and the main goals were the continuation of the family line and the provision of future economic security for both partners and any children they might have. Marriage was used to unite powerful families, quell feuds, and increase the wealth and holdings of a kinship group.

Thus the main considerations in the choice of a mate were rank, wealth, and family affiliations. The past deeds and ancestors of the families involved were particularly critical because not only did marriage affect a family's socioeconomic status, it also formed a spiritual link to the luck and honor of the two clans, which affected everyone in both kinship groups. Still, the consent of each of the prospective spouses was considered necessary to complete the bargain, and few cases in which the relatives coerced a marriage against the inclination of one or both parties turned out well in the end.

The sealing of a marriage bargain involved a complicated and extensive exchange of gifts between the couple and their families. The bride brought a dowry consisting of a substantial sum—this represented her share of the family inheritance—as well as the bed, linens, furniture, dishes, and other household goods. Although her husband and his family had the use of this gift throughout the marriage, it was the woman's property and reverted to her possession in case of divorce or her husband's death.[1] The husband, in turn, made a hefty monetary gift to the bride's family to compensate them for the loss of a valuable member. The man made a further substantial gift to his wife the morning after their wedding night, designed to ensure her economic future.

A couple's ability to acquire all the wealth necessary for a respectable wedding proved that they were capable of supporting themselves and a family. However, the giving of gifts reflected more than a financial exchange; it also had the spiritual effect of linking the energies of the two parties together in a holy bond. Accepting the marriage gifts promoted close spiritual ties and enhanced the status and reputation of the parties concerned.

A woman hungered for love in her marriage, and she knew that only a man of worthy deeds and honor could win her respect. Thus maidens, as well as their kinfolk, judged their prospective suitors by their wealth, their honor, and their fame rather than valuing good looks or flashy clothes.[2] A man was equally concerned with the honor and family heritage of his prospective wife because, as the mother of his descendants, her ørlög and soul would become part of his entire family line for generations to come. The woman was the bearer of spiritual power, of the ancestral soul, from one generation to another, and hence the husband and his family were equally concerned with a potential mate's courage, strength, wisdom, wealth, and ancestral line.

Overcoming Obstacles to True Love

So Heathen marriage was founded on love after all, but that love did not manifest itself until after the final gifts had been duly exchanged. However, once the gifts were given, love could not fail to grow. The modern idea of the romantic hero or heroine pining away for unrequited love would not have seemed romantic to Heathen Germanics but rather would have been regarded as a sign of mental imbalance. Because of this, it is hard to imagine how the situation of star-crossed lovers in need of Lofn's aid could arise. However, human nature being what it is, love often defied both economics and custom, as a number of sagas and verses testify.

Many types of obstacles might arise to thwart a couple's wishes. Problems in obtaining wealth enough to ensure a proper and desirable wedding might affect either member of the pair. The family of one person might not be considered to have enough rank or fame to suit the other family, or there might be a skeleton in someone's closet, projecting its ill luck throughout the family line and warning off suitors. A feud or a murder involving members of either family would make an alliance seem impossible. Even a random incident, like a storm at sea or a sudden journey, might intervene to frustrate a romance. With so many potential obstacles beyond a person's control and with so much at stake, it makes sense that there would be a deity to intercede in such situations.

The first step in many Germanic marriages was taken by the couple themselves, who undoubtedly began dropping hints to their families regarding who they might wish to wed. The young man often would send an aunt or another female relative to visit his intended's family to find out if she was free to be betrothed and to feel out how they might regard him as a son-in-law. In almost every society where choice of a mate rests with parties other than the lovers themselves, the figure of the clever matchmaker appears in stories and folklore. The more restrictive a society is toward its young people, the more cunning and ruthless this figure becomes.

Almost all of Greek and Roman comedy, and later Commedia dell'arte, centers around the adventures of young lovers who thwart their fathers, usually with the aid of devious servants or concubines. This comic theme is continued in Shakespeare's England, Molière's France, and even crops up now and then today. This rebellion of youth against age and authority must have been a common one to have been so widely represented in drama through the ages. Another common aspect of these stories is an almost universal sympathy for the lovers and ridicule and contempt for the old people. Despite the standards of society, people seem to instinctively recognize the folly and error of age in trying to meddle in young love. It is almost like the archetypal battle of youth and age, summer and winter, that surfaces so often in old rituals.

In this light, Lofn appears both as a conventional goddess concerned with marriage and love and as a firebrand revolutionary, bucking authority and the rules of society to promote the aims of individualism and freedom. Interestingly, she is said to win permission from both Frigg and Odin for her lovers. It is unusual to see Odin in the position of matchmaker. His connection with Lofn could be due to the fact that, as the leader of the gods, he represents the ruling powers and therefore would have to be consulted before overruling their authority. He might be included because he is Frigg's husband and together they represent the happily married couple that the besieged lovers hope to become. On the other hand, as a god of deceit and cunning, an unraveler of knots and a breaker of boundaries, his presence might indicate the rebellious and individualistic nature of Lofn's work.

 **Trance**

I see a woman sitting by an indoor pool in Frigg's hall. She stirs the water with a stick, moodily; her face seems to shift and change from moment to moment. As she looks into the pool, she sees events happening in the world of humans, and what she sees upsets her.

A mistress of craft and cunning, Lofn does not hesitate to resort to sneakiness and trickery to help the lovers she chooses to protect, for she knows they work under a disadvantage and must use all means in their power to triumph. She is an expert at disguise and intrigue. She is young, in her early twenties, with a pale face and wide-set blue eyes. Her hair is dark red, or auburn, hanging about her, luxurious and straight. Of medium height and build, she is stronger than she looks. She wears a dark cloak and a light gown and carries a concealed dagger.

Lofn smiles when she sees me; her face becomes very animated as we talk. "It's so rare and wonderful to find someone you can truly love that one must fight with all one's might to keep that love." She is passionate—a champion of the individual against authority, youth against age—and empathetic to the sorrow of others. Her emotions are strong and sudden—she is quick to decide and quick to act. I see Snotra following behind her with a small smile, as Lofn, now clad in brown breeches and tunic, strides purposefully off on another mission, eyes blazing and the wheels of her mind clacking away on another scheme.

Note how Lofn's use of the pool to view events happening in Midgard is similar to Hlidskjalf, the high seat from which Odin and Frigg can see all that goes on in the Nine Worlds. Notice also the reappearance of Snotra, acting in her preferred role as helper and perhaps exercising the skills in matchmaking that an accomplished woman should possess. Lofn appears as archetypal youth—rebellious, passionate, idealistic, rash, moody, strong, and noble. She seems like a mix of girl and warrior, of lovestruck maiden and Machiavellian plotter.

Interestingly, another woman with whom I had shared my ideas concerning using tranceworking to flesh out the stories of the Norse goddesses experimented with Lofn before I worked on her. Whether this woman's results influenced mine or whether we were both tapping in to the same source is hard to say, but we both recorded similar motifs relating to Lofn, notably the dagger, the red hair, the clothing, the youth, and the fearlessness of the goddess.[3] This is an example of how recurring images tend to surface in the workings of different individuals, and these overlapping symbols are especially potent to use in invocation. Their recurrence is suggestive that they are collective images and not merely individual whims.

Easing the Way, Even Today

One might perhaps think that today, with sexual freedom and a fair amount of autonomy for adults, we don't have much need for a Lofn. However, the course of true love is still often rocky. Parents no longer have life and death power over their grown children, but anyone who has brought home a potential mate for family inspection knows that it's much easier to say you don't care what your parents think than to actually endure their objections. There are also all kinds of potential issues affecting any love relationship—problems of money, distance, time, social mores, and even legal difficulties—all of which can hinder a pair of lovers. Lofn seems particularly effective when invoked by people who truly desire to be together in peace; I know a number of couples who have asked her for help and gotten remarkably prompt and efficient results.

Although she is very much a goddess of youth, Lofn can be invoked by lovers of any age and sex. She would be called on specifically to remove obstacles of any kind preventing people who are already interested in each other from being together; she is not the one to ask for help in attracting lovers or inspiring passions. These obstacles can include objections from parents and other family members, legal difficulties stemming from previous marriages or problems with obtaining a marriage license, troubles concerning the marriage ceremony itself and any accompanying celebrations, issues involving money or travel, and societal objections to the relationship. Snorri's description of Lofn's ability to get leave for both men and women to marry is plural in the original and could therefore be interpreted as including same-sex unions, so Lofn might be called on by gay or lesbian couples for special assistance.

Ritual

An altar to Lofn might be draped in strong, vibrant, passionate colors, such as red or purple, and many candles would be used to create an atmosphere of energy and light. A dagger might be included as a symbol of the goddess and also of the power to cut down obstacles. Because one would often have a specific reason to invoke Lofn, pictures or symbols of the loved one or the couple involved could be included, as well as representations of the problems preventing the union. These obstacles could then be ritually burned or otherwise destroyed during the ritual to symbolize the removal of the hindrances in real life. At the close of the ritual a small celebration might be included, with special food and drink, to commemorate the successful resolution of the situation. Bits of poetry, literature, or drama appropriate to the qualities Lofn represents might be read, preferably ones with happy outcomes (Keats's "The Eve of St. Agnes" rather than Shakespeare's *Romeo and Juliet,* for example).

Call to Lofn

Hail Lofn—defender of lovers—beloved of youth,
*   You who have the ear of Frigg and Odin . . .*
Beloved winner of leave to live!
Lady of fire,   watcher in the pool,
Dagger-cunning and heart-soothing.

Cloaked in love, you lift the latch
*   That bars the way to wedding;*
Cheat of old age,   wealth-scornful,
Lady of lying tongue and whole heart.

Come to us, Lofn of love-luck—

Break our bonds,
Clear our course,
Smooth our sailing,
Aid our love!

Give us boldness and blessing, shelter and safeguard,
Be our champion and our luck—
Be true to us, who are true to each other.

Lofn—Beloved Champion—Come!

15

Sjofn

The Peacemaker

 Lore

Sjofn (ON Sjöfn) is another goddess who is only mentioned in passing in the Eddas and skaldic lore. According to Snorri (Gylfaginning,
ch. 35), the word *sjafni* ("love, affection") was derived from her name.
She is said to be greatly concerned with turning the minds of both men
and women to love.

It is all very well to dismiss a deity with the comfortable label "love
goddess" and leave it at that. Certainly love seems to be an important
function of many of the Northern goddesses, but that does not mean
that they are all the same. Rather than dimissing a goddess like Sjofn
as a redundant and therefore unimportant aspect of Frigg, one should
try to discover why a separate goddess evolved for this function and
what particular aspect of that function she might represent. If there
are several goddesses of love, what kinds and aspects of love do each of
them oversee? In Sjofn's case, as with Frigg and all her associates, the
love she inspires is not casual; it is love that leads to relationships and
commitment.

When the Gylfaginning states that Sjofn turns people's minds to
love, the actual word used for "mind" is *hugr,* which is a broader term,
encompassing consciousness, intuition, and emotion, as well as the

intellectual processes. Sjofn's power does not merely create a passing infatuation; it affects a person at the deepest level of being, touching all facets of the soul. Guerber states that Sjofn (or Vjofn, as she calls her) reconciles quarreling spouses and keeps harmony and peace among people in general.[1] Although written from a nineteenth-century perspective, this does indeed seem to catch the quality of Sjofn's work. The love she creates is more than physical or even romantic love; rather, it is real frith, that broader and more all-encompassing love and harmony that binds people together socially at the deepest level, the love of family, tribe, nation, and even of the world and life itself.

Cultivating Frith

Frith is an old Saxon word meaning "fruitful peace, joy." It is hard to accurately describe the concept today, when so much of the original Germanic culture has been destroyed. Frith was a condition that automatically existed from birth between all members of a kinship group and that could be created between other people through bonds such as marriage, blood brotherhood (or possibly sisterhood), allegiance between a chieftain and his followers, and friendship. Frith reflects the Germanic view of a person as essentially a social being, incomplete unless part of a close-knit group. Kinfolk were united by mutual self-interest and self-sacrifice, bound in loyalty, peace, support, and joy.

This love meant more than passively refraining from doing one's fellows harm; it required one to actively support and protect each kin member. Frith was the loyalty, love, and goodwill with which kindred folk lived together; it was the very core of the soul, the seat of a person's humanity and the wellspring of all her thoughts, feelings, and desires.[2] Kinfolk felt a deep love for each other; this love carried strong notes of intimacy and joy. Humans were seen as intrinsically social, and the greatest joy and peace arose from being in one's own home among one's family and trusted friends. This is the love Sjofn seeks so strongly to inspire in the minds of men and women. It is the basis of society, of humanity itself; without it, the worlds of order would fall back into chaos.

As mentioned earlier, there were unions other than blood kinship in which a state of frith could exist between people, but these could only happen through the giving of gifts. To the Heathen Germanics, all important agreements and relationships depended on the exchange of gifts to create the same love that automatically existed between members of a family. In giving a gift, a person gave a part of her soul to the other, and the gift itself became a physical manifestation of love and goodwill.

The kind of love born from the exchange of marriage gifts was more than romance; it was real frith, a sharing of honor and ørlög between husband and wife that also united the families involved. Friendship sprang from exchanging gifts too, as did the bond between a chieftain or war leader, who was often referred to as "ring giver," and his sworn followers. The paying of *wergild,* a monetary compensation for manslaughter, carried with it the promise of real reconciliation, as it pledged the two feuding families to peace.

These, then, are the two sources of love and frith—kinship and gifts. So Sjofn must be connected to both. She would be involved not only in creating love where it did not exist before—new unions, such as marriage, friendship, social and political alliance, and treaty—but also in restoring the state of frith in situations where it has been strained or broken.

Trance

I see her in the garden behind Frigg's hall, Fensalir, leaning on the trunk of a tree. She seems rather plain for a love goddess, with a kerchief edged in dark blue embroidery on her head. Her hair is a kind of ordinary brown. Her voice is soft, light, and quick, and she has a subtle, worldly sense of humor. She puts her arm around me and guides me through the door or gate leading out of the garden.

We go to various homes in the world of men. In one there is a quarreling couple. She talks with each in turn, both husband and wife, sitting them down at the table and putting her arm around each one. She understands and empathizes equally with them both. Afterward she goes outside to a meadow and sits beside a young girl under a tree. Sjofn talks to her of boys, and her manner is now teasing and coy; she takes off her kerchief and is suddenly more beautiful. Her hair is a tawny light brown or dark blond, with just a tiny hint of red highlights, and is wavy and full. Her mouth is strong and sensual, her eyes gray-green and striking. She wears embroidered clothes in a sort of European peasant style.

I see her next goes to an outsized hall and sits with great leaders of nations and armies at a large table; she tries to reconcile their differences, acting as a diplomat. She is like a chameleon, her appearance and manner changing from moment to moment. Her manner is warm and kindly, but uncompromising; she has empathy with old and young, men and women, rich and poor.

I see her on a rooftop during a festival for the new year, holding a wine cup. I sense the great love she feels for the crowd below, and for the stars and the very air, and her great joy. She keeps running one hand through her hair. I see now that she is in her late twenties or early thirties; she is sometimes fair, sometimes plain, depending on who she is with at the moment. Her love is a love of gentleness, not lust. She is quiet, with deep humor and strong charisma.

Suddenly we are back in the garden, at the tree—it is an apple tree. She pulls off an apple and bites it, and laughs.

Both the few facts known about Sjofn and my impressions of her in trance point to the broader aspects of love—the sense of camaraderie and loyalty that holds societies and clans together, the closeness and warmth that bind families, the joy of life that makes our time on this planet worthwhile. In this promotion of peace and joy, Sjofn is similar to Frey and some of the other Vanir, at whose celebrations weapons were put aside. This is also true of the German goddess Nerthus, whose festival is described by Tacitus in his *Germania* (ch. 40).

Sjofn is a goddess for all, rich and poor, ugly and beautiful, foolish and wise. She has a broad understanding of and sympathy for humanity and the mortal condition. Adaptable, tolerant, and empathetic, she is capable of many moods and able to deal with an infinite variety of situations. The love she inspires is the glue that holds society and the ordered world together, the very spirit that makes us human.

 ## Ritual

With this in mind, a ritual to Sjofn could be performed for any situation where a little harmony and concord is desired, including disruptive homes, bad situations at work, meetings of kinfolk with differing ideas, or even worldwide political conditions. One can call her to help you maintain and celebrate good relations and situations in your life as well. Sjofn can also be asked to help in the selection of gifts and to bless them before they are distributed.

Muted colors, especially blues and greens and other shades considered to promote harmony and calm, might be used as altar decorations or clothing. I think Sjofn probably prefers an understated and subtle yet aesthetic altar, evoking the same effect as a Japanese tea ceremony, with a few beautiful objects to please the mind and eye rather than a clutter of fancy paraphernalia. Try to reach a state of peace and contentment beforehand. Think of all the individuals, groups, places, activities, and things you love, things that make you glad to be alive. You could put some symbols of these on your altar. You might also want to gather together some people for whom you have particular affection, to join you in this rite, if possible.

Helping Those Who Help Themselves

If you are doing the ritual to remedy some unpleasant condition or situation, take a few moments at some point during the ritual to clearly identify what the actual problems are and try to see what you can do to make things better. Visualize the situation as you want it to be, harmonious and friendly. Don't expect Sjofn to magically turn things around if you don't formulate a plan to implement some changes and actively do your part, for Sjofn is similar to the gods Tyr and Forseti in that she is a goddess of justice and fairness. Similarly, don't visualize the situation being remedied by yourself gaining power over everyone else and putting them under your thumb, because Sjofn does not embrace vengeance or power trips.

You should also not invoke Sjofn out of misplaced idealism or a desire to feel virtuous in situations where you don't really want to love the others involved. If you truly think that your obnoxious neighbors are truly dreadful, don't play the "turn the other cheek" game and ask Sjofn to help you be a better person and "love" them. Sjofn will only work for real love, love that is—or at least once was—there. She will also promote a love that could be there with a little help—that person at the office who irritates you, but for no real reason that you can pinpoint, and might become a friend with the proper attitude and actions; or the spouse who was once special but whose habits are grating in times of stress or hardship; or the fellow kindred full of good enough folk who unfortunately don't see eye-to-eye with your group on some issues. This does not mean you cannot feel a certain level of kinship with even strangers at times—at a parade or on New Year's Eve—the bond of being human and alive on the same planet. But don't use Sjofn as a chance to play the goody-two-shoes and feel self-righteous about your supposed tolerance and goodness of heart.

If others do the ritual with you, share some food and drink at the end. If you are alone, call or write loved ones afterward. Go do something celebratory where there will be lots of people, like a fireworks exhibition, a walk in a public park, a crafts show, a dance, or a play. Try to pick something where you will be likely to enjoy being with others (a ride on a crowded subway probably is not a good choice, however).

Besides her important functions of maintaining goodwill, harmony, and love between spouses, families, friends, and coworkers, Sjofn seems to encompass a sort of world spirit, a reveling in the experiences of life and in being human; as such, she is a valuable ally in combating boredom, frustration, despair, and the "blues" in general. She is the specialness in everyday events, the joy of being in the present, the richness of contact with one's fellows. She is both carnival and bedtime story, reveler and sister, joy and comfort, plenty and peace.

Call to Sjofn

Goddess of the gateway,
    the open ear, the open heart, the open mind;
Goddess of the kind heart,
    love-glad, joy-proud, life-strong;
Goddess of the wise heart,
    bringer of frith, keeper of peace, mender of vows.

Goddess of the two sides, goddess of the table,
    Friend to men and women,
        Goddess of love,
        Goddess of the world—
            Sjofn, we need you now.
            Sjofn, Love Goddess,
            Sjofn, we need you now.
            Sjofn, Peacekeeper,
            Sjofn, we need you now . . .

16

Var

The Hearer of Oaths

 Lore

Var (ON Vár, "beloved," perhaps "spring"), listed by Snorri as the ninth of the Aesir goddesses (Gylfaginning, ch. 35), is yet another of Frigg's attendants. According to the *Prose Edda,* she heard all oaths made by people, particularly vows and promises between men and women, and took vengeance on those who broke their promises. The word for vows (*várar*) is thus said to come from her name. Because of this function, Var was called on to bless and witness marriage and betrothal rites. In the Þrymskviða (st. 30), when the giant Thyrm thinks that the disguised Thor is actually the goddess Freyja, his would-be bride, he calls his attendants to bring him Thor's hammer to lay in the bride's lap and wed them together in the name of Var.

In Old Norse society the oath or vow was seen as a deeper, more significant and magical act than modern people usually regard it. The keeping of one's word was bound with the all-powerful honor and luck of a person and her family, the ørlög or fate that grew from past actions. When a person swore on a holy object, such as a sacred stone, sword, or ring, the power of her words was greater, forming a vow that could not be rescinded. Vilhelm Grönbech, author of *Kultur und Religion der Germanen* (The Culture of the Teutons), talks of how the

word was seen to go on ahead, carving out a path for the deed to follow, drawing the speaker with it. If the word was not upheld, the luck
and even part of the very soul of the speaker would be involved in the
loss of honor.[1]

The formal exchange of gifts implied a sort of oath between the parties involved, since it was believed to create the same kind of troth and
trust. A gift was traditionally accompanied by words indicating in some
way that the giver's goodwill and luck accompanied it. To the Germanic
people, the custom of giving gifts amounted to not merely an exchange
of worldly goods but also an exchange of luck and fate between the givers, a joining of lives and kin; thus, gifts were not accepted casually. If a
gift was accepted, a gift had to be given in return to seal the friendship.
Even when trading or bargaining, members of the Norse culture could
not quite accept the transactions as mere commerce; some exchange of
luck still took place.

Because people felt that a part of one's soul was considered to be
passed along with a gift, the act of giving ensured that loyalty and love
would naturally follow and create a bond and obligation. The power of
both gift and vow bound together the honor and the fate of the participants, altering the very nature of their wills and feelings toward each
other. Once a gift had exchanged hands, no earthly power could stop its
effects and no one could resist its spiritual pull.[2]

Marriage was seen as the ultimate exchange, uniting in blood two
distant families or kinship groups who would ever after share each other's honor, luck, and fate. A person married not only her spouse but also
his entire family, and in earlier days such bargains were made with great
care by both the couple and their kinfolk. Because all true bargains were
sealed with gifts, the husband gave a bride gift to the head of the bride's
family, as well as gifts to the woman herself. She, in turn, gave him
gifts as well, usually weapons. Finally, in Heathen times a marriage was
not fully valid until the groom presented the bride with her morning
gift on the day following their union, which fully established the reality
promised by their first night together. If later the bargain, or marriage,
was broken, the wife left the man and returned to her former home and

the gifts reverted to their former owners. Even today there is a kind of repugnance aroused when we hear of people keeping engagement rings or wedding gifts after a match has been broken off, although we are not always fully aware of why we feel that way. The primary significance of the marriage gifts lies in the spiritual power and troth they symbolize. They are concrete manifestations of the trust, the loyalty, the love, and the vows between the parties involved, and they are tangible proof of the sincerity of the givers.

Bargains were also sealed by the sharing of drink and food, and marriage vows were traditionally pledged over sacred drink in the presence of all the kin and friends. Today it is still common to toast the bride and groom at the reception, often in a traditional and formal manner. Throughout Old Norse literature, we find evidence of sacred ceremonies where vows were pledged over drink. The *bragarfull,* the sacred cup over which oaths were pledged during the Yule season, is one example. Thus, wedding toasts carried the weight of sacred oaths, and the whole process was considered a holy ritual.

Today we tend to treat promises and agreements casually, but the underlying power of our words still exists, whether or not we acknowledge it. Between any people swearing oaths to each other a type of troth exists, the same kind of loyalty that is shared by kin. This means that they are true to each other in all their actions, fulfilling all obligations, whether large or small. A person's honor lies in the strength of her word. A person's soul grows in honor and might every time her actions match her words. Conversely, each time one fails to uphold one's words with deeds, the soul is weakened. When a person loses honor, she loses frith, and hence a bit of her humanity.

All lies and broken promises weaken the power of your word, not only among the people with whom you have dealings but also with the gods and with yourself. If you always tell the truth and habitually carry out everything you say you will do, your words develop a power of their own and a momentum that aids in their actually becoming true. If you tell lies and break your vows in everyday life, then when you speak words in ritual or in magic they will have little force to influence the universe. In addition, within your deepest soul, you yourself will doubt your own ability to carry out your will.

Moreover, the breaking of a vow dishonors not only the oath-breaker but also the person to whom the vows were made. The soul-might exchanged whenever oaths are given is of such power that it inextricably binds the honor and fate of the two parties: their honor becomes one; hence, one person's failure taints the other. This is one reason that the breaking of oaths is such a serious matter; it inflicts real harm on the injured party, just as much as if she had been physically assaulted.

By accepting a gift or an oath, then, you are essentially putting your-self in the other person's power. Not only does your well-being depend on your own care in fulfilling your obligations, but it now equally depends on the conscientiousness of the other person. Exchanging oaths and gifts is a risky business, but a necessary one, since all meaningful social relations rest on such oaths. Recognizing the danger inherent in exchanging promises and vows should not keep us from making any commitments but rather should motivate us to use care and caution in choosing the obligations we do accept.

Overseeing Honesty in Love

Var, in her role as hearer of vows, bears a resemblance to Tyr, the god of the Thing who hears oaths at lawmaking ceremonies. Other gods who preside over oaths include Ull, the god of winter, and Thor. However, Var differs from these other deities in that she hears not only formal and public oaths but also private and informal agreements. The descrip-tion of her in the *Prose Edda* implies that she listens to the private talk between men and women. This would seem to imply not only marriage or betrothal agreements but also all those careless assurances and prom-ises made in many a bed, hayloft, and backseat from the beginning of time through the present. What this really seems to mean is that the act of love itself is an exchange of gifts and that both parties owe a certain honesty and trust to one another. This doesn't necessarily mean that all romantic encounters should be viewed as lifelong commitments, but it does mean that you should not try to deceive the other person about your feelings or intentions.

As the one who punishes broken vows, Var should be seen not as an avenging fury flying around after the culprit and crying for her blood but rather as akin to the mighty Norns, the three goddesses who govern the fate of the whole universe. To break an oath is to set in motion a series of events, a pattern of cause and effect, that will ultimately bring down the offender's luck and thus blight her fate. When you break promises and vows, you yourself cause the retribution by damaging your own honor. You weaken your soul-might and taint the way you view yourself. With every promise left unfulfilled, you send a message to the universe that your words have no power and that you are incapable of carrying out your will. In that case, gradually all your enterprises will begin to falter and fail.

 ## Trance

I see a smallish, slender, youngish woman in her late twenties or early thirties. She has an elfin face: round high cheeks, pointed chin, broad wide forehead. Her hair is dark—black—long and straight and parted in the center. Her eyes are pale gray, almost clear, and startling, a little intimidating. Her skin is very pale, her eyelashes and brows very dark. She is solemn, stern, serious. She wears a small jeweled cap, similar to those worn in Tudor England, as well as a purple cloak and a light-gray, or sometimes dark, dress. I see her standing behind people—at an altar during a ceremony, alone in a bed at night—always behind them, listening when they least expect her.

She brooks no breaking of vows and holds all accountable for their promises, showing no mercy. "Why should I have mercy on them, when they have none?" she says. "When they learn to be kind, then I will."

If two people are faithful and honest in their vows, her blessings can change a mere love affair into something exquisite. She is a goddess of marriage, a goddess of commitment.

"But sometimes it is hard, or even impossible, to keep some oaths," I remind her.

"Then don't make them in the first place," she replies, with a slight smile.

I see her in halls, entering from a side or a back door, standing in the shadows. She has a small ash casket that holds many lovely gold and jeweled rings; these represent all vows that have been kept. But she shows me a large treasure room she has underground where there are many, many huge chests containing tarnished rings—these are all the broken oaths. She returns to the upper rooms, to a big, empty chamber similar to one that might be found in a medieval castle. It is stone, with high, Gothic-shaped windows through which the late-afternoon sun streams. Var sits on the floor with her lovely rings all in her lap, running her hands through them with pleasure.

The picture of Var I saw in trance dovetails nicely with her function as a hearer of vows. She is not the grand hierophant, swearing the participants to fealty and promising dire consequences if the oaths are not kept. Rather, she is a silent witness, keeping to the background, a reminder to the oath makers, who are the real performers of the rite, of their promises and of the holy presence bound up with their words. The rings I saw are reminiscent of the gifts that the Heathen Germanics gave to seal their commitments. Like the tarnished jewelry, a gift whose promise has been broken is dimmed, bereft of meaning and power.

Var's personality is stern, harsh, and unyielding; unlike some of Frigg's gentler attendants, she is not soothing or motherly. She expects you to deliver what you say you will or not make the promise to begin with. She is a reminder, in this age of easy bargains and casual promises, of a time when a person's word was the only assurance needed to seal an agreement.

Ritual

Var is one of those deities who should not be approached glibly or without good reason. The most obvious rituals to her would be those seeking her as a witness to oaths, particularly marriage vows. However, you'd better be prepared to make good on any promises you make to her, so she should be called on sparingly and with caution. Another type of ritual to Var would be one asking for enlightenment on the mystical meaning of oaths in an attempt to develop oneself spiritually. For this sort of rite, Var could be petitioned more readily, as she is undoubtedly only too happy to give anyone a better understanding of her holy trust.

An altar to Var would probably be stark, using either dark or muted colors, or else white or light gray. Any sacred object on which oaths could suitably be sworn, whether or not you intend to swear on them at this particular time, could be placed on the altar—among them, sacred stones, rings and other jewelry, knives, swords, or other weapons. When swearing serious oaths, it is always best to do so in the presence of some trusted witnesses—people you know well, who hear your words and join with you in acknowledging your intentions. In a wedding rite, Var would probably be only one of several gods and goddesses addressed, but the actual vows should be made to her and sealed with gifts and a sacred toast.

In performing a ritual to Var for personal growth and wisdom, you can set up the altar, make the invocation, and perhaps meditate on the nature of promises, and then think of situations when you kept or did not keep your word and the consequences you encountered as a result. Realize that all your deeds and vows, broken and kept, have created your present world and condition but also that your deeds now can shape your future. Understand that you have the power, at each given moment, to create the future you want, step by step and act by act. Var is a stern taskmaster, but only because she knows the vital importance of the vows she guards. She wants those who call on her to choose to be victorious and strong and glad.

Call to Var

Lady of Vows,   mighty Var—
Witness of weddings,   loather of lies,
Hearer of oaths,   teacher of truth.

Lady of the purple cloak,
Lady of rings,
Keeper of honor,
Harsh lady—

Be with us, great hearer of vows—
You are the witness of our deeds,
*   the warder of our words.*
You watch our makings and our unmakings.
We ride on the rush of our words toward our fate,
*   the future where you wait,*
*   bright or clouded,*
The soul of our truth.

Hail, Var! Hear us, and come!

17

Fulla

The Sister

 ## Lore

Fulla (ON Fulla; also called Folla, Volla, Fylla) appears as the goddess closest to Frigg and, like Eir and Gefjon, seems to have a more well-defined existence than some of the others. Her name means "full" and is usually taken to refer to fullness or abundance. The word *full* was also the term used for the *blót,* or ritual, cup. Fulla is listed by Snorri as the fifth Aesir goddess and appears in several myths as one of the goddesses seated as judges in the high seats in the great hall at Asgard.

Like many of the other Asynjur, Fulla is described as one of Frigg's attendants; however, she appears to be the most constant, most favored, and most intimate attendant, a sort of maid of honor to the queen. In the "Second Merseburg Charm," Volla (Fulla) is called the sister of Frija (Frigg). Grimm speculates that Fulla might have been associated with the full moon, both because her name is similar to the Gothic word *fullips* and the Lithuanian Pilnatis and because Frigg is often connected with the constellation Orion. In addition, Frija and Volla are followed in the charm by another pair of goddesses, Sunna (the sun) and her sister Sindgund.[1] However, this reasoning seems a little strained, particularly since the moon is a male deity in Germanic mythology.

Fulla is described as a beautiful young girl wearing her long golden hair loose, restrained only by a golden band, circlet, or snood. Indeed, one of the skaldic paraphrases for gold was "snood of Fulla" (Skáldskaparmál, ch. 32). The unbound hair indicates Fulla's status as a maiden; unmarried girls wore their hair loose in Old Norse society. The golden circlet is a sign of nobility. Like Thor's wife, Sif, Fulla and her flowing hair can be seen as symbolic of the ripening grain, the golden band representing the binding of the harvested sheaf. In this guise Fulla represents the fullness and bounty of the earth. Grimm compares her to the German female fertility figure Dame Habonde, or Abundia.[2] De Vries sees her as merely a personification of the abstract idea of dispensing prosperity, based on Roman models,[3] although Scandinavia was far less influenced by classical ideas than continental Europe and Britain. It is more likely that she was originally a fertility or agricultural deity.

Frigg's Confidante

Fulla's main role seems to be as Frigg's chief companion, confidante, and advisor. Fulla has custody of the queen of the Aesir's ashen casket, presumably containing her jewels and other treasures. Mythologically, however, this casket could symbolize the container of the divine mother's blessings, prosperity, and fertility, and Fulla would thus be the one in charge of preserving this power until Frigg is ready to dispense it.

Fulla is also said to be in charge of Frigg's shoes. Although this sounds rather mundane to us now, in earlier times shoes were rarer and more expensive, as much a symbol of wealth and prestige as jewelry or fine cloth. The foot has connotations of fertility. Early rock carvings picture the imprints of feet alongside fertility symbols. The foot has traditionally had important symbolic meaning in Germanic and Celtic lore; for example, the word *foot* was often used symbolically to indicate the penis and hence fertility and prosperity. Footwear might also signify travel and journeys, and indeed Fulla is often seen as Frigg's messenger in a number of myths.

As described on pages 56–57, Frigg and Odin, disguised as an old peasant couple, raise two boys who have been shipwrecked on an island. Odin taunts Frigg that his favorite, Geirrod, is a king while hers is a nobody. Frigg accuses Geirrod of being inhospitable and miserly, some of the most terrible charges one could make in Norse society. She then sends Fulla to Midgard to trick Geirrod. Fulla tells the king to beware of an evil magician in a blue cloak who can be recognized by the fact that dogs will not bark at him. This description, of course, fits Odin, who is so badly treated when he arrives at Geirrod's court that he revokes his favor to the king. In Saxo's *Gesta Danorum* (book 1, ch. 7)—a much later text that is sometimes confused with the myth of Freyja and the Brisingamen jewel—Fulla enlists the aid of a dwarf to help Frigg prevent Odin from finding out that his queen had stolen a piece of gold from one of his statues to make herself a necklace. In both of these myths we see Fulla as Frigg's close friend and helper, sharing with the queen her traits of cleverness, strategic acumen, and cunning. As Frigg's helper, Fulla is similar to Loki in his role as Odin's helper and partner in deceit.

Fulla is a goddess of rank and stature. This is implicit in her inclusion with other prominent Asynjur on important occasions. For example, she is named among the lawgivers of the Aesir in the Skáldskaparmál (ch. 1) in the *Prose Edda*. In the "Second Merseburg Charm" she is paired with her sister Frija, the wife of the Aesir's leader, and is among those called on to try to heal Balder's foal. Because of the similarity of her name to the god Phol, an obscure god who is also mentioned in the charm, some have suggested that Volla, or Fulla, might have been one half of a god and goddess pair, similar to Frey and Freyja.[4] Phol is often regarded as another name for Balder. There is also a Prussian god of plenty with a similar name, Pilnitus.[5]

Fulla appears again in a Balder myth in the Skírnismál of the *Elder Edda*. In this story Balder's wife, Nanna, sends back gifts from the Underworld to Frigg and Fulla—Fulla receives a golden finger ring. At the same time Balder sends back Odin's magic ring, Draupnir. Just as Odin's ring, which reproduced itself every nine nights, is often seen as representing wealth and prosperity, so might Fulla's ring be a symbol of the abundance and riches she is said to dispense. Coming as it does from the world of the dead, it might also be a symbol of the link between life and death. Grimm speculates on its having magical powers, perhaps invisibility. He goes on to point out that Aventiure, Frau Ehre's messenger, has such a ring. Earlier I compared Aventiure to Saga because of their association with poets and history, but Aventiure is also similar to Fulla in that each functions as her queen's messenger.

Fulla's inclusion in these stories hints at some sort of possible relation between this goddess and Balder, although what that might be is not clear. As Frigg's closest friend, Fulla would certainly share Frigg's love and concern for her son, and the fact that she is Frigg's sister would make her Balder's maternal aunt. Fulla's connection with the harvest might also link her with a god who by his own death symbolizes cyclic change. At any rate, Fulla was obviously considered to be closely connected to Frigg and important enough to be petitioned, along with her, for help and to be equally honored with a gift.

 ## Trance

She is small, roundish, buxom, solid. Her hair is blond, her cheeks red. Dressed in rose colors, she is shining, fresh smelling, energetic, bustling. I see her at night, lying in bed with her sister Frigg, both of them naked together, laughing and exchanging secrets.

I fly or sail to Valhalla. As I go to Frigg's hall, Fulla meets me in the garden between Fensalir and Valhalla. "We don't need to bother with all that formality this time," she tells me. She is very chatty and perky, wearing a medieval-style, rose-colored gown. She braids my hair back away from my face and gives me one of her gold chains to make a circlet for my brow like hers. She makes me look pretty as we sit at night in the garden. We walk along with our arms around each other's waists. We stop in Fensalir to say hello, and we find Frigg and the other goddesses all busy doing various tasks. Fulla takes me up to Frigg's bedroom and shows me Frigg's things. The famous footgear is all magical—"Why do you think they have someone guarding a lot of old shoes?" she asks. "One pair makes you swift, one gives endurance, one makes you invisible, one lets you dance all night, one leads you to a lover!" Fulla giggles uproariously at the last pair. She then shows me Frigg's jewels. At first she starts to show me the notorious piece said to be made from a jewel she and Frigg purloined from one of Odin's statues, but she changes her mind at the last minute. Each piece has a story, and Fulla knows them all.

Just then Frigg comes in looking worried. She says she is a bit upset because Odin is on one of his journeys and has been gone longer than expected. Fulla decides we should all have a fancy dinner to cheer us up. She dresses Frigg in her finest clothes and lays out a gorgeous table for dinner—"Just for us," as she puts it. Just then Odin comes in—a tall, handsome man in his early to mid-forties, dusty and worn-looking from travel, with very acute, sharp blue eyes (or eye, in his case). He sort of smiles at the sight of our party and asks who's joining us for dinner. "Maybe it's a secret lover," Fulla teases him. Frigg interrupts to say that she and Fulla were just about to have dinner together. "Well," says Odin, "I won't disturb you then," and he makes as if to leave. Fulla hops up, saying no, she's changed her mind and isn't eating, so she supposes he might as well stay. We leave Odin and Frigg together, smiling at each other.

Fulla then decides we should climb out the window and down the trellis and leave the house in secret to "go on an adventure." We travel by boat down a river, Fulla rowing. As we float by the shore, we see various pairs of women of many different ages who are all fast friends—first two little girls playing together on a dock. Next we see two young girls in their early teens walking in the woods. "How sad," says Fulla. "They will soon quarrel over a boy, and he is not worth the loss of their friendship." I see myself and a close friend of mine, representing women in young adulthood. I am surprised to see myself. Fulla says, "Why? You're a part of this too. You are and have friends."

Fulla talks of the importance of women having women for friends—even the ability to later be a lover stems from the ability to be a "best friend," she tells me. "Women's friendship—this is the secret kept in my ashen casket." I next see my mother and her sisters on the shore, having lunch. I complain about the fact that I have no sisters. "Make your own sisters, being sisterless!" Fulla tells me.

We return to Fensalir and go in through the front door this time, finding all the other goddesses sitting together in the main hall. Fulla laughingly admits to sneaking out earlier. I then leave. As I go, I turn to see Fulla and Snotra standing arm in arm in the doorway, waving good-bye.

In my trancework Fulla exhibited not only the traits of loyalty, support, generosity, friendship, and sisterhood, which might have been expected from reading the myths, but also a great deal of vitality, fun, and, yes, mischief. She seems to be the archetypal best girlfriend and particularly devoted to women and their friendships. Although she appeared outwardly girlish, frivolous, and fun-loving, there was an undercurrent of power, an ability to manifest and manage things, and a hidden side of secrets that was only revealed in brief glimpses.

Though neither distant nor unfriendly to men, Fulla seems to be especially concerned with women and their relationships with each other, as sisters and friends; this complements Frigg's role as wife and mother. Fulla is the best friend, always ready to help, trade secrets, discuss love affairs and life goals, and share a good time. Unlike some goddesses, who remained relatively distant until I had worked with them for some time, Fulla was immediately friendly and intimate; moreover, she began reappearing spontaneously in other tranceworkings afterward. She evoked in me a feeling for old childhood friends so strong that I felt moved to call some of them after my first ritual to her. Fulla is the part of every woman that remains young and an individual, despite the many other roles and responsibilities created by family and work obligations that overlay the original personality.

In her role as confidante, loyal family member, and skilled strategist, Fulla is a good source of advice and help on various enterprises, particularly where cunning and subtlety are involved. As messenger and advisor to Frigg, she would be good to enlist as an emissary to the queen of the Aesir when one is seeking that goddess's aid. As a repository of various secrets and cosmological gossip, Fulla is a valuable source of wisdom and enlightenment, although her light and whimsical manner of imparting knowledge makes it a challenge to find the kernel of truth within. She might also be of help in improving or enhancing one's physical appearance and in giving parties, dinners, or other gatherings, as well as in injecting some fun and pleasure into one's life in general.

 Ritual

An altar to Fulla might be decorated with bright colors, such as rose, bright blue, leaf green, or gold. Flowers, fruits and grains, or jewels and baubles could also be used. One might wear one's hair loose with a golden circlet, ribbon, or band like Fulla's, or put a circlet on the altar as a symbol of her. Fulla can be invoked as a means of obtaining Frigg's help and favor, to aid in mischievous and fun-loving endeavors, to promote a prosperous harvest, and to initiate or deepen friendships, particularly with women and most especially between women. For harvest rituals or celebrations, offerings of fruits, breads, and other food and drink might be exhibited on the altar or consumed during the course of the rite. Music, songs, dancing, games, and other diversions are pleasing to Fulla and in keeping with her character; these may be included during or following the ritual. You might want to put pictures of close women relatives or friends on the altar or wear gifts of jewelry or clothing from beloved women in your life. After the ritual, try calling or writing a close female relative or friend for a chat.

Fulla is a complex and unpredictable figure. My experience of her was that she was very easy to contact but difficult to fully grasp or keep up with. In one sense she is the archetypal companion, best friend, younger sister, or cunning servant—helpful, clever, a little cheeky, and lots of fun. Underneath this supportive and frivolous layer there is an undercurrent of something mysterious and unpredictable, and a little unsettling. Fulla is easier to reach than Frigg, and yet, at another level, she is less comprehensible and less comfortable to work with. She is truly Frigg's sister, the flip side of the wife, mother, and queen—the wild, irresponsible, unfettered maiden, ripe with promise and yet to be harvested.

Call to Fulla

Fulla, Volla, Fylla, Abundia—
Sister of Frigg, maid of honor—Hail!

Lady of the chamber,
Mistress of wealth,
Guardian of treasures—
    Bring us abundance.

Wearer of the ribbon,
Lady of the ash,
Keeper of the casket,
    Adorn our lives.

Keeper of jewels,
Keeper of shoes,
Keeper of secrets,
    Ward well our dreams.

Come with gift and greeting,
Come with fun and folly,
Come with lore and laughter—
Sweet sister of the gods—Come!

18

Hlín

The Protector

 ## Lore

Hlin (ON Hlín) is probably the most accessible of the Asynjur. Snorri names her twelfth on his list of Aesir goddesses, and she also appears as one of Frigg's attendants; in fact, Hlin is often thought to be identical to Frigg herself. Her name comes from the ON word *hlína* ("to hide or protect"), and she has the special task of protecting those people Frigg wants to save from danger; thus there was a saying that one who escapes peril "leans" or finds refuge (*hleinir*). Hlin is also a sort of intermediary between Frigg and humankind, listening to the desires and problems of mortals and aiding Frigg in deciding how best to respond to their needs. In addition, Hlin is sometimes presented as a goddess of consolation, one who comforts the grieving.[1]

Hlin's close identification with Frigg comes from several lines in the Völuspá of the *Elder Edda* (st. 53), when the spirit of the dead wise-woman predicts the events of Ragnarok, the end of the world, and tells of Odin's death:

> *Then comes to Hlin*   *yet another grief,*
> *When Odin goes out*   *to fight with the wolf,*

> *And Beli's bright slayer*   *battles with Surt;*
> *Then will fall*   *Frigg's beloved.*
> VÖLUSPÁ, ST. 53

The first hurt implied here is generally assumed to be the murder of Balder, Frigg's dearest son. Because Hlin is supposed to experience sorrow from the deaths of Balder and Odin, some have speculated that Hlin and Frigg are the same goddess. This may be true, and like all twelve Asynjur who are the attendants of Frigg, Hlin shares many of Frigg's characteristics and functions.

Another interpretation is that since it is Hlin's main duty to protect those in whom Frigg takes particular interest, and because the queen of the Aesir would naturally want her own son and husband kept safe, Hlin's ultimate failure to keep these loved ones from harm would certainly be a source of great sorrow to her. For all her might, Hlin cannot withstand the power of the Norns and of fate; she cannot fulfill what she has promised to her queen, cannot preserve her kin from destruction. Perhaps that is why she is so sympathetic to those weighed down by grief and despair.

Traditionally, the protective abilities of mothers were considered to be particularly powerful, and Hlin embodies this function of the mother goddess Frigg, the fierceness of the mother guarding her young. The skills of weaving and sewing, which are other important aspects of Frigg's might, are also related to protective magic. Items made by a mother or sister for a family member could be magically empowered to preserve that individual from harm. In several of the Grimms' tales a young girl must make shirts to save her brothers from enchantment. The *Orkneyinga saga* (ch. 11) tells how the mother of Jarl Sigurd made him a magical raven banner to bring him victory in battle.

Women of the early Germanic tribes typically accompanied their men to the battlefield, where they encouraged and incited them during the fighting and used their prophetic powers to aid them in their military strategy. It is also likely that some of these women worked spells of warding and protection. Certain women are shown as magically faring forth into battle to protect and aid their favorites, such as Sigrun, described as a "Valkyrie," in Helgakviða Hundingsbana I (sts. 31 and 56).

The image of Hlin following Frigg's favorites and keeping them from danger is reminiscent of the *fylgja,* or fetch, an attendant spirit protecting an individual or a clan. This being often appeared in the form of a woman or an animal and was said to show herself in times of stress or danger, especially before the death of the individual she was attached to. The fylgja often accompanied not just one person but a whole family, passing from one member to another through many generations. Similar to the *fylgjur* were the dísir, tutelary goddesses who were attached to a neighborhood, family, or individual and were responsible for fertility and protection. Hlin functions almost like a dís or fylgja of Frigg's family, lending her aid and protection to the favored ones throughout the generations. Frigg's activities in the realm of Midgard here mirror those of Odin, who also often lends his favor and protection to various kings and warriors throughout the myths and sagas. Like Odin, Frigg takes a keen interest in politics and the affairs of kings and nobles, and through the offices of Hlin, her delegate, she lends power to those she supports.

Despite these weighty activities, however, Hlin's strongest image is as a very personal, very approachable, very comforting mother figure. The first time I contacted this goddess, I wasn't even trying to reach her; I was merely doing an ecumenical pathworking on the "Dark Mother" at a large festival. The presence I felt was nonetheless very striking and strong; it wasn't until much later, when I chose to embark on these journeys to meet Frigg and her twelve companions, that I saw Hlin once more and recognized that I knew her.

 ## Trance

I sit in a dark egg, covered with heavy, black, soft material, perhaps velvet, but coarser, like felt or soft wool. A gaunt, regal woman somewhere between thirty and two thousand sits rigidly, her dark garments blending with part of

the tapestry. She stares into the distance. Her face is made of sharp bones and sharp features, with piercing, deep-set, gray-blue eyes. She is playing a stringed instrument, like a lute or a dulcimer, and I am sitting at her feet, leaning my head on her right knee. I think of the qualities of rest and comfort. I remember sitting and leaning on my own mother, my head on her breast, in my old rocking chair in my room at home, of the times she comforted me when I was unhappy or frightened. I remember how my mother was then and I begin to cry now, feeling the tears course down my cheeks—only two tears, one from each eye—slow, dignified tears. The dark lady picks me up and lets me rest my head on her breast while she rocks, as my mother did back in my childhood. She puts her lute to one side, where it continues to play by itself. She rocks me, but her eyes still look off into the distance. When I finally feel free of emotion, I pull away from her and look into her face. She now looks at me, and her eyes meet mine for the first time—they are piercing and bottomless. I smile gravely at her and she smiles back. . . .

Later I see Hlin sitting in a chair in dark robes, her head hooded. Her hair looks gray at first, but I soon see it is dark brown. Her eyes are light, and kind. She lets me rest my head on her knees. She puts her hand on my back and wraps her cloak around my shoulder. . . .

I climb on Sleipnir, Odin's horse, but he fidgets until I fall off and have to remount; he is very impatient. We bypass Valhalla entirely, and I go to Fensalir directly through the garden. On my way through it I see Fulla in a nook, giggling; she is in the bushes with the god of mischief, Loki, of all people. She giggles and waves at me; he leers from the shadows.

Frigg meets me at the door to her hall. Most of her ladies are in the main hall, relaxing; no one is working today. Hlin, in dark robes, is sitting on a high, thronelike chair. She has straight, dark-brown hair, parted in the center, and very light, china-blue eyes. Her face is squarish and strong; she wears a hood over her head. Sitting on her chair, she hears the wishes of everyone throughout the worlds, especially those who are sad or in trouble. People come to her at their lowest ebb, their worst point; they are like children when they seek her. Because she sees people like this, she is best able to advise Frigg how to help them. People try to be respectable, proper, and strong when they approach Frigg, but when they approach Hlin, nothing is hidden. Each one rests her head *on Hlin's knees, and she pats their shoulders. She sits in her chair most of the time, except when one of her charges is in danger. Then she whirls down from Heaven, her billowing cloak acting like a protective shield, repelling evil forces. She plays her lutelike instrument, which soothes people. While she lets people talk themselves out to her, she remains silent—she lets, and makes, people solve their own problems, leads them to their own discovery of a solution, rather than giving them the answer herself. "You need to go beyond feelings, to be yourself in spite of them," she says. She talks little; her hands are cool; her eyes are very beautiful.*

Hlin appears as a goddess both comforting and remote. The image of her using her cloak to protect people reminds me of the story of Hadding's visit to the underworld in Saxo's *Gesta Danorum* (book 1). In this tale the hero Hadding meets a woman bearing fresh herbs in the middle of winter. When he agrees to go with her to see the land from which they came, she wraps her cloak around him and draws him under the earth. Notice how the cloak here is used not only as protection but also as a means of traveling between the worlds.

The picture of Hlin as a goddess of comfort and consolation may seem a little out of keeping with a people noted for their stoicism and cheerful optimism in the face of difficulty. But the outward show of strength does not mean the Norse people did not feel, and feel deeply. The old literature has many examples of real and terrible grief. There is the *Sonatorrek,* a poem written by the famous Icelandic skald Egil Skallagrimsson to mourn the loss of his son at sea. An even better example is a scene from the Guðrúnarkviða I from the *Elder Edda* (sts. 1–14) in which Gudrun sits inconsolably beside the body of her murdered husband, Sigurd, killed by her own brother Gunnar. Gudrun has been unable to weep for Sigurd, and one by one all her father's warriors and then their wives try to offer her some comfort that will allow her to express her grief. Finally, a woman named Gullrond simply uncovers the dead man's face and bids Gudrun to look, after which the tears run down Gudrun's cheeks like rain. So even the fierce Vikings realized the need to express deep emotions at appropriate times.

However, they also recognized that grief should have its limits, and prolonged sorrow and depression were looked upon as both unhealthy for the grief-stricken one and harmful to the loved ones being mourned. One legend tells of a young mother who lost her only child. She would not be comforted but wept at his grave every night. On the night before Twelfth Day (during Yule) she saw Berchte's train of children pass by. At the end of the procession came a little boy carrying a jug of water that was so heavy he couldn't keep up with the others; the shirt he was wearing was soaking wet. The woman recognized him as her son and ran to help him over a fence. He asked her not to cry so much, because he had to carry all her tears in his jug and it was already full. After that, the mother stopped weeping.[2] This folktale is similar to a scene in Halgakviða Hundingsbana II in the *Elder Edda* (sts. 43–44), where the dead Helgi tells his wife Sigrun that the reason he is damp with hoarfrost is because each tear she sheds falls like icy blood on his breast.

Certainly people who grieve too much or too long can harm their own physical and emotional health, as well as hurting all the other people in their lives, but these stories indicate that the souls of the dead themselves are also affected by excessive mourning among survivors. This may even suggest that mourners can somehow hold their loved ones back with their grief, preventing the dead from continuing their progress in the afterlife. The dead want to be remembered and honored by their families and friends and to have their deeds recalled and their fame sung, but they don't want life to come to a screeching halt just because they've left it. Hlin is a goddess who helps people to recognize and experience their feelings of grief and loss but who also encourages them to stop after an appropriate interval to work through their emotions and get on with their lives.

Hlin may be a goddess of comfort; however, she is a goddess for private and real grief, not large groups engaging in wailing sessions or individuals grappling with trivial discomforts. She is a very personal and private consoler of great grief, of despair, of the difficult experiences that occur in every life, no matter how successful. She not only comforts, she also inspires the realization that these problems are not the end of the world, that you can and should overcome them. Her own dignity offers both comfort and inspiration. She is a goddess of total honesty, plumbing the depths of the personality, forging the fears and weaknesses into a strong core of steel with her fires of the soul.

Ritual

Hlin can be invoked for the comfort and protection of oneself and of others. Rituals to her lend themselves to intimacy and privacy because of the strong emotions involved; a couple, a family, or a few very close friends might join for a rite to Hlin, but very large groups are probably not advisable. Comfort would generally be sought for a particular occurrence of grief or unpleasantness, such as the loss of a loved one. Protection could be sought either for a specific danger, such as protecting a loved one who is embarking on a journey, or for the general safety or well-being of a person or a place. Another way to honor Hlin would be to comfort and protect others who are going through rough times; as the goddess herself once said to me, "It's not always about you."

Hlin's altar would be dark and muted, with dark grays or blues or black predominating, and a few simple adornments. Pictures of loved ones being mourned or for whom protection is desired might be included. If you are doing the ritual to Hlin to purge yourself of a specific grief or comfort yourself in the face of a particular sorrow, allow enough time to fully experience the emotions you call up, to deal with them, and then to rise above them and return to a calm and centered state. You should feel rested and comforted afterward, not worried and frazzled; remember, the purpose of the ritual is to feel better, not to feel emotionally drained and unhappy. It is not unusual to experience some sort of realization and understanding of your inner state, of how you have arrived at this point and what you can do in the future. After the ritual, treat yourself to a glass of fine wine or hot cocoa, a warm bath, a night's rest on clean sheets and a wooly blanket. Be kind to yourself.

Whether as an avenging spirit, a comforting mother, or a wise advisor, Hlin is both mysterious and otherworldly, and yet very personal and accessible. She is a source of inner strength to be called on throughout life, a force that echoes and resonates with each individual's strongest and best self.

Call to Hlin

Hlin—goddess of refuge,
Goddess of the comforting cloak,
Defender of Frigg's beloved—

You comfort mourners,
You dry tears,
You soothe grieving hearts.

You who have your lady's ear,
 Give us aid.
Goddess of Protection,
 Ward us well.

Hlin, goddess of comfort, soothe us.
Hlin, goddess of mourners, dry our tears.
Hlin, goddess of refuge, keep us safe.
Hlin, Frigg's guardian, be with us now.

19

Syn

The Guardian

 Lore

Syn (ON Syn), the eleventh goddess in Snorri's list (Gylfaginning, ch. 35), is another protective deity, and her name means "denial" or "refusal." She is also one of Frigg's attendants, and it is Syn's job to guard the door of the hall, warding it against those who should not enter. Frigg, in her role as wife and mother, is the goddess of the home and the hall, and Syn, her companion, functions as the guardian of the inner sanctum of the family, of its most private and holy places.

Syn's second function is as public as her first is private. She is one of the deities of the Thing, the lawgiving assembly of Old Norse culture.

Many modern ideas of democracy are derived not from classical models but rather from the social practices of the Old Germanic peoples. In early times most northern European societies were divided into a number of loosely associated clans. A chief became king through nomination by the other chiefs, "the first among equals," and his authority and power were limited by the assembly of the people.[1] This assembly, or Thing, as it was called in Scandinavia, was an annual gathering of all free men of an age and status to bear weapons (and this included nearly everyone except the very lowest class of thralls). It was usually held in the summer. The people met to proclaim the laws and put them into effect, pass judgments, settle suits, worship their gods, engage in contests of strength and skill, and buy and sell various goods. Each district would have its own Thing and, later, as society became more complex and centralized, there would be a larger Althing for the whole land. The laws of Norse society were retained by custom and transmitted orally each year by the elder members of the Thing, the law-speakers. The law was set down in an alliterative form to help people remember it, combining law, poetry, and magic into one.[2]

The distinction between civil and criminal law that we have today did not exist at that time. All complaints were brought by an individual or family against another, and all required some sort of personal restitution. Murder and acts of violence, as well as other injuries, were resolved according to a scale of compensatory payments.[3] Though judgment was delivered by means of the Thing, enforcement was usually left to the individuals and families involved, and, if no reconciliation could be reached, the injured parties were obligated to recapture their honor through acts of vengeance.

Any injury, from murder to insult, was viewed as damaging the honor, and hence the luck and personal power, of the offended individual, and through him, his family and his entire clan. Restitution for a wrong had to be made to heal the injury. Because the injured luck of one individual could eventually enfeeble the entire group of people to which he was attached, society took it upon itself to redress wrongs and restore the balance. Thus, the spirit of Teutonic law was characterized by sympathy for the offended party; the Thing declared itself at one with the injured person and committed itself to procuring restitution for him, renouncing his opponent.[4]

Defender of the Accused

Into this setting the home-loving goddess Syn appears, entrusted with the defense of the accused. She is said to protect people against unjustified charges, defend against any legal actions she wishes to contest, and preside whenever anyone denies something under oath. In Old Norse society, when people rejected charges against themselves and pled not guilty, the usual formula was to say, "Syn is set forward" (Gylfaginning, ch. 35).

The law at that time rested on the principle that an accusation made in proper form was enough to tarnish a person's honor and luck and therefore compelled him to defend himself before the Thing. If he was not ready to nullify the charges by his own oath and those of character witnesses willing to swear on his behalf, he was as good as guilty. The mere accusation itself allowed guilt to enter into a person unless he hurled it back with his oath and freed himself.

Syn, then, like Tyr, Thor, Ullr, and Var, is a deity of oaths. Where other gods of the Thing represent society and its values and concerns, Syn stands on the side of the individual, protecting him against unjust charges and accusations. The fact that Syn refutes only those cases in which she chooses to involve herself implies that she does not support all defendants but only unjustly charged people. Truly guilty parties have already lost their luck by virtue of their deeds.

 ## Trance

When I begin my journey to Fensalir, I find Sleipnir grazing peacefully. After passing over Bifrost, I dismount and walk. I bypass Valhalla and go straight to Frigg's hall. I find the door locked and the entire house dark downstairs, but there are lights in the windows above. I walk around to the back and knock. A woman's stern voice, with a sort of Texas country accent, asks sharply who it is. I state my various names and begin to expound on the great and esoteric reasons I am there. I hear the woman chuckle, and she opens the door a crack. She is large, though not fat—a tall, big-boned woman with large, muscular arms that are visible under her short, rolled-up sleeves. She wears dark, plain peasant clothing and a shawl. Her reddish blond, or ash-blond, hair is worn in a loose bun on top of her head like a Gibson girl, but with stray strands coming down. Her gray or green eyes are set in a face with angular, strong cheekbones and a squarish jaw. She takes me to her chair, which is by the kitchen hearth, and gives me some tea. On her chair she has some knitting, some papers, and some books. We sit and talk. She shows me her knitting; it's a neck-scarf with a design on

it. *"It's for himself, to keep from catching cold on all those wanderings." I ask her about the design, and she holds it up saying, "It's a DNA molecule"—and so it is.*

Someone pounds on the door. Syn talks through the door with whoever it is for a minute, then lets in a young woman carrying some things in bundles; the young woman hastens upstairs. Later we hear another pounding at the door. The voice sounds similar to that of the young woman who previously entered, but Syn decides that whoever it is this time may not come in. The voice wheedles, then pleads, then threatens. As the voice gets angrier and angrier, it becomes apparent that it belongs to a giant. Syn rebukes him sharply and lifts a huge bar into its place across the door, her arms rippling with muscle. There is furious pounding and pushing on the door, so hard that the wood strains inward slightly—but the door holds. Unconcerned, Syn returns to her chair by the fire. "When you're in here with your door shut, you just forget about anything out there," she says. She also tells me that I need to finish the things I start, to resolve unfinished business and relationships or else I'll have to carry all this leftover "stuff" around all my life.

After a while Syn puts on her "good shawl," as she calls it, and goes to a large assembly of law—a trial, or lawmaking body of some sort. The politicians and legislators and lawyers greet her with outward courtesy, but one can see that they really wish she wasn't there. They view her as troublesome, a nuisance. She stops some of their bills, or decisions, and refutes them. The politicians are conciliatory at first, then openly angry, but Syn remains calm and firm— "What's right is right, and what ain't right, ain't," she tells them. I leave her there with the sullen and angry lawmakers, like a nursemaid with sulky children.

My vision of Syn was surprisingly homely and down-to-earth, a countrywoman, a yeoman-like figure. At first glance there appears to be some discrepancy between Syn's function as a hearthside doorkeeper and her position as an oath taker at the law assembly. One answer to this paradox comes from another look at Old Norse thought. One of the most dreaded punishments in Norse society was outlawry, or banishment; it isolated people from family and clan and left them without legal rights. Worse, it cut them off from their family power and luck and from their family's protecting spirits, cut them off from the fabric of life itself, in this world and the next.

But a pronouncement of outlawry by the legal assembly carried no real weight as long as a person was still supported and acknowledged by his kin. If they rejected the court's decision and agreed to retain the condemned individual in their clan, he could remain safe and protected at the family homestead. True, this might lead to a feud between the accused's family and that of the offended party, but the defendant was safe from the ultimate isolation, the living death, of being a true outlaw. Since the deeds of all family members contributed to its ørlög—to the luck and fate of everyone in the family—it is not likely that a clan would risk its future and its ultimate prosperity to protect a truly guilty individual. But an innocent or unjustly punished individual would be able to count on his family's support.

This is the tie between Syn's function at the law assembly and in the home—she represents the family hall, the inner reaches of the homestead, where the family sits united behind strongly barred doors, protecting its own from the vagaries of the outside world. In Norse society one's home and kin were the ultimate defense against all attacks.

Moreover, the center of the home was considered to be the seat of the greatest frith, where a family's luck and holiness were strongest. Women, since they dwelt in and worked closest to this inner refuge, were filled with the greatest frith. Therefore, no man of sense would disregard what the women of his house advised on any serious matter but rather regarded their speech as reflecting their close ties to the family's luck and therefore of great significance. In this context, Syn is the voice of the higher self, speaking from the inner place of holiness within us all to guard and guide us.

Today, with our modern systems of impersonal law enforcement, where wrongdoers are usually accused by the state and pay restitution, if any, to society at large instead of to the people they have actually wronged, perhaps Syn's function is not as clear as it used to be. However, surely a goddess can adapt to changing legal systems if people can, and there are still unjustly accused individuals today, as in the past. Today we must rely on the goddess to work through lawyers and legislators as well as through family honor and clan interrelationships.

 ## Ritual

Syn could be invoked by any people accused of wrongdoing, both those involved in formal legal proceedings and those blamed for mistakes on a more informal level—a person being unjustly blamed for an error at work, for example. Syn could also be of help on a broader level, defending against laws or decisions in the various executive, legislative, and judicial branches of government. For example, you could ask her to help reject the licensing of a potentially harmful industrial site or veto an unjust law in Congress.

Syn can also be invoked for protection, especially protection of the home and of holy places. You could do a ritual to her to bless a new dwelling or to offer extra protection any time you feel you might be threatened in your home. She can also be invoked to protect a ritual circle or *hof* (temple) any time you do a ceremony. As the guardian of the door to the hall, she, along with Heimdall, the guardian of the rainbow bridge to Asgard, is a natural choice to call on to protect and keep sacred holy places and rites.

Despite her more exalted functions, Syn seems to be a down-home kind of goddess. In my dealings with her I hear her speak with an accent similar to country dwellers of the area where I grew up. Therefore, her altar should be rather cozy and homely, with simple, cheery, homemade decorations, if possible. A quilt or shawl on the altar would be appropriate, and you might add any little knickknacks or family "heirlooms" that remind you of home (even ugly or tacky ones—Syn is one of the few Asynjur who would probably be willing to sacrifice aesthetics for sentiment). For rites of defense, you might use various symbols to help purify and protect the area—salt, water, fire, incense, sacred stones or other holy objects, special weapons, flaxseeds, or vinegar, to name just a few. Including a knife, sword, or other weapon on the altar is particularly useful. In such rituals I have often incorporated the image of a giant wooden door slamming shut and Syn's strong arms lifting an enormous bar in place to secure it, with a loud slamming noise added for good measure.

If you're doing a rite to invoke Syn's aid in your defense against unfounded charges, first make sure the charges are, indeed, unjust; you need to handle the things of which you are guilty yourself. However, even if you are guilty, Syn can still be invoked to ensure that you get fair treatment. State in the ritual the facts and details of the case and give your oath on a stone, weapon, or other sacred object. You might want to charge a small object or talisman in the ritual and carry it with you when you face your accusers. Realize that it is up to you to fight as hard as you can in your own defense in the physical world; Syn will then lend her power to support your actions. Your deeds also serve to cleanse your spirit of any ill luck or guilt that might linger as a result of the accusation.

Call to Syn

Syn, mighty goddess, guardian of Fensalir,
> *You who bar the door against the intruder,*
> *You who forbid ill luck to enter,*
> *You of the strong will and the strong arm.*

Syn, goddess of the Thing,
> *defender of the blameless,*
> *keeper of the kin,*
> *guardian of the luck.*

Goddess of truth and light,
> *Syn the incorruptible.*
Be with us now,
> *Ward well our hall,*
> *Keep fast our honor.*
Mighty Syn, Come!

20

VOR

The Wisewoman

 ## LORE

Vor (ON Vör), the last of the Aesir goddesses associated with Frigg, is the most enigmatic of the group. Her name might mean something like "the careful one," but this etymology is dubious. Snorri lists her tenth in his enumeration (Gylfaginning, ch. 35) and otherwise offers scant information about her. She is said to be of a wise and searching spirit and has foreknowledge of all that is to happen. Like Odin, she is constantly seeking wisdom and nothing can be hidden from her. The saying that a woman became "aware" of what she learned derived from Vor's name (perhaps referring to the Norse belief that women had special abilities to sense the otherworld and divine the future), and she is particularly associated with the wisdom and lore of women.

Vor seems to have much in common with the Norse völva, a type of shamanic seeress once common in Norse society. A völva practices a type of magic called *seiðr,* which is generally characterized by activities such as soothsaying and faring forth into other realms of existence in order to work magic and to learn from contact with other beings. Unlike rune magic and *galdr,* which emphasize control and will, *seiðr* involves submerging one's consciousness into altered states and experiencing other worlds of reality. It is also concerned with natural substances, such as animals, herbs, stones, and crystals.[1]

Seiðr includes a type of divination performed by a class of trained seers, both men and women, who act as go-betweens for the human race and the various other worlds. The völva's spirit travels forth from her body while she remains in a trance state, aided by chanting, dancing, or drumming. She might wear a symbolic costume of animal furs or feathers and is helped by various animal spirits. The purpose of the rite is traditionally to find out the answers to questions dealing with the well-being of the entire community, such as the causes of disaster or sickness or the answers to matters involving spiritual lore, but questions are also asked regarding the fortunes of individuals.

Images of the old Norse völva appear in various sagas and other literature. The Völuspá of the *Elder Edda* is a long poem presented as the predictions of a dead völva foretelling the future of the gods and the universe; the title literally means "Prophecy of the Völva." *Eiriks saga Rauða* includes a detailed description of a völva and the ceremonies she performs. She dressed in animal skins, including calfskin boots, a lambskin hat, and catskin gloves. Before the ceremony she ate a special meal made from the hearts of various animals. During the rite she sat on a high platform while other women chanted special spells to draw the spirits near so that the seeress could learn hidden things from them. After the main rite, the völva answered important questions regarding the welfare of the community at large, then predicted the individual destinies of some in her audience.

These seeresses are usually associated with Freyja rather than Frigg and are traditionally consulted chiefly on matters that are also the prime concern of the Vanir—the prosperity of the community and the fertility of the people. The typical völva traveled around the countryside, going from community to community and attending the great feasts, just as the priests of the chief Vanir god, Frey, did. There is some evidence that these seeresses might have once traveled in groups in earlier times; perhaps they only later became solitary workers when the old traditions were being broken down.[2]

Intuitive Wisdom, Magical Power, and Dreaming

Vor ties in with Frigg's function as a seer of destinies. However, while Frigg is not given to speaking her predictions, Vor, if she is at all like her human counterparts, is more likely to share her services with the human community. Vor represents the kind of intuitive wisdom and magical power often associated with women in older Germanic cultures, where women were thought to be particularly in tune with spiritual forces, given to prophetic dreams and empathic predictions, and greatly respected and heeded by community leaders.

Women in early Norse society were ordinarily considered to possess a higher degree of holiness than men under normal circumstances and to be in closer contact with the family's luck. This was because a family's frith and luck were believed to be concentrated most strongly at the heart of the home, where the activities of the women were centered. Thus, women were thought of as being closer to the other worlds and more readily able to perceive the patterns of ørlög in the web of the universe. A woman's premonitions and her knowledge of what-is-becoming is born of an overflowing of luck from the depths.[3]

Therefore, a woman's counsel was highly regarded, particularly when it seemed she was prophesying, and no wise man would disregard her advice on an important matter. Tacitus describes a woman whose prophecy led her German tribe, the Bructeri, in their battles against the Romans. She was rewarded by receiving the best of their plunder and was regarded as nearly divine.[4] Vor's powers of foreseeing, then, while related to seið-magic, are more representative of the spiritual gifts typical of women in general than they are to the specialized practices of a worker of magic.

Another source of wisdom is found in dreams. Dreams often offer a glimpse into the future, allowing a person to be aware of events before they happen, to see the workings of the web of *wyrd*. The fylgja, that guardian female spirit, often appears in dreams to give warning or advice. Dreaming is also one of the ways a person can contact dead ancestors for wisdom and blessing. In earlier times a person would sometimes sleep on top of a barrow, or burial mound, to contact the dead and draw on the might of the past.

Dreams can give us valuable insight into our lives and ourselves. They provide information about the physical world that we were too busy or distracted to consciously register at the time as well as hints regarding any subconscious, emotional reactions that we may have repressed. Dreaming can also give clues to understanding how we feel about ourselves and our inner world, opening a channel of communication between the higher self and the conscious mind.

Many people have trouble remembering their dreams and may even think they don't dream at all. Often, if we don't consider our dreams important or feel we don't have time to deal with them, we inhibit our memory of the dreamworld; it's as if the subconscious mind gets discouraged and gives up trying to communicate. One good way to get more out of dreams is to write them down. Not only will this help you remember the details, but it will also emphasize the fact that you consider your dreams important and will thus help stimulate recall. To start, you might write down whatever you are thinking when you first awaken, whether or not it seems to be a dream. When you do record your dreams, write quickly without trying to organize the events or edit your writing. Finally, be sure to do something with each of your dreams, even if it's only a brief analysis.

Lucid dreaming is a particularly powerful form of dreamwork. During a lucid dream you become aware of the fact that you are dreaming and have the opportunity to affect and shape your own dreamworld. The lucid dream is thus a curious blend of the conscious mind and the world of the subconscious, and such dreams are often particularly vivid and heightened. Some people fall into lucid dreaming quite easily and naturally, without really trying. Sometimes lucid dreaming occurs when a dreamer experiences something so odd and inconsistent with reality that she is shocked into awareness.

If you are not lucky enough to experience lucid dreaming easily, there are still methods you can use to train yourself to do it. One way is to pick an object or simple action, which, when it occurs in a dream, will signal you that you are dreaming. For example, Carlos Castaneda, in his book *Journey to Ixtlan,* describes how his teacher, Don Juan, instructed him to look at his hands in his dreams to trigger the lucid state. You can program yourself to use anything as your signal. You might also check your notes on any spontaneous lucid dreams you have had and try to pinpoint common images that might be used as triggers in future dreams.

The only danger in lucid dreaming is that too much dream control might reduce the richness of the spontaneous dream imagery and interfere with the messages coming from the subconscious. If you constantly change your dreams to make them turn out the way you want, you may be missing out on the chance to work out your inner conflicts and resolve your problems. The goal is to learn to confront problems in dreams, and shape and use these energies, rather than control them.

Trance

I have a hard journey to Asgard. Sleipnir is slow and sleepy. We travel to the root of the world tree that lies by Urd's well. I see a figure there in a brown cloak. We next travel across some plains and then across Bifrost, the rainbow bridge. We pass by Valhalla, Odin's hall, and turn to Frigg's dwelling, Fensalir. All of Frigg's goddesses appear briefly, in the order in which I have met them. Syn, the last, pops her head out of the kitchen and motions me out the back door. I again see a figure wearing a brown cloak—mud-brown and coarsely spun, and tattered and worn as well—seated on a stone bench, or a rock. I come to the bench and see that a woman sits there. She is very slight and fragile looking, with long, honey-blond hair. At first she seems very young; then I think she must be in her early forties. She seems ageless.

We go to a snowy wood; the snow is not deep, but similar to that found in early fall or late spring—patches of snow here and there. We walk through the forest together. She is a companion and a teacher to me, quietly wise and simple—a nature woman. At last Vor puts an arm around my shoulders and guides me to sit on a rock. She is very quiet; she bids me to listen to nature, to watch and hear things in the woods. She motions me to stop my inner and outer

chattering and experience the woods, myself, the moment—to be, to listen to
how the world is and how I feel, not to plan everything so rigidly. Vor makes
plans in terms of centuries or ages, not in days or weeks. I move toward her
across a slushy, icy patch in the path. As my foot steps on that icy patch, I fall
through the ground and awaken with a jerk in my own world.

My experiences with Vor were cloudy and difficult to interpret.
Perhaps that is in keeping with her nature as a seeress and wisewoman.
The kind of wisdom she offers is not immediately accessible. It is an
experiential knowledge that grows and develops slowly. She governs the
ability to interpret unspoken motivations and subtle actions, to sense
what is really going on. Vor can be invoked for help in acquiring this
type of wisdom, for shamanic-style workings, or for any type of divination, tranceworking, or dreamwork. She could also be useful for "wom-
en's mysteries"—rituals for puberty, marriage, pregnancy, and birthing.

Ritual

An altar for Vor might be covered in dark materials, or even consist of a
bare stone; outdoor workings are also desirable. Various natural objects,
such as rocks, leaves, flowers, or feathers, would be appropriate symbols,
as well as any tools for scrying or divination—crystals, a dish of water,
a set of runes, and the like. Vor is not one to be consulted for a specific
problem, like some of the other goddesses, but rather for general wisdom and enlightenment. However, you might want to call her before
performing a specific divination or shamanic ceremony.

Similarly, any type of scrying, meditation, tranceworking, or dreamworking can be performed after calling on Vor, both as an act designed
to please her and to give her the opportunity to impart any wisdom she
cares to offer you at the time. You should carefully record any dreams
you have after doing a working to Vor and try to discern any special
message she is giving you. Vor could also be summoned by women who
want to awaken their femininity and recapture some of the holiness and
power that was once specifically theirs in the past.

Ultimately the worship of Vor, becoming "aware," is an ongoing process, not just an isolated ritual but a way of life. She is a goddess whose might and aid work over the long term, granting the kind of wisdom and power that can only come from age and experience.

Call to Vor

Vor, wise one,
Watcher in the woods,
Ever waiting—
You know all that is to be in all the worlds.

Goddess of the wise and searching spirit—
From you nothing is hidden.

Goddess of faith—
in oneself,
the inner spirit,
the inner self,
the inner ear,
the inner voice.

Goddess of wisdom,
Teacher of women,
Walker in dreams—
Goddess of awareness,
Goddess of listening,
Goddess of the inner heart.

Vor—Wisewoman—Come!

Afterword

When I began making these journeys to the other worlds, I was only looking for a little information to enable me to include lesser-known deities in my rituals. What I found, however, was a rich and boundless source of power and wisdom and a means to establish real and meaningful relationships with my gods and goddesses. I also discovered that it is possible to build skills in right-brain enterprises, like scrying and tranceworking, just as it is with cognitive or physical activities.

I have shared my personal experiences with these goddesses mainly because there isn't any other way to fully explain this kind of experiential knowledge. I have tried to be clear about what information I derived from written sources, which conclusions I arrived at by musing over that same information for possible meanings, and which ideas came from my personal tranceworking and ritual experiences. None of the details drawn from my trances is meant to be a definitive description of the goddesses in question, and indeed many people get varying pictures of these beings when they contact them in trance and dream.

When I first became involved in the Heathen community years ago, it seemed that no one was using things such as tranceworking to gain information about the other worlds (or at least, no one was admitting to it). Many gods and goddesses, particularly the latter, were ignored because Heathens had no information about them. People seemed locked into the sparse facts available from the few "legitimate" sources left to us, sources that are themselves mostly post-Heathen writings filled with contradictions and inaccuracies. I wanted to share some of the alternative methods I'd been working with and encourage people to be more open to nonliterary sources of information as well as scholarly ones.

Now, it seems, a number of people are eager to dabble in faring forth, becoming so excited by their experiences that they get angry and defensive when others don't immediately accept their findings. The problem today for many is trying to learn how to evaluate and use information received in dreams and trances, and how to reconcile contradictory versions of reality.

Despite the problems inherent in using experiential, subjective techniques, I still believe it's better to try them than to remain starving for spiritual lore and contact. If people can feel free to explore ideas fully, using all the avenues available to them, and to share these ideas and impressions with each other without feeling as if there must be a "right" answer, we can eventually begin to regain our spiritual heritage and reforge the lost links of kinship with our gods and goddesses and our kin.

> *The gods meet on the Ida-plain,*
> *and speak of the world worm,*
> *And there call to mind   the mighty doom,*
> *and the High God's ancient runes.*
>
> *Then will be found,*
> *Left behind in the grass,*
> *The wondrous tables of gold*
> *Which the gods had owned in olden days.*
>
> VÖLUSPÁ, STS. 61–62

Mother Holle

Translated from "Frau Holle,"
by Jacob and Wilhelm Grimm

A widow had two daughters, one of whom was beautiful and industrious, the other ugly and lazy. But she much preferred the ugly and lazy one, because she was her real daughter, and the other had to do all the work and be the scullion in the house. The poor girl had to sit daily at a well by the great road and spin so much that her fingers bled. Now one day the spindle was so completely bloody that she bent down to the well in order to wash it; but it slipped out of her hand and fell down in the well. She wept, ran to her stepmother, and told her about the misfortune. But the mother scolded her severely and was merciless enough to say, "If you have let the spindle fall down the well, you can fetch it back up again." Then the girl went back to the well and didn't know what she should do, and in her great anxiety she jumped into the well to fetch the spindle.

She became unconscious. When she came to, she was in a lovely meadow where the sun shone and many thousands of flowers stood. Out of this meadow she went forth and came to a baking oven that was full of bread; but the bread cried, "Oh, pull me out, pull me out, or else I will burn. I'm already done enough!" So she stepped up to it and with the bread peel (a shovel-like tool used by bakers to slide baked goods into and out of an oven) lifted the loaves out, one after the other. After that she went on farther and came to a tree. The tree hung full of apples and called out to her, "Oh, shake me, shake me, my apples are ripe, one and all!" So she shook the tree and the apples fell like rain, until no more were overhead. When she had placed them all together in a heap, she again went on farther.

Finally, she came to a small house, out of which peered an old woman, but since the woman had such big teeth, the girl was frightened and wanted to run away. But the old woman called after her, "What are you afraid of, my child? Stay with me. If you do all the work in the house neatly, things will go well for you. You must only take care that you make my bed well and shake it out diligently, for then it snows in the world. I am the Mother Holle." Because she spoke so kindly, the girl took heart, consented to stay, and set to work at her employment.

The girl took care of everything to the old woman's satisfaction and always shook the feather bed powerfully so that the feathers flew around her like snowflakes. For her work, the girl always had a good living, with stews and roasts every day and never a harsh word.

Now she had been with Mother Holle for a year when she became sad. At first she didn't know herself what was lacking, but finally she realized that she was homesick. Even though she was a thousand times better off than she had been before, she still had a longing for her home. Finally, the girl said to Mother Holle, "I've gotten homesick, and though it goes ever so well with me here, I can't stay any longer. I must go back up again to my own people." Mother Holle said, "It pleases me that you long to go home again, and because you have served me faithfully, I will bring you back up myself." Then she took the girl by the hand and led her up to a great gate. The door was opened, and just as the girl stood under it, an enormous shower of gold fell, and all the gold remained hanging on her so that she was covered both over and under with it. "That you shall have, because you have been so hard-working," said Mother Holle, and she also gave her back the spindle that had fallen in the well.

With that, the gate was closed and the girl found herself above in the world, not far from her mother's house. And as she came into the courtyard, the cock was sitting on the roof and called, "Kikeriki! Our golden girl is here again." Then she went inside, and because she arrived all covered with gold, she got a good reception from her mother and sister.

The girl told of all that had befallen her, and when the mother heard how the girl had come to such great wealth, she wanted the other, the ugly and lazy daughter, to obtain the same good fortune. The ugly sister had to sit by the well and spin. So that the spindle should become bloody, she pricked herself in the finger and thrust her hand in the thorn hedge. Then she threw the spindle in the well and jumped in herself.

She came, as the other girl had, to the lovely meadow and went forward on the same road. When she reached the oven, the bread cried again, "Oh, pull me out, pull me out, otherwise I'll burn. I'm already baked enough!" But the lazy one answered, "I have no desire to make my hands dirty," and went off down the road. Soon she came to the apple tree, which cried, "Oh, shake me, shake me. My apples are ripe, one and all!" But she answered, "That's all very well, but what if one should happen to fall on my head?" and she went on farther.

When she came to Mother Holle's house, she wasn't frightened because she had already heard about the big teeth, and she accepted employment at once with the old woman. On the first day she set mightily to work, was very industrious, and did whatever Mother Holle told her, because she was thinking of all the gold that the old woman would give her. But on the second day the girl already started to be idle; on the third day she was even lazier, so that she wouldn't even get up in the morning. She also didn't make Mother Holle's bed as she was supposed to and didn't shake it well so that the feathers flew all around. Therefore, Mother Holle soon became tired of her and told her the employment was over.

The lazy one was entirely pleased with this and supposed that now the shower of gold would come. Mother Holle led the lazy girl to the gate, just as she had done with her sister, but when the girl stood under it, instead of gold, a great kettle full of pitch poured out. "That is to reward you for your service," said Mother Holle, and shut the gate.

Then the lazy one came home, but she was completely covered with pitch, and the cock on the roof, when he saw her, called, "Rikeriki! Our dirty girl is home again." But the pitch remained stuck to her and would not come off as long as she lived.

This story is typical of all we know of Frau Holde and Berchte. The goddess rewards the clean and industrious girl but severely punishes the lazy and rude one. Holde also approves of the girl's loyalty to her family, showing her interest in preserving social relationships. Holde's connection to the weather is reflected in the fact that making her bed causes snow to fall in the world.

The Three Spinners

Translated from "Die Drei Spinnerinnen,"
by Jacob and Wilhelm Grimm

There was a girl who was lazy and would not spin, and despite what her mother might say, the older woman could not get her daughter to do it. Finally, one day, the mother, overcome with anger and impatience, gave her a blow, whereupon the girl began to weep loudly. Now just then the queen was being conducted through the neighborhood, and when she heard the weeping she ordered her party to stop, stepped into the house, and asked the mother why she hit her daughter so hard that one could hear the crying out in the street.

Then the woman was ashamed to reveal her daughter's laziness and said, "I cannot fetch her away from her spinning, she will always and perpetually spin, and I am poor and cannot procure the flax." Then answered the queen, "I like to hear nothing better than spinning and am never more amused than when the wheel purrs. Let your daughter accompany me to my castle. I have flax enough, and there she shall spin as much as she likes." On hearing this, the mother was very content, and the queen took the girl away with her.

When they arrived at the castle, the queen led the girl up to three small rooms full of flax from top to bottom. "Now spin this flax for me," the queen said, "and when you are finished, then you shall have my eldest son as your husband. Even if you are poor, I care nothing for that.

Your indefatigable industry is dowry enough." The girl was inwardly terrified that she could not spin the flax if she were to live to be three hundred years old and sat at it each day from morning until evening. When she was all alone she began to weep and sat that way for three days without stirring a hand to work.

On the third day the queen came, and when she saw that as yet nothing was spun, she was surprised. But the girl explained that because of the great distress brought on by leaving her mother's house, she had not yet begun to spin. That pleased the queen, but she said as she went away, "Tomorrow you must begin to work."

When the girl was again alone, she wasn't able to think of any way to help herself, and in her distress she stepped over to the window. There she saw three women coming down the road. The first had a broad flat-foot, the second had such a large lower lip that it hung under her chin, and the third had a broad, broad thumb. They remained standing in front of the window, looked up, and asked the girl what she was in need of. The girl poured out her trouble to them, after which they offered her their help, saying, "If you will invite us to your wedding, not be ashamed of us, and call us your cousins, and also seat us at your table at the wedding feast, then we will spin your flax, and do it in a short time." "With all my heart," the girl answered, "only come in now and begin the work at once."

Then she let the three strange women in and made a space in the first chamber, where they could sit down and set up their spinning wheel. One drew out the thread and treaded the wheel, another moistened the thread, and the third turned it and struck the table with her finger, and as often as she struck, a skein of the most finely spun yarn fell to the ground. Whenever the queen came, the girl hid the three spinners and showed her the quantity of spun yarn, for which she got no end of praise. When the first chamber was empty, they went on to the second, and then finally to the third, and it too was soon empty. Now the three women took their leave, saying, "Don't forget what you have promised us. It will bring you good luck."

When the girl showed the queen the empty chambers and the great heaps of yarn, the queen arranged for the wedding, and the bridegroom rejoiced that he should obtain such a skillful and industrious wife, and praised her enormously. "I have three cousins," said the girl, "and since they have done me much kindness, I would not like to forget them in my good fortune. Please permit me then to invite them to the wedding and let them sit with us at the head table." The queen and the bridegroom said, "Why shouldn't we allow this?"

Now when the feast began, the three spinners stepped in wearing strange costumes, and the bride said, "Be welcome, dear cousins." "Oh," said the bridegroom, "how do you come to have such ugly kin?" Thereupon he went to the first, the one with the broad flatfoot, and asked, "From what do you have such a broad foot?" "From treading," she answered, "from treading." Then the bridegroom went to the second and said, "From what do you have such a long, underhanging lip?" "From licking," she answered, "from licking." Then he asked the third, "From what do you have such a broad, broad thumb?" "From turning thread," she answered, "from turning thread."

Then the king's son was frightened and said, "Then my dear bride shall never again so much as touch a spinning wheel!" And with that the girl was free forever from the dreadful flax-spinning.

This story reminds me of Frigg and the German goddesses because of the emphasis on spinning. Unlike most Germanic folk stories, the lazy spinner is eventually rewarded, rather than punished, for her behavior. Perhaps the three goddess figures take pity on her because, despite her laziness at home, she was not responsible for the unreasonable behavior of the adults who got her into the predicament—her mother's ambition to raise her daughter's social station and the queen's unrealistic expectations about how much flax even a good spinner could be expected to spin. Maybe the goddesses felt the girl's friendliness and kindness toward three strange and ugly women outweighed her lack of industry in this instance. At any rate, the ugly women are reminiscent of Holda and Berchte in their wild aspects, and the fact that their ugliness is caused by spinning is even more fitting.

The other characters in the story also exhibit Frigg-like characteristics. The mother's insistence on her daughter's spinning, the queen's passion for spinning and her approval of the girl's longing for her home and mother, the royal family's easy willingness to let the girl's relatives sit at the head table at the feast, and the groom's highly understated reaction and politeness to his bride's rather hideous kinfolk—all exemplify the kind of courteous, socially cooperative, and practical behavior associated with Frigg.

Queen Olga

Retold from the *Russian Primary Chronicle*

During the tenth century Igor was king of the Rus and ruled in the city of Kiev with his queen, Olga. One year he led his troops against the Derevlians in order to gather tribute. As he and his army were returning from this successful expedition, he suddenly decided to send his army on ahead while he and a few followers returned for more booty. The Derevlians, who now far outnumbered him, were able to slay him and all his troops.

The Derevlians then said, "Now that we have killed the prince of the Rus, let us marry his wife, Olga, to our own prince Mal; in that way we will obtain possession of her young son, Svyatoslav, and influence him according to our will." They therefore sent twenty of their best men to Kiev by boat, and they arrived on the shores of the Dnieper River below the heights of the city.

When Olga heard that the envoys had arrived, she welcomed them into her presence and asked why they had come. They replied that they had been sent to report that they had slain her husband because he was as crafty and greedy as a wolf but that their own prince was good and so Olga should come and marry their prince Mal.

Olga replied, "Your proposal pleases me, and indeed my husband is dead and cannot rise again. But first I want to honor you before my people. Therefore return to your boat and remain there with an attitude of arrogance. Tomorrow I shall send for you, and you shall say, 'We will go neither by horse nor on foot. Carry us in our boat.' And you shall be carried, and everyone will see how you are honored." Thus the Derevlians returned to their boat and did as she bade them.

Now Olga commanded that a large, deep ditch be dug in the hall of a castle she had that stood outside the city. On the next day she sat in that hall and formally sent for the envoys. The Derevlians responded as the queen had instructed them and demanded that they be carried to the audience in their boat. The people of Kiev lamented that their prince was dead and now their queen intended to marry Prince Mal and make them all slaves, but they carried the Derevlians as they were ordered. The envoys sat in their finest robes all swollen with pride. When they were carried into the hall, the Kievans dropped both boat and envoys into the deep ditch. Olga leaned over and asked if they found this honor to their liking. They answered that it was worse than the death of Igor. With that Olga commanded that they should be buried alive, and thus she avenged her husband's death.

Olga then sent a message to the Derevlians, saying that if they truly wished her to come there, they should send a party of their most prominent men to escort her in honor, for otherwise the people of Kiev would not let her go. When the Derevlians heard this, they gathered together their best men and sent them to her. When the second party of Derevlians arrived, Olga ordered a bath to be made ready and invited the representatives to refresh themselves before appearing before her. When the bathhouse was heated and the Derevlians went in to bathe, Olga's men closed the doors behind them, and the queen ordered the doors to be set on fire so that all the Derevlians were burned to death.

Olga then sent another message to the Derevlians, saying that she was now coming to them and asking them to prepare quantities of mead in the city where her husband had been killed so that she could honor him with a funeral feast. When the Derevlians received this message, they did as she asked. Olga journeyed to Dereva with a small escort, and when she arrived at Igor's grave, she wept for him and had her followers build him a grave mound and then commanded that a funeral feast should be held. When the feast was ready, the Derevlians sat down to drink and Olga had her followers wait on them. The Derevlians inquired after the envoys they had sent to her earlier, and she replied that they were following with her husband's bodyguard. When the Derevlians were drunk, Olga ordered her men to attack them. She herself went among them urging them on, and they killed five thousand of the Derevlians. Meanwhile, Olga returned to Kiev and gathered an army to attack the survivors.

Olga and her son, Svyatoslav, gathered a large and courageous army and attacked the country of the Derevlians, who came out to meet her forces. When both sides were ready for battle, Svyatoslav cast his spear over the Derevlians, but because he was just a child, his spear fell short and struck the horse on the leg. But Olga's men cried out, "The prince has already begun battle. Forward after the prince!" And they conquered the Derevlians, so that the remnants of the Derevlian forces fled back to their cities and barricaded themselves inside.

Olga besieged the city where her husband had died but was still unable to conquer it for more than a year, for the Derevlians now realized that she would show them no mercy. Finally, the queen thought of a plan and sent this message to the town: "Why do you continue to hold out? All your other cities have surrendered and paid tribute and now plow their fields in peace, but you would rather starve than submit." The Derevlians replied that they would pay tribute gladly, but they feared it was revenge she was after. She answered, "Since I have already three times avenged my husband's death, twice when your messengers came to Kiev, and a third time at my husband's funeral feast, I do not desire more, but I do request a small tribute. After we have made our peace, I will return to my home again."

The Derevlians asked what she wanted of them, offering her honey and furs. Olga responded that by this time they probably had neither honey nor furs, but because she knew their resources were exhausted by the siege, she asked only one small token gift, three pigeons and three sparrows from each house. The relieved Derevlians collected the birds from each house as she asked, sending them to Olga with their greetings. Olga then told them to return to their city and promised that she would depart for her own capital on the next day. The Derevlians returned to their city with the news and all the people rejoiced.

Then Olga gave a bird to each of her followers and ordered them to tie a piece of sulfur wrapped with cloth to each of them. At nightfall she had them release the pigeons and sparrows, which returned to their nests in the Derevlian houses and thus set all the roofs on fire. With so many houses afire at once, the people could not put them out and fled from the city, where Olga's troops were waiting for them. Thus she took and burned the city and captured its elders; some she killed, some she gave as slaves to her followers, and the rest she left behind to pay a heavy tribute.

Olga ruled for many years, until her son, Svyatoslav, was old enough to become king. His people had flourished under his mother's reign, and she had reared him to be a great and powerful prince, with the courage of his father and the cunning of his mother.

I chose this story because it shows a successful Germanic queen in action, and Olga possesses many abilities and personality traits I tend to associate with Frigg. First, all her actions throughout the story are designed to protect and empower her son, whom she intends to rear to be the next king in his father's stead. She is also trying to ensure the social order of her nation, which would not fare well if the country came under the control of its enemies, and to preserve her husband's inheritance for his heir. She has the complete obedience and respect of her followers, an uncanny knowledge of human nature, and a great supply of cunning and energy.

Throughout the story she turns the virtues expected of an obedient wife to her own ends—she appears only too willing to give up the burden of rulership to a strong husband, acts the eager and gracious hostess to all the ambassadors, plays the part of the grieving widow at her husband's gravesite, and is utterly reasonable and conciliatory in her request for a suitable wergild for her husband's loss. When the

Derevlians continually take her at face value and fall into her trap, she is ruthless and efficient about annihilating her enemies. But, above all, she is a queen and a mother; she knows in her gut that the Derevlians mean no good to her son or her realm, and she exerts all her strength and energy over a period of many years to achieve her goals.

Notes

CHAPTER 1.
THE IMPORTANCE OF MYTHOLOGY

1. Doty, *Mythology*, 6.
2. Lowry, *Familiar Mysteries*, 15.
3. Bolle, *Freedom of Man in Myth*, 38.
4. Eliade, *Myth and Reality*, 19.
5. Bolle, *Freedom of Man in Myth*, 109.
6. Doty, *Mythology*, 23.
7. Lowry, *Familiar Mysteries*, 3.
8. Ibid., 4.
9. Doty, *Mythology*, 48.
10. Eliade, *Myth and Reality*, 19.

CHAPTER 3.
DEFINING TRANCE AND ITS
MANY MANIFESTATIONS

1. Merriam-Webster's Collegiate Dictionary: *trance,* defined as "stupor, daze," "a sleeplike state (as of deep hypnosis) usu. characterized by partly suspended animation with diminished or absent sensory and motor activity," and "a state of profound abstraction or absorption."
2. Butler, *Magician*, 114.
3. Harner, *Way of the Shaman*, 21.
4. Gundarsson, *Teutonic Magic*, 211–12, 290.

CHAPTER 4.
HOW TO DO TRANCEWORK

1. Thorsson, *Northern Magic,* 161.
2. Price, *The Viking Way,* 174.

CHAPTER 7.
THE INFLUENCE OF THE QUEEN
OF THE GODS ON GERMANIC CULTURE

1. De Vries, *Altgermanische Religionsgeschichte,* 2:303.
2. Ingham, *Goddess Freyja,* 123.
3. De Vries, *Altgermanische Religionsgeschichte,* 2:306.
4. Ibid., 2:304.
5. Gundarsson, *Teutonic Religion,* 41–42.
6. Grimm, *Teutonic Mythology,* 1:270 n.
7. Guerber, *Norsemen,* 38.
8. Davidson, *Gods and Myths of Northern Europe,* 111; and Turville-Petre, *Myth and Religion of the North,* 72.
9. Guerber, *Norsemen,* 43.
10. Ibid., 51.
11. Grimm, *Teutonic Mythology,* 1:285; and Guerber, *Norsemen,* 57.
12. Guerber, *Norsemen,* 51–53.
13. Ibid., 53–54; and Ingham, *Goddess Freyja,* 191–92.
14. Grimm, *Teutonic Mythology,* 1:275; and Ingham, *Goddess Freyja,* 203.
15. Grimm, *Teutonic Mythology,* 1:276–77.
16. Ibid., 1:429 n.
17. Ibid., 1:277–78.
18. Ibid., 4:1370.
19. Ingham, *Goddess Freyja,* 206.
20. Grimm, *Teutonic Mythology,* 3:1162.
21. Ibid., 1:280.
22. Ibid., 4:1368.
23. Ibid., 1:271–72.
24. Ibid., 1:269.
25. Ibid., 4:1370.
26. Ibid., 1:269n.

27. Ibid., 4:1370.

28. Ingham, *Goddess Freyja,* 176.

29. Grimm, *Teutonic Mythology,* 1:274.

30. Ring of Troth, *Our Troth,* 121.

31. Ibid.; and Gundarsson, "The Spinning Goddess and Migration Age Bracteates," 7.

32. Grimm, *Teutonic Mythology,* 1:275–76.

33. Ibid., 1:273.

34. Ibid., 2:632.

35. Ingham, *Goddess Freyja,* 185.

36. De Vries, *Altgermanische Religionsgeschichte,* 1:451.

37. Grimm, *Teutonic Mythology,* 3:925–26.

38. Ingham, *Goddess Freyja,* 210–11; and Grimm, *Teutonic Mythology,* 1:252.

39. Grimm, *Teutonic Mythology,* 1:304.

40. Danaher, *Year in Ireland,* 14.

41. Ibid., 27–28.

42. Ström, "King God and His Connection with Sacrifice," 714.

43. Grimm, *Teutonic Mythology,* 4:1780.

44. Gundarsson, *Teutonic Religion,* 49.

45. Grönbech, *Culture of the Teutons,* 2:164.

46. Ibid., 2:165.

47. Stokker, "Folklore of Butter," 19.

48. Ibid., 20.

49. Wiesner, "Spinning Out Capital," 234.

50. Ibid., 234–35.

51. *The Viking,* 195.

52. Wemple, "Sanctity and Power," 146.

53. Bauschatz, *Well and the Tree,* 13–14.

54. Grimm, *Teutonic Mythology,* 4:1369.

CHAPTER 8. FRIGG—THE ALLMOTHER— AND A SAMPLE GODDESS RITUAL

1. Davidson, *Lost Beliefs of Northern Europe,* 117.

2. Gundarsson, *Teutonic Religion,* 240.

3. Ring of Troth, *Our Troth,* 494.

4. Ibid., 123.

5. Lucas, *Common and Uncommon Uses of Herbs,* 3.

6. Grieve, *A Modern Herbal,* 1:266.

7. Ibid., 1:267.

8. Ibid., 2:864.

CHAPTER 9. EIR—THE DOCTOR

1. Tacitus, *The Agricola and the Germania,* 107.

2. Grimm, *Teutonic Mythology,* 3:1163–64.

3. Ibid., 3:1165.

4. Ibid., 3:1173.

5. Mason, "Folk-Lore of British Plants," 325–26; and Grimm, *Teutonic Mythology,* 4:1812–13.

6. Ibid., 3:1166.

7. Ibid., 3:1188.

8. Ariel, "A Morning's Meditation," 5–6.

9. Davidson, *Gods and Myths of Northern Europe,* 62.

10. De Vries, *Altgermanische Religionsgeschichte,* 2:316–17.

11. Snorri Sturluson, *Edda,* 157.

CHAPTER 10. SAGA—THE STORYTELLER

1. Steblin-Kamenskij, *Saga Mind,* 26.

2. Grimm, *Teutonic Mythology,* 3:911.

3. Ibid.

4. Suchenwirt [Suchenwirth] cited in Grimm, *Teutonic Mythology,* 3:911.

CHAPTER 11. GNA—THE MESSENGER

1. Guerber, *Norsemen,* 48; and Anderson, *Norse Mythology,* 239.

2. Grimm, *Teutonic Mythology,* 2:896.

3. Ibid., 2:897.

4. Guerber, *Norsemen,* 252.

CHAPTER 12.
GEFJON—THE WORKER

1. Davidson, *Gods and Myths of Northern Europe,* 113.
2. Grimm, *Teutonic Mythology,* 1:264.
3. De Vries, *Altgermanische Religionsgeschichte,* 2:330.
4. Ibid., 2:293.
5. Ellis, *Road to Hel,* 75; and Ring of Troth, *Our Troth,* 129.
6. Ring of Troth, *Our Troth,* 129.
7. Ibid.
8. Grimm, *Teutonic Mythology,* 1:311.
9. Ring of Troth, *Our Troth,* 129.
10. This stanza is taken from a poem by the ninth-century Norwegian skald, Bragi Boddason the Old, which is quoted in both the Gylfaginning (ch. 1) of the *Prose Edda* and the *Ynglinga saga* (ch. 5).

CHAPTER 13.
SNOTRA—THE PRUDENT ONE

1. Ring of Troth, *Our Troth,* 303–4.
2. Wicker, "Nimble-Fingered Maidens in Scandinavia" 884; and Spurkland, *Norwegian Runes and Runic Inscriptions,* 144–45.

CHAPTER 14.
LOFN—THE CHAMPION

1. Gundarsson, *Teutonic Religion,* 246.
2. Grönbech, *Culture of the Teutons,* 2:62.
3. Snow, "Lofn," 9.

CHAPTER 15.
SJOFN—THE PEACEMAKER

1. Guerber, *Norsemen,* 49.
2. Grönbech, *Culture of the Teutons,* 1:53, 1:59.

CHAPTER 16.
VAR—THE HEARER OF OATHS

1. Grönbech, *Culture of the Teutons,* 2:125.
2. Ibid., 2:58.

CHAPTER 17.
FULLA—THE SISTER

1. Grimm, *Teutonic Mythology,* 1:308.
2. Ibid.
3. De Vries, *Altgermanische Religionsgeschichte,* 2:328.
4. Ibid., 2:171.
5. Grimm, *Teutonic Mythology,* 1:308.

CHAPTER 18.
HLIN—THE PROTECTOR

1. Guerber, *Norsemen,* 47. Guerber is the only source that mentions this, but it does fit in with the protective, motherly aspect of Hlin's activities.
2. Grimm, *Teutonic Mythology,* 3:932.

CHAPTER 19.
SYN—THE GUARDIAN

1. Brondsted, *Vikings,* 241.
2. Ibid., 242.
3. Ibid.
4. Grönbech, *Culture of the Teutons,* 1:90.

CHAPTER 20.
VOR—THE WISEWOMAN

1. Thorsson, *Northern Magic,* 159.
2. Davidson, *Gods and Myths of Northern Europe,* 120.
3. Ibid., 121–22.
4. Grönbech, *Culture of the Teutons,* 2:122.

Glossary of Terms

Aegir (Ægir): A jotun, husband of Ran; ruler of the deep sea.

Aesir (Æsir, sing. áss): The race of gods and goddesses, including Frigg, Odin, and their kin; particularly associated with air and fire, consciousness, intellectual knowledge, magic, and war.

Althing: A Thing (a legal assembly) with a constituency covering a wide area, such as a nation.

Asatru (Ásatrú): Literally "true to the gods"; a modern term used by some for the original pre-Christian religion of the people of northwestern Europe, particularly Scandinavia.

Asgard (Ásgarðr): The home of the Aesir gods.

Asynjur (Ásynjur, sing. ásynja): The Aesir goddesses.

Balder (Baldr): An Aesir god, called "the Beautiful"; son of Odin and Frigg, brother of Hod, and husband of Nanna; accidentally killed by his brother Hod; said to return to rule Asgard at the end of the age; symbol of the heroic warrior, a god of masculine potency, regeneration, transformation, wise counsel, and goodness.

barrow: A burial mound.

Berchte, or **Perchta:** German goddess similar to Frigg and nearly identical to Holda; associated with spinning and other crafts, children, the Yule season, and the Wild Hunt; worshipped in southern Germany.

Bifrost (Bifröst): The rainbow bridge of fire, air, and water that links the world of the gods to the other worlds.

blót: "Blessing" or "sacrifice"; a religious ceremony in which offerings (nowadays usually intoxicating drink, but traditionally sacrificial animals) are made to the gods and in return their power is distributed in the world of humans.

bragarfull: "Promise cup"; in a sumble or other ritual, the toast over which one makes a vow or promise.

Bragi: An Aesir god, son of Odin and husband of Idun; god of poetry and poets (called skalds), fame, and hospitality.

Brisingamen (Brísingamen): "Necklace (or Belt) of the Brisings"; Freyja's treasure, made by four dwarves; it embodies the life force of which Freyja is mistress.

byname: A nickname or alias, often used by gods and others traveling between worlds.

dísir (sing. dís): Ancestral female beings with powers of protection and fertility.

Draupnir: The gold arm-ring of Odin, which produces eight rings of equal worth on every ninth night.

Edda: Either of two important works in Icelandic lore dealing with Norse myths and legends. The *Elder Edda,* or *Poetic Edda,* is a collection of poems preserved in the Codex Regius on the Norse religious and heroic traditions. The *Prose Edda,* or *Younger Edda,* was written by Icelander Snorri Sturluson between 1222 and 1235 and includes Norse cosmology, legends, and poetic traditions.

Eir: Aesir goddess of doctors, healing, and childbirth.

faring forth: Engaging in out-of-body travel.

Fensalir: Frigg's hall in Asgard.

Ffraed (Ffræd): Welsh goddess of poetry, fire, and healing.

Fjörgynn (f)/**Fjörgyn** (m): An earth or fertility deity; the name appears in both feminine and masculine form.

Forseti: Son of Balder and Nanna; a god of civil law, cooperation, compromise, peace, reconciliation, and fairness.

Frau Gode, or **Frau Wode:** "Mrs. Odin"; German goddess connected to the Wild Hunt and the harvest.

Frey (Freyr): Njord's son and Freyja's brother, who gave up his sword and his horse to win the jotun maiden Gerd for his wife; god of male potency, fertility, peace, prosperity, joy, and kingship.

Freyja: The foremost Vanir goddess, Njord's daughter, and Frey's sister; goddess of love and beauty, eroticism and sensuality, war, death, magic, clairvoyance, wealth, independence, and the life force itself.

Frigg: Odin's wife and queen of the Aesir; goddess of the home and family, motherhood, domestic affairs, crafts and craftspeople, divination, social order, and relationships.

frith: Peace, with connotations of freedom and fellowship.

full: The ritual cup or toast in a Germanic ceremony.

Fulla: Frigg's sister and keeper of her secrets and treasures; Aesir goddess of abundance, fruitfulness, and generosity.

fylgja: A guardian spirit, often seen as a semi-independent part of the soul, which usually appears in the shape of an animal or a female.

galdr: Magical song or chanting, especially used in rune magic.

Gefjon, or **Gefjun:** Aesir goddess of farming and agriculture, fruitfulness in potential, young women, and merrymaking.

Gerd (Gerðr): A beautiful jotun maiden who married the Vanir god, Freyr, after a difficult courtship; represents the untilled earth.

giants: *See* jotun.

Gna (Gná): Frigg's messenger who travels through the different worlds on her horse Hofvarpnir.

Grid (Gríðr): A jotun-wife, mistress of Odin, and mother of the god Vidar. She lent Thor her magic gloves, girdle, and staff to fight the giant Geirrod.

Gunnlod (Gunnlöð): A jotun maiden, guardian of the mead of poetry, who was seduced by Odin when he came to recapture it; possibly the mother of the god Bragi.

hawk dress: A magical dress or cloak owned by Frigg (also attributed to Freyja), which enables the wearer to fly between the worlds in the form of a hawk.

Heathen: A follower of a Pagan (non-Abrahamic) religion, specifically a Germanic religion.

heimchen: The train of children who follow Berchte in her procession; said to be the souls of dead and/or unborn children.

Heimdall (Heimdallr): The Aesir guardian of the bridge leading to Asgard; forefather and teacher of humans and shaper of the various classes of society; a god of wisdom, holiness, order and stability, and fertility.

Hel, or **Hela:** Daughter of Loki and the female jotun Angrboda; the goddess of death and the Underworld.

Helheim, or **Hel:** One of the Nine Worlds—the Underworld—realm of the goddess of death, Hel.

Hermod (Hermóðr): Called "the Bold"; the Aesir god who, at Frigg's request, rode to Hel to try to ransom his brother Balder.

Hlidskjalf (Hliðskjálf): Odin's high seat in Valhalla from which he and Frigg can see all that happens in the Nine Worlds.

Hlin (Hlín): Attendant of Frigg; Aesir goddess of protection.

Hod (Höðr): The blind Aesir god who was tricked by Loki into accidentally killing his brother Balder. He was later killed by Vali to avenge Balder's death and joined his brother in Hel.

Holda: German goddess similar to Frigg and nearly identical to Berchte; associated with spinning, children and childbirth, the Yule season, and the Wild Hunt; worshipped in northern Germany.

hof: A temple or ritual area.

Huginn: "Thought"; one of Odin's raven messengers.

hugr: The rational part of the soul; consciousness, mind, intellect.

Huldra: Scandinavian goddess with similarities to Frigg; associated with cattle, herding, and dairies; fond of music and dancing.

huldrefolk: Norse elves or nature beings, usually found in the mountains. They are led by the goddess Huldra.

Idun (Iðunn): Bragi's wife, who guards the golden apples of youth; Aesir goddess of youth, spring, and rebirth.

Jarnsaxa: "Iron Sword"; the jotun mistress of the god Thor and the mother of his two sons, Magni ("Might") and Modi ("Courage").

Jord (Jörð): An earth jotun, mistress of Odin and mother of Thor; a Norse version of Mother Earth.

jotun (jötunn, pl. jötnar): A being of great age, strength, and knowledge, associated with the forces of chaos and primal energy; often in conflict with the gods and humans; sometimes called "giants."

Jotunheim (Jötunheimr): The realm of the jotuns.

kindred: A word used by many modern Heathens to mean a group of people who gather regularly to study the Germanic Pagan religion and to perform rituals and other religious observances.

law-speaker: Among the ancient Norse, a public official with the duty of memorizing the laws and publicly reciting them at prescribed intervals.

Lofn: Frigg's attendant; an Aesir goddess who can remove obstacles from the paths of lovers.

Loki: A jotun considered one of the Aesir by virtue of his blood-brotherhood with Odin; god of change, mischief, and deception.

Lyfjaberg: A hill of healing inhabited by the goddess Menglod and her attendants.

Menglod (Menglöð): "Necklace Glad"; a supernatural maiden dwelling on the Lyfjaberg, a place of healing, with her attendants; often associated with the goddess Freyja.

Midgard (Miðgarðr): "Middle World"; the home of humans; the physical realm of existence.

Mimir: The wisest of the Aesir; Odin gave up one of his eyes for a drink from Mimir's well of wisdom; after Mimir was killed by the Vanir, Odin preserved his head and from it receives advice and occult wisdom.

Muninn: "Memory"; one of Odin's raven messengers.

Nanna: Balder's wife, who died at his funeral so that she could follow him to the Underworld.

Nerthus: An early Germanic fertility goddess.

Nine Worlds: In Germanic cosmology the universe is divided into nine worlds or realms of existence.

nisser (sing. nisse): House ghosts; protective beings who delight in order and industriousness and who help protect and care for the house and its grounds.

norns (pl. nornir): Female beings who shape ørlög or fate; the three great Norns who shape ørlög for all the worlds are Urd, Verdandi, and Skuld.

Odin (Óðinn): Frigg's husband; leader of the Aesir, who gave up one of his eyes for wisdom; he shaped the world, along with his brothers Vili and Ve; a god of poetry and the creative arts, magic, ecstasy, inspiration, magic, wisdom, conflict, war, death, communication, travel, and commerce.

ørlög: Literally meaning "primal layers"; loosely defined as "fate." It refers to the past actions that shape the present and the future.

Ragnarok (Ragnarök): The final battle between the gods and the forces of chaos, which marks the end of the current age.

Rig (Rígr): A god, usually assumed to be Heimdall, who fathers the three different social classes of people.

Rind (Rindr): A princess who was tricked by Odin into bearing his son Vali, Balder's avenger.

Saga (Sága): Aesir goddess of history and storytelling, old lore, and ancestral memories.

saga: Old Norse word for story or history; usually refers to part of a body of literature recorded in Iceland in the twelfth and thirteenth centuries, dealing with historical and legendary themes.

seiðr: A magical technique involving trance states, prophesying, shamanic traveling, and talking to spirits.

shape-shifter: A magician who can travel out of the body in the shape of an animal or another being.

Sif: Thor's wife; her golden hair symbolizes ripe grain; a goddess of fertility and fruitfulness.

Sigurd (Sigurðr): Famous hero of the Volsung tribe; slayer of the dragon Fafnir.

Skjold (ON Skjöldr, OE Scyld): One of the first of the legendary Danish kings who founded the Danish royal line with the goddess Gefjon; he appears in the opening of Beowulf as that hero's father.

Sjofn (Sjöfn): An attendant of Frigg; Aesir goddess who turns the thoughts of men and women to love.

Skirnir (Skírnir): Frey's attendant who traveled to Jotunheim to woo the jotun maiden Gerd for him.

Skuld: One of the three great Norns who shape ørlög; her name means "That Which Should Become."

Sleipnir: Loki's child; Odin's magical, eight-legged horse that can travel between the worlds.

Snotra: An attendant of Frigg; Aesir goddess of moderation, known for her wisdom, gentleness, and prudence.

Sokkvabekk (Sökkvabekkr): "Sinking Brook"; the name of the goddess Saga's hall in Asgard.

sumble (OE symbel, ON sumbl): A formulaic Germanic drinking ritual.

Sunna, or **Sol** (Sól): The Germanic sun goddess.

Syn: Frigg's attendant; Aesir goddess who guards the door of the hall and keeps out intruders; also called on at law assemblies to defend the accused.

Thing: Old Norse assembly for legislative, legal, religious, and social purposes.

Thor (Þórr): The son of Odin and the jotun-wife Jord (earth); the red-bearded Aesir god of thunder and the defender of Asgard and the earth from chaos; a god of strength and physical courage, physical power, force and energy, fertility, and oaths, and protector of the home and temple.

thrall: A bond servant, the lowest class of Old Norse society.

troth: "Truth"; a pledge or oath; loyalty, faithfulness.

Tyr (Týr): An Aesir god who lost his right hand in order to bind the wolf of chaos and keep an oath; thought by many to be the original Indo-European sky father; god of honor, law and contracts, rational judgment, oaths, the Thing, warriors, service, and sacrifice.

Ull (Ullr): The winter god of hunting, archery, skiing, and skating; a god of oaths and single combat.

Urd (Urðr): One of the three great Norns who shape ørlög; her name means "That Which Is."

Valhalla (Valhöll): "Hall of the Slain"; Odin's hall in Asgard, where the souls of many of the battle-dead and those pledged to Odin go after death.

Vali (Váli): Son of Odin and Rind; Aesir god who avenges Balder's death by killing Hod.

Valkyrie (valkyrja): "Chooser of the Slain"; a female supernatural being attending Odin, god of war; the Valkyries help decide the outcome of battles and conduct the chosen slain to Valhalla.

Vanaheim: The home of the Vanir gods.

Vanir (sing. vanr): The race of gods, including Freyja, Frey, and their kin; particularly associated with prosperity, fertility, eroticism, nature, and hidden wisdom.

Var (Vár): Frigg's attendant; Aesir goddess who listens to the vows and contracts made between men and women.

vatni ausa: "Sprinkling with water"; Norse naming ritual in which a child is accepted into the family and given an ørlög.

Ve (Vé): "Holy Place"; Aesir god who, along with his brothers Odin and Vili, shaped the world.

Verdandi (Verðandi): One of the three great Norns who shape ørlög; her name means "That Which Is Becoming."

Vidar (Víðarr): An Aesir god noted for his silence and his strength.

Viking (noun): A Scandinavian warrior-adventurer and seafarer; Vikings raided and traded on the coasts of Europe from the eighth to the tenth centuries.

viking (verb): To go on an expedition of discovery, trade, and raiding.

Vili: "Will"; Aesir god who, along with his brothers Odin and Ve, shaped the world.

völva: A female magician who specializes in divination and prophecy.

Vor (Vör): Frigg's attendant; an Aesir goddess said to be so wise that nothing can be hidden from her.

wergild: In Anglo-Saxon and Germanic law, a monetary compensation paid to the kin of a slain person.

wish maiden (öskmær): Another name given to the Valkyrie; she aids Odin in carrying out his will in his function as dispenser of gifts and granter of wishes.

wood wife: Female land-wight, a wild, elflike dweller in the deep woods; wood wives sometimes give advice and help to humans in exchange for gifts and favors.

wyrd: "Fate"; also the OE form of the proper name Urd, the Norn who represents "That Which Is."

Glossary of Runes

RUNES

STAVE	NAME	SOUND
ᛈ	*fehu* ("cattle," movable wealth)	f
ᚢ	*uruz* ("aurochs," wild ox)	u
ᚦ	*þurisaz* ("thurs," giant)	th
ᚠ	*ansuz* ("áss," god)	a
ᚱ	*raiðo* ("riding," "wagon")	r
ᚲ	*kenaz* ("torch") or *kaunaz* ("sore")	k
ᚷ	*gebo* ("gift")	g
ᚹ	*wunjo* ("joy")	w
ᚺ	*hagalaz* ("hail")	h
ᚾ	*nauþiz* ("need")	n
ᛁ	*isa* ("ice")	i
ᛃ	*jera* ("year," harvest)	j, y

STAVE	NAME	SOUND
ᛇ	*eihwaz* ("yew")	ei, i
ᛈ	*perþro* (meaning unknown, possibly a joy in the hall, lot-cup)	p
ᛉ	*elhaz* ("elk's sedge," "elk," protection)	z, -R
ᛋ	*sowilo* ("sun")	s
ᛏ	*tiwaz* ("Tiw," Tyr)	t
ᛒ	*berkano* ("birch," the birch goddess)	b
ᛖ	*ehwaz* ("horse")	e
ᛗ	*mannaz* ("man," human being)	m
ᛚ	*laguz* ("water") or *laukaz* ("leek)	l
◇	*ingwaz* ("Ing," possibly Frey)	ng
ᛞ	*dagaz* ("day")	d
ᛟ	*oþala* ("odal lands," estate, hereditary property)	o

Bibliography

Anderson, Rasmus B. *Norse Mythology: Or, The Religion of Our Forefathers*, 7th ed. Chicago: Scott, Foresman and Co., 1901.

Arent, A. Margaret, trans. *Laxdoela Saga*. Seattle: University of Washington Press, 1964.

Ariel. "A Morning's Meditation." *The Runestone*, no. 49 (Fall 1984): 5–6.

Bauschatz, Paul C. *The Well and the Tree: World and Time in Early Germanic Culture*. Amherst: University of Massachusetts Press, 1982.

Bellows, Henry Adams, trans. *The Poetic Edda*. New York: American-Scandinavian Foundation, 1923.

Bidgood, Ruth. "Hymn to Sant Ffraed." *The Anglo-Welsh Review* 69 (1981): 5–11.

Bolle, Kees W. *The Freedom of Man in Myth*. Nashville: Vanderbilt University Press, 1968.

Branston, Brian. *Gods of the North*. New York: Thames and Hudson, 1980.

Brondsted, Johannes. *The Vikings*. Harmondsworth, UK: Penguin, 1965.

Burland, C.A. *The Vikings*. London: Hulton Educational Publications, 1959.

Butler, W. E. *The Magician: His Training and Work*. North Hollywood: Melvin Powers, Wilshire Book Co., 1959.

Byock, Jesse L., trans. *The Saga of the Volsungs: The Norse Epic of Sigurd the Dragon Slayer*. Berkeley: University of California Press, 1990.

Castaneda, Carlos. *Journey to Ixtlan*. New York: Simon & Schuster, 1972.

Chadwick, Eileen. *The Craft of Hand-Spinning*. New York: Charles Scribner's Sons, 1980.

Cross, Samuel Hazzard, and Olgerd P. Sherbowitz-Wetzor, trans. and eds. *Russian Primary Chronicle*. Cambridge, Mass.: Mediaeval Academy of America, 1953.

Crossley-Holland, Kevin. *The Norse Myths*. New York: Pantheon Books, 1980.

Danaher, Kevin. *The Year in Ireland*. Cork, Ireland: Mercier Press, 1972.

Davidson, H. R. Ellis. *Gods and Myths of Northern Europe*. New York: Penguin Books, 1964.

———. *Lost Beliefs of Northern Europe*. New York: Routledge, 1993.

Doty, William G. *Mythography: The Study of Myths and Rituals*. Tuscaloosa: University of Alabama Press, 1986.

Dumézil, Georges. *Gods of the Ancient Northmen*. Berkeley: University of California Press, 1973.

Eliade, Mircea. *Myth and Reality*. New York: Harper & Row, 1975.

———. *Shamanism: Archaic Techniques of Ecstasy*. Princeton: Princeton University Press, 1972.

Ellis, Hilda Roderick. *The Road to Hel*. Cambridge, U.K.: Cambridge University Press, 1943.

Gordon, E. V. *An Introduction to Old Norse*, 2nd ed. Revised by A. R. Taylor. Oxford, U.K.: Clarendon Press, 1980.

Graham-Campbell, James, and Dafydd Kidd. *The Vikings*. New York: Metropolitan Museum of Art, 1980.

Grieve, Mrs. M. *A Modern Herbal: The Medicinal, Culinary, Cosmetic and Economic Properties, Cultivation and Folk-lore of Herbs, Grasses, Fungi, Shrubs and Trees with All Their Modern and Scientific Uses*. New York: Dover Publications, 1971.

Grimm, Jacob. *Teutonic Mythology*. Translated by James Steven Stallybrass. New York: Dover Publications, 1966.

Grimm, Jacob, and Wilhelm Grimm. *Kinder und Hausmarchen*. Berlin: Wilhelm Herz, 1899.

———. *Selected Tales*. Translated by David Luke. Harmondsworth, U.K.: Penguin, 1982.

Grönbech, Vilhelm. *The Culture of the Teutons*. London: Humphrey Milford, 1931.

Guerber, Helene A. *The Norsemen*. New York: Avenel Books, 1985.

Gundarsson, Kveldúlf. *Teutonic Magic: The Magical and Spiritual Practices of the Germanic People*. St. Paul, Minn.: Llewellyn, 1990.

———. "The Spinning Goddess and Migration Age Bracteate." *Idunna* 5, no. 4 (1993): 6–9.

———. *Teutonic Religion: Folk Beliefs and Practices of the Northern Tradition.* St. Paul, Minn.: Llewellyn, 1993.

Harner, Michael. *The Way of the Shaman: A Guide to Power and Healing.* New York: Harper & Row, 1980.

Hecht, Ann. *The Art of the Loom: Weaving, Spinning, and Dyeing Across the World.* New York: Rizzoli, 1989.

Hollander, Lee M. *The Skalds.* Ann Arbor: University of Michigan Press, 1968.

———, trans. *Poetic Edda,* 2nd ed. Austin: University of Texas Press, 1986.

Ingham, Marion Frieda. *The Goddess Freyja and Other Female Figures in Germanic Mythology and Folklore.* Ann Arbor, Mich.: University Microfilms, 1987.

Lowry, Shirley Park. *Familiar Mysteries: The Truth in Myth.* New York: Oxford University Press, 1982.

Lucas, Richard. *Common and Uncommon Uses of Herbs for Healthful Living.* New York: Ace Books, 1959.

Magnusson, Magnus, and Hermann Palsson, trans. *Njal's Saga.* Harmondsworth, U.K.: Penguin, 1960.

Mason, James. "The Folk-Lore of British Plants." *Dublin University Magazine* 82 (September 1873): 313–28.

Palsson, Hermann, and Paul Edwards, trans. *Orkneyinga Saga: The History of the Earls of Orkney.* Harmondsworth, U.K.: Penguin, 1981.

Price, Neil S. *The Viking Way: Religion and War in Late Iron Age Scandinavia.* Uppsala, Sweden: Department of Archaeology and Ancient History, Uppsala University, 2002.

Ring of Troth and Other True Folk. *Our Troth.* Edited by Kveldúlf Gundarsson. Seattle, Wash.: The Ring of Troth, 1993.

Saxo Grammaticus. *The History of the Danes.* Cambridge: D.S. Brewer, 1979–1980.

Snorri Sturluson. *The Prose Edda.* Translated by Arthur Gilcrist Brodeur. New York: American-Scandinavian Foundation, 1916.

———. *The Prose Edda of Snorri Sturluson: Tales from Norse Mythology.* Translated by Jean I. Young. Berkeley: University of California Press, 1954.

———. *Edda.* Translated and edited by Anthony Faulkes. London: J. M. Dent; Rutland, Vt.: Charles E. Tuttle, 1987.

———. *Heimskringla: History of the Kings of Norway.* Translated by Lee M. Hollander. Austin: University of Texas Press, 1991.

Snow, Madeline. "Lofn." *Runestone,* no. 43 (Spring 1983): 8–9.

Spurkland, Terje. *Norwegian Runes and Runic Inscriptions.* Translated by Betsy van der Hoek. Woodbridge, Suffolk, U.K.: Boydell Press, 2005.

Steblin-Kamenskij, M. I. *The Saga Mind.* Translated by Kenneth H. Ober. Odense, Denmark: Odense University Press, 1973.

Stokker, Kathleen. "Folklore of Butter." *Viking* 91, no. 10 (1994): 19–22.

Ström, Ake V. "The King God and His Connection with Sacrifice in Old Norse Religion." In *The Sacral Kingship: Contributions to the Central Theme at the 8th International Congress for the History of Religions* (Rome, April 1955), 702–15.

Studies in the History of Religions, vol. 4. Leiden, The Netherlands: Brill, 1959.

Sweet's Anglo-Saxon Primer, 9th ed. Revised by Norman Davis. Oxford, U.K.: Clarendon Press, 1980.

Tacitus. *The Agricola and the Germania.* Translated by H. Mattingly, revised by S. A. Handford. Harmondsworth, U.K.: Penguin, 1970.

Taylor, Paul, and W. H. Auden, trans. *The Elder Edda: A Selection from the Icelandic.* London: Faber and Faber, 1973.

Thorsson, Edred. *Futhark: A Handbook of Rune Magic.* York Beach, Maine: Samuel Weiser, 1984.

———. *Runelore: A Handbook of Esoteric Runology.* York Beach, Maine: Samuel Weiser, 1987.

———. *Northern Magic: Mysteries of the Norse, Germans and English.* St. Paul, Minn.: Llewellyn Publications, 1992.

Turville-Petre, G. *Myth and Religion of the North.* Westport, Conn.: Greenwood Press, 1975.

Wicker, Nancy L. "Nimble-Fingered Maidens in Scandinavia: Women as Artists and Patrons." In *Reassessing the Roles of Women as 'Makers' of Medieval Art and Architecture,* edited by Therese Martin, 865–902. Leiden, The Netherlands: Brill, 2012.

The Viking. New York: Crescent Books, 1975.

Vries, Jan de. *Altgermanische Religionsgeschichte.* Berlin: De Gruyter, 1956–57.

Wemple, Suzanne F. "Sanctity and Power: The Dual Pursuit of Early Medieval Women." In *Becoming Visible: Women in European History,* 2nd ed., edited by Renate Bridenthal, Claudia Koonz, and Susan Stuard, 131–51. Boston: Houghton, Mifflin, 1987.

Wiesner, Merry E. "Spinning Out Capital: Women's Work in the Early Modern Economy." In *Becoming Visible: Women in European History*, 2nd ed., edited by Renate Bridenthal, Claudia Koonz, and Susan Stuard, 221–49. Boston: Houghton, Mifflin, 1987.

Index